M. Ali Kettani is Director General of the
Islamic Foundation for Science, Technology
and Development, Jeddah. Born in Fes and
educated on four continents, he received the
PhD in electrical engineering from the
Carnegie Institute of Technology,
Pittsburgh. For several years he lectured at
the universities of Pittsburgh and Riyadh
before joining the University of Petroleum
and Minerals, Dhahran, where he was made
Professor and Chairman of the Department
of Electrical Engineering.

In the general field of energy he is a world
renowned authority on solar energy and has
written more than one hundred articles for
scientific journals and published five books:
*Direct Energy Conversion, Plasma
Engineering, Energy and Development,
Heliotechnique and Development* and *Solar
Energy in the Arab World.*

From his early years Dr Kettani has held
an intense interest in the plight of Muslims
throughout the world, especially those
living as minorities, and has travelled
extensively to study their problems. He has
developed a strong feeling of identity with
them and a commitment to their struggle to
survive and to grow into strong, self-reliant
communities. His earlier books on the
subject, written in Arabic, are *Muslims in
Europe and America* , two volumes, and
*Muslims in Communist States.*

D1034195

Institute of Muslim Minority Affairs
Monograph Series Number 2

# Muslim Minorities
in the World Today

*By the same author*

*In English*
Direct Energy Conversion
Plasma Engineering
Energy and Development
Heliotechnique and Development
Solar Energy in the Arab World

*In Arabic*
Muslims in Europe and America
Muslims in Communist States
Travels of Ibn Battoutale (ed.)

Institute of Muslim Minority Affairs

# Muslim Minorities in the World Today

*M. Ali Kettani*

*With a foreword by Syed Z. Abedin*

Mansell Publishing Limited, *London and New York*

First published 1986 by Mansell Publishing Limited
(A subsidiary of The H. W. Wilson Company)
6 All Saints Street, London N1 9RL, England
950 University Avenue, Bronx, New York 10452, U.S.A.

British Library Cataloguing in Publication Data

Kettani, M. Ali
  Muslim minorities in the world today.— (Institute
  of Muslim Minority Affairs monograph series; no. 2)
  1. Muslims—Non-Muslim countries
  I. Title   II. Institute of Muslim Minority Affairs   III. Series
  305.6'971      BP163

  ISBN 0–7201–1802–6

Library of Congress Cataloging in Publication Data

Kettani, M. Ali
  Muslim minorities in the world today.
  (Institute of Muslim Minority Affairs monograph
  series; no. 2)
  Includes index
  1. Muslims—Non-Muslim countries
  I. Title   II. Series
  BP52.5.K47   1985      305.6'971      85–15478

  ISBN 0–7201–1802–6

Printed in Great Britain by Whitstable Litho Ltd., Whitstable, Kent

*In the name of God, Most Gracious, Most Merciful*

This book is dedicated to my parents
Mohammed Muntasir Kettani and Oum-Hani Fassi-Fihri
who raised me in the love of Islam and the Ummah.

It is also dedicated to my wife Nuzhah and children, Hasna, Hasan, Hamzah and Hussein, hoping that they will carry on the same tradition of concern for Muslims in the world.

And it is dedicated to all those Muslims across the centuries and continents who are soldiers in the defence of the *ummah* and who have struggled and continue to struggle in the way of God by word and deed, or at least keep the spirit of struggle ablaze in their hearts.

# Contents

# List of Tables and Figures

*Tables*

## Figures

# Foreword

*Muslim Minorities in the World Today* is in many respects a seminal work. It treats of a subject that is still, in a manner of speaking, in its infancy. 'Minorityness' for Muslims is, according to Ali Kettani, a comparatively new experience. There were, no doubt, small communities of Muslims that established themselves outside the heartlands of Islam right from the outset. But these communities were by and large the beneficiaries of what may be termed the *watasima* syndrome (a lone woman entrapped in the distant stretches of an alien and hostile land confidently and successfully invoking the power and might of the Caliph of Islam). Kettani prefers to call this phenomenon the 'prestige and power of established Islam', which allowed these communities, however small or remote, to be viewed as enclaves of the Muslim world on alien soil.

It is against this backdrop of history that we can more fully appreciate Kettani's contention that 'minorityness' in its sociological sense is the product of overall Muslim decadence and subjection. There are two key concepts involved in his analysis; one is the concept of 'established Islam', but the other more crucial concept is of 'Consciousness of Community' or Ummah. This concept becomes more central to Kettani's thinking as he moves along, recounting the 'long, continuous and glorious epic of struggle for survival against heavy odds' of Muslim communities in different parts of the world. To the point that one is led to the conclusion that more than political power, the *watasima* syndrome was the reflection of the 'Consciousness of Community' that infused the world of Islam in its ascendant phase.

Such being the case Kettani sets about through this book to

revive the 'Consciousness of Community' among present day
Muslims. Muslim minorities, he claims, are 'those parts of the
Muslim Ummah living outside its sovereignty'. He wishes to instill
among them the feeling that they are part of the Ummah. He
wants to build bridges between them and Muslim majorities. He
argues that for a Muslim, minority status is limited not only by
space, but by time as well. 'Minorityness' is thus a transitory
phase, a redressable accident of history. A Muslim is not supposed
wilfully to acquiesce in it.

As a logical corollary to this approach, Kettani makes specific
demands on Muslim majority communities. Their first priority
should be to support Muslim minority communities 'morally, culturally and politically'. Even the nature of their relationship with
non-Muslim states should be determined by these states' treatment
of their Muslim minorities. To Kettani the degree of commitment
of Muslim majorities toward Muslim minorities is the index of the
strength of the consciousness of community among majoritarian
Muslims. Without it not only would Muslim minorities lose their
distinct identity, but Muslim majorities themselves would most
likely cease to exist.

It is this clear conviction that makes Kettani lament the fact that
no overall philosophy of dealing with Muslim minorities has been
developed in the Islamic world.

The discussion in *Muslim Minorities in the World Today* to this
extent is persuasive, erudite and well-documented. Nonetheless, it
tends at times to reflect the classic Muslim majoritarian approach
to 'minorityness'. This should not be all that surprising. For with
his origins in Morocco and his long standing and distinguished
service in the cause of the Ummah, Kettani *is* a majoritarian
Muslim. But he is at the same time also acutely aware of 'how the
other half lives'. During the first years of his life, he tells us, he
went through experiences similar to those of members of minority
communities. It is this encounter perhaps which has induced him
to pursue an alternate current of thought in *Muslim Minorities*,
which provides the book with a more challenging and realistic aspect.

Acknowledging the fact that some minority communities may be
a long way away from becoming majorities (which yet remains the
only acceptable *raison d'etre* for Muslim 'minorityness'), Kettani is
careful to point out that Muslim communities should avoid being
looked at by their non-Muslim compatriots as foreign bodies in their
midst. They are warned from cultivating political relationships
with Muslim majority communities. Islamically, they are even

permitted to absorb certain characteristics from their environment, in terms of 'language, dress and minor social habits'.

For consciousness of community and also perhaps for reasons of physical security Muslim minorities are encouraged to reside in areas of high Muslim concentration. But Kettani is also clearly aware of the drawbacks of a 'ghetto-like mentality'. He forcefully argues that Islam is not attached to any piece of land; its principles could meaningfully blossom in any environment.

Among these principles Kettani particularly underscores the cardinal tenet of Islamic belief, *Tawhid*, which is the belief in the Oneness of God. But argues Kettani, 'if God is One, humanity is one as well'. It is therefore against the tenets of Islam for Muslims whether living as majorities or minorities to raise up barriers of discrimination among the children of Adam.

Kettani thus offers two alternate models for Muslim minorities to choose from, depending on their circumstances. The first is the classic model of 'Makkah'. In this model the Muslim minority subject to cruel and unrelenting pressure is constrained to opt for *hijrah* or belligerence and warfare. For a long time this option was in traditional Muslim majoritarian thinking invested with the status of inevitability and exclusive viability. But the unique distinction of *Muslim Minorities in the World Today* lies in its cognition of an alternate model — the 'Abyssinian model'. Here at last for the believers is the assurance of a future *with* others. Kettani characterizes it as a state of 'tolerance, peaceful coexistence and exchange of ideas'.

That Kettani, writing from the vantage point of a majoritarian and committed as he most assuredly is to the resurgence of the Ummah, could still acknowledge and trace the contours of an alternate model is what makes this book so very valuable for Muslim minorities. This is the closest that any 'committed' majoritarian Muslim scholar has, to my knowledge, come in the avowal of a pluralistic reality.

It is necessary to point out that minority living, being a cooperative endeavour whichever model Muslim minorities choose, would to a significant extent depend upon the attitudes, predilections and policies of the majority constituent of any particular social order. 'Abyssinia' is thus a challenge not only for Muslim minorities but also and more fundamentally for the non-Muslims among whom they reside.

Institute of Muslim Minority Affairs　　　　　SYED Z. ABEDIN
*London*　　　　　　　　　　　　　　　　　　*Director*

# Preface

•

Minorities are those groups of people who for one reason or another become the first victims of the despotism of the state or of the community that constitutes the majority and thus the human base on which the state rests. Quite often they are relegated to the obscurity of insignificance. They are the ones whose history remains unwritten, their condition of existence remains unknown, and their ideals and aspirations remain unappreciated. They are those whom the *Holy Quran* seems to refer to as '*Al-Mustadafin fi al-Ard*' (the despised through the land):

> Call to mind when ye
> Were small in numbers
> Despised through the land,
> And afraid that men might
> Dispoil and snatch you;
> But He (God) provided a safe asylum
> For you, strengthened you
> With His aid, and gave you
> Good things for sustenance:
> That ye might be grateful. (Chap. 8, Verse 26)

Most of these minorities are inclined to degenerate and lose their identity. Few care to support their struggle for survival. When they vanish, hardly anyone cares to shed a tear at this tragedy. Some of these minorities try to compensate for their weakness in numbers by the strength of their ideals. If their dedication to their ideals and values is a deep and sincere one and is coupled with maturity, constructive vision and energy, then it is likely that those ideals will ultimately triumph.

Islam, which embodies the Message of God to humanity in its perfect form through His last Messenger Muhammed ibn Abdallah, itself started as a minority religion. It attracted the *'Mustadafin fi al–Ard'* (the despised through the land) in a world that was ruled by the forces of evil and darkness. Its roots are deep with those 'few in numbers' who, across the centuries, had to carry the burden of being the victims of despotism in its myriad forms. Across the centuries and across the continents, Muslims have formed a single world brotherhood, an indivisible *ummah* irrespective of whether they were living in countries where they were in the majority or minority.

While many books have been written about minorities in general, or one or another minority in particular, no book has been written about the Muslim minorities of the world. True, there are a multitude of books written about Muslims in one country or another or in one continent or another, but often these books were written by special categories of people: anthropologists, Christian missionaries, European colonial officers, Communist propagandists. All of these have one characteristic in common: a complete lack of identity of feeling between the writers and the subjects of their writing. Thus, it seemed worthwhile to this writer to see, and subsequently to present the situation of the Muslim minorities as it appears to a Muslim, to someone who quite professedly shares their world-view and beliefs, and identifies with their desire to carve for themselves a meaningful future. The author who grew up in a Muslim country while it was under colonial rule, went to colonial schools and has been subjected to anti-Islamic propaganda from an early age, experienced during the first years of his life the same feelings that the members of minority communities experience. In his adolescence and early youth, he continued his studies in Europe and America, to discover more about the distortion Islamic ideals receive at the hands of the media in these countries. This enabled him to gain greater empathy with those Muslim communities which have to live in similar situations. After completing his studies, he embarked on studying the situation and problems of the Muslims across the globe. The experience was a fascinating one and it increasingly became a passion with him, becoming the major preoccupation after his professional work as a scientist and engineer. As time has passed, he has felt more and more a duty towards his people. The sorry state of affairs prevailing in the Muslim countries in general has also driven him increasingly towards the Muslim minorities. He

has felt inspired and thrilled by the idea that some of these minorities might one day produce those sons and daughters of Islam who
might change the whole course of events of the entire Muslim
*ummah*. This dream has sustained him in his study, and above all,
in his striving to extend a helping hand to those who, if not taken
care of, might be cast aside into complete obscurity.

The aim of this book is, therefore, to present the truth about
these minorities, to depict the epic of their struggle against oppression, injustice, cruelty and of their longing to live as self-
respecting men and women, and as Muslims. The book has been
written primarily for them for two purposes: to help them realize
the fact that the minority status is limited by space and possibly by
time as well. It has also been written to help them recognize that as
members of a world community of more than a thousand million
people scattered over all the continents of the world they should
not feel alone in their struggle for survival. The book is addressed
to all enlightened and sensitive human beings, regardless of their
racial, geographical and religious affiliations. It is addressed especially to all members of the Muslim *ummah* who happen to live
in states where they form a majority. One would wish that they
were able to see the importance of the Muslim minorities and the
importance of the role of the Muslims living in majority areas as
the guarantors of Islamic universality. It perhaps need not be
emphasized that any Muslim majority might become reduced to a
minority if it forgets the basic rule of allegiance to the *ummah* and
its loyalty to God, to His Messenger (peace be upon him) and to
the ideals of Islam. Finally, the book is written for all those in the
world who care to know the truth and to free themselves from the
stereotypes and from the ignorance which underlies the intoler-
ance, the racism, and the oppression which make this world unnec-
essarily a worse world to live in. Ultimately, if this book helps in
building bridges between minorities and majorities, in converting
hatred and rancour into respect and sympathy, and in dispelling,
even if partly, the fog of falsehood which blurs and distorts our
vision, then the effort will not have been in vain.

The book has been divided into ten chapters, each chapter being
sub-divided into ten sections. From the beginning, it was found
that the sub-division of the world into regions, as far as Muslim
minorities were concerned, was difficult. However, after careful
thought, it was found that the best division would be that which
took account of the numbers involved in the minorities as well as
of the geographical divisions of the world. Thus, the first chapter

attempts to define certain terms followed by a study of the problems relating to the genesis and survival of minorities in general
and of Muslim minorities in particular. It includes also a plan of
action for the minorities to follow in order to help them in their
struggle for survival. This is combined with an effort to point out
the forces which erode their vital rights. The eight subsequent
chapters deal with minorities in different parts of the world from
those in Europe to those in the Pacific. In each of these chapters
the history of each major minority community has been traced; its
numerical strength has been assessed, as well as its present situation, in terms of organization and the treatment meted out to it
by the majority. Chapter 10 gives a general view of the distribution
of Muslims in the world, as well as a sketch of the basic ideals
of Islam, stressing those ideals which are scarcely known in the
secular or communist media. These are meant to provide an introduction to those open-minded readers who might want to seek the
truth on their own.

The different chapters include a number of tables and maps. A
list of footnotes and references has been added at the end of each
chapter, but it is not basic to the gathering of the information. In
fact most of the information gathered is first-hand information
obtained from the minorities themselves by the author. The
author, during the last ten years, has extensively visited Muslim
minorities in Europe, Asia, Africa, the American continent,
Australia and the Pacific islands. He sat with their leaders and
discussed their problems. He also developed a bank of information
which is being continuously updated. The author also met a great
number of the leaders of refugees from countries where Muslims
are oppressed and discussed with them their situation in their
respective countries.

One aspect of the Muslim minorities most difficult to come by
is their numbers. Official censuses usually under-estimate the
numbers of minority communities. Often Muslim communities are
completely ignored. When offical censuses are reasonably reliable
their figures have been used. Sometimes, official censuses are
corrected on bases explained in the text. When official censuses
are non-existent or obviously erroneous, other means have been
resorted to in order to obtain the necessary data. For instance, to
estimate the Muslim population of Sao Paulo, the author found no
other way but to ask the caretaker of the Muslim cemetery how
many Muslims were buried each year. Another example is the
deduction of the number of Muslims in Sweden from the census of

the different foreign immigrants by their countries of origin; and so on and so forth.

The author's professional field of specialization is electrical engineering. More specifically, he has been interested in problems relating to energy, particularly solar energy and more recently in establishing the Islamic Foundation for Science, Technology and Development. The writing of this book has been a spare-time activity which was possible only because of the encouragement of many people. First of all, my wife Nuzhah and children Hasna, Hasan, Hamzah and Hussein who sacrificed a very great part of the time which I owed them. Thanks and acknowledgement are also due to my dear friend, Dr Zafar I. Ansari, of the University of Petroleum and Minerals who read the entire manuscript, corrected almost every page, and gave encouragement at the end of every chapter. Thanks are also due to Mr Rustoom Sadri for his suggestions on the two chapters dealing with the Soviet Union and China, and to Mr Chennur M. Azmatullah who carried out the typing of the different versions of the manuscript with a sense of mission that equals that of the author. Finally, thanks are due to all the friends around the world who supplied me with information and encouragement. But for their assistance, and above all, without God's help and succour, the writing of this book would have remained an unfulfilled dream.

Praise be to God the Lord of the Worlds.

# 1 Introduction

## What is a Muslim Minority?

In order to ensure conceptional clarity from the very beginning, it seems necessary to define first the terms 'minority' and 'Muslim' separately, and then the appellation 'Muslim minority'.

Webster's *Seventh New Collegiate Dictionary* defines a 'minority' as 'a part of a population differing in some characteristics and often subjected to differential treatment'. However, this definition is not enough to explain the coming into existence of a new minority. For instance, it is clear that the factor that leads to the formation of a minority is the existence among a group of people of 'different characteristics'. However, if those who possess these 'different characteristics' are not aware of them, nor have achieved any solidarity because of their awareness of them, such a group of people can hardly be termed a minority merely because of the existence of those 'different characteristics'. Nevertheless, if the majority becomes aware of their different characteristics and starts meting out 'differential treatment' to those who share them, the chances are that such an action on the part of the majority would induce an awareness among them of the 'different characteristics' that they possess, leading to the coming into existence of a minority. The characteristic might be a physical one such as the colour of the skin. For instance, since a differential treatment was meted out by the majority in the US to those who share the blackness of the colour of their skin, a black minority has indeed come into being. The same characteristic is considered completely irrelevant in a Muslim environment and a black minority in Morocco, for instance, does not exist, although many Moroccans are black. Similarly, that characteristic might be a linguistic one. In a truly

Muslim environment, the difference in language too is irrelevant. For instance, in the early days of the Ottoman Empire, this principle was strongly adhered to and hence there could be no talk of linguistic minorities. However, as the European-inspired nationalism started competing for the allegiance of Muslims with the Islamic identity, linguistic minorities began to emerge, leading eventually to the break-up of the Muslim Ottoman State. On the other hand, a group of people might still be considered a minority even though it possesses numerical majority in a country or region if somehow it has become overwhelmed by others and is subjected to differential treatment by a smaller but more influential group which has characteristics different from its own.

In this study the word 'Muslim' is used to denote all those who affirm Muhammad, the son of Abdullah (peace be upon him) to be the last messenger of Allah and hold his teachings to be true, irrespective of the extent to which they know about those teachings, or the extent to which they are able to live according to them. This affirmation naturally engenders a feeling of identity with all who share the same beliefs. For the purposes of this discussion a person would be considered a Muslim as long as he feels, even vaguely, to be part of the overall Muslim *ummah* wherever he might be. There is no other possible definition of 'Muslim' in a study dealing with Muslim minorities, especially in view of the extremely severe conditions which have confronted these Muslims in the past and are confronting them now.

Going back to the dictionary definition, one may say that a 'Muslim minority' is 'a part of a population which differs from the rest of the population because its members affirm Muhammad, the son of Abdullah to be the last messenger of Allah and hold his teachings to be true, and which is often subjected to differential treatment by those who do not share the above-mentioned belief.' Or in a shorter form and retaining the definition of the word 'Muslim', one may say that a 'Muslim minority' is 'a part of a population differing because its members are Muslims and are often subjected to differential treatment'. Therefore, for such a minority to be in existence it is necessary that those who share the 'different characteristic' of being Muslim should be aware of such difference and should have attained a degree of solidarity because of it. Otherwise there can be no 'Mulsim minority'. Finally, one could conclude that a Muslim community might be numerically inferior but superior politically, or socially. Such a group is not a minority. This would apply, for instance, to the Muslims of

Moghul India. On the other hand, a Muslim community might be numerically superior to the non-Muslims but might be relegated to a position of insignificance and ineffectiveness by the more powerful non-Muslims even though the latter might be numerically inferior. In this case, the Muslims should be considered a minority. Today, many countries of the world fall into this category: Albania, Ethiopia, Tanzania, are some examples.

## Genesis of a Minority

Islam itself began as a minority, a minority of one person, namely that of the Prophet Muhammad (peace be upon him). But the quality of that Allah-chosen man made that minority grow despite all resistance, and even persecution. This minority had already turned into a majority in Arabia before the death of Muhammad in a span of about a quarter of a century.

Islam discourages a Muslim to acquiesce wilfully to a state of minority if he cannot exercise his right to worship the One True God. In this case the Muslim is required to emigrate to a land more congenial to the practice of his faith, with the intention of returning to his original homeland and securing his right to live according to the teachings of Islam. Emigrating for the protection of one's belief is an act of religious merit; in some cases it is even a religious duty. Such a man is a *muhajir*, but not a refugee. He is required to work hard to prepare for his return, and the Muslim community at large is required to help such *muhajirs* even if there might be no other way for them to return except by resorting to force. This is the case of the first Muslim wave of emigrants from Mecca to Abyssinia during the Prophet's lifetime. This is the case in a more drastic way of the emigration of the Holy Prophet Muhammad from Mecca to Medina with the entire Muslim community. So important was this event for the Muslims that it became the starting point of the Muslim calendar. The Prophet returned to Mecca with the Muslims when they were able to fight their way back to their homeland. Therefore, when the right of a Muslim to practise his faith is denied by any power, he must either fight back in self-defence, and become a *mujahid*; or if he cannot fight or fails in this fight, he should emigrate and become a *muhajir*. If he can do neither one nor the other, he should keep his faith, even secretly if he has to, and try his best to pass it on at least to his descendants. A Muslim may also emigrate either in search of knowledge or of material benefits, etc., as long as his faith is not endangered. In this case he should try to present the example of a good Muslim and should also be the carrier of the message of Islam to the people around him.

The first Muslim minorities came into being as a result of the Muslim merchants settling down in foreign ports for commerce. In the beginning these merchants were ambassadors of a strong state and carried all the prestige that it implied. These were the first Muslim communities on the coast of India, Sri Lanka, China, East Africa, the Indonesian and Philippines archipelagos and the islands of the Indian Ocean. In the course of time these merchants married local women and the second and third generations became a part of the land. Often local populations were converted to the new faith giving numerical strength to the Muslim community. In several areas these conversions happened on such a large scale that what appeared in the beginning to be insignificant minorities became, in the course of time, fully fledged majorities as in the case of Malaysia and Indonesia.

The Muslim state expanded dramatically after the death of the Prophet Muhammad. For over a century the Muslims remained organized as one political entity, but later this broke into several fragments. Despite political fragmentation, the Muslims were held together by a common religious outlook, a common standard of moral evaluation and a common legal system. Moreover, their religious idealism provided them with the impetus to develop one of the greatest civilizations of human history so that for many centuries they remained the leaders of all mankind in all branches of life. But the success of no nation abides for ever, and eventually the civilization of Muslims was also subjected to decline. This manifested itself, among other things, in the shrinking of the Muslim states and the conquest of Muslim territories by non-Muslims. The result was that many Muslim majorities were brought under non-Muslim powers. The development usually follows the following pattern. First a community is reduced to ineffectivity despite its numerical majority because of non-Muslim occupation, and when the occupation lasts long enough, the majority is transformed into a numerical minority because of large scale expulsion of Muslims, immigration of non-Muslims, and low rates of natural increase among Muslims owing to abnormally difficult conditions. In this category fall the minorities of the Soviet Union, occupied Palestine, Thailand, Ethiopia, and Bosnia-Herzegovina in Yugoslavia, etc.

There is another type of Muslim minority which is slightly

different from the one mentioned above. This is the case when Muslim rule in a land does not last long enough, or the efforts to propagate Islam are not vigorous or effective enough to transform the Muslims into a numerical majority in the lands which they ruled. As soon as their political power collapses, the Muslims find themselves reduced to the status of a minority in their own country. This applies in the case of India and the Balkans.

A third type of Muslim minority might come into existence. And this is by the conversion of a certain number of non-Muslims in a non-Muslim environment. If these new converts become aware of the importance of their Islamic beliefs and assign to it priority over other characteristics and attain solidarity with each other because of sharing those beliefs, a new Muslim minority comes into being. Usually, the immigrant stream and the converted stream fuse together to establish a Muslim minority well adapted to the local culture and yet well attached to the Muslim *ummah*. An example of such a case is the Muslim community of Sri Lanka which is actually the fusion of Muslim immigrants from South Arabia and converts from the island. Culturally, however, these Muslims adopted the Tamil language which is also used by Muslims of South India, rather than the Singhalese language, but kept the *Shafii madh-hab* of the Arab immigrants.

## Organizational Problems

As mentioned above, many Muslim minorities came into being by individual actions; either by the emigration of an individual Muslim to a non-Muslim land, or the conversion to Islam of a non-Muslim in a non-Muslim land. By such an individual action a different characteristic comes into being: that of not following the religion of the majority. However, the existence of Muslims in a country does not imply the existence of a Muslim minority, unless an awareness takes place leading to solidarity among them as a result of trying to keep this different characteristic in existence. Organization can be defined as such a solidarity-inducing action. Without organization, in one form or another, there can be no Muslim minority, and the Islam of the different individuals is likely to be eroded with the lapse of time and would die out with the death of its carriers.

Therefore, the fact that Islam has no clergy should not create any misunderstanding. Islam is a way of life as well as a religion. When Muslims find themselves outside *dar-al-Islam*, it becomes their duty to organize themselves in order to be able to safeguard as much as possible of this way of life. Most Muslim minorities have done this by electing their own *qa'id* and nominating their own *qadis*.

The organizational action has, perforce, to start with the initiative of certain individuals. Such leaders of the community emerge usually from among those Muslims who have some leadership qualities and a higher perception of the need of solidarity-inducing action for survival. The quality of the organization depends on the quality of the leaders and on their knowledge of Islam and its principles.

Once a Muslim finds himself in a non-Muslim environment it becomes his Islamic duty to get organized with other Muslims. The Prophet commanded organization by stressing that even if two Muslims go on a journey, they should choose among themselves an *amir*. The Prophet is also reported to have said that if a Muslim dies without binding himself in loyalty and obedience to an *amir* he will have died a *jahili* death. Of course, the choice of the *amir* is to be understood as an organizational set-up for the Muslims in a given land, and this will naturally be in consonance with the circumstances in which they have to take solidarity-inducing action as Muslims.

Islam is a social religion in the sense that a person cannot become a Muslim unless he actively cares about his Muslim brothers. In this respect, many sayings are reported from the Prophet: 'None among you can become a [true] believer unless he desires for his brother what he desires for himself'; 'Muslims are like one body; if a part of the body hurts, the whole body becomes sick'; 'If any of you sees a wrong being done, he should change it with his hand; if he cannot, then with his tongue; if he cannot do that, then with his heart, and that is the weakest state of faith'. Therefore, it is the Islamic duty of every Muslim, especially in a non-Muslim environment, to become organized with other Muslims.

The organizational set-up should be aimed at establishing a viable Muslim community. For this, the set-up has to be based on Islamic principles. It should also be effective and efficient. The general principles on which such an organizational set-up should be based are the following: The organization should express the Islamic identity of the Community, and this identity alone should underly their collective identity and organization; The Islamic principle of *shura* (mutual consultation) should be fully observed; The limit of the organization should be a given political entity.

The first condition implies that the organizational set-up should be open to all those who are Muslims (as defined above). The organization should not be an elitist gathering consisting of those who are high quality Muslims. Neither should it be a partisan gathering consisting only of those who have identical or similar political views. It should not be a sectarian gathering consisting only of those who follow a certain *madh-hab* (theological or legal school). It should not be a national or ethnic gathering consisting only of those who have the same national origin. It should not be a racial gathering consisting only of those who belong to the same race. Neither should it be a professional gathering consisting only of those Muslims who belong to the same profession. It should be an organization that would throw its doors wide open to all Muslims in recognition of the fact that they are Muslims and disregarding everything else.

However, talking about organization implies sub-grouping within an overall system. What should then be the basis of the sub-grouping? In principle, the only Islamically acceptable basis would be geographical. What we mean by this is that all the Muslims of a town, or part of a town, or a county would form one *jamaat* (association), all the *jamaats* within a state or a region would form a council and all the councils of a given country should form a federation. Each association would have its Mosque (as defined in the time of the Prophet); the Mosque being a fully-fledged Community Centre, a place of worship and education, etc.

The Muslims within each association could be divided into several chapters if the community comprises several linguistic groups. There seems nothing objectionable from the Islamic viewpoint if people sharing the same language decide to form a chapter in the association, or even a fully-fledged association within the council.

The second condition is that the principle of *shura* (mutual consultation) should be fully observed. In this connection we have to bear in mind the following directive of the Prophet. 'There may be no obedience to any creature if that entails disobedience of the Creator'. The *shura* must be implemented within the limitation of the safeguard of Islam. In other words, the Muslims should have complete freedom to choose their leaders and decide upon policies and courses while remaining within the limits set as *halal* or *jaiz* by the *Quran* and the *Sunnah*. Therefore, the Muslims should elect among themselves their office bearers and leaders, and should be able to change them whenever they wish to do so. For this, constitutions which are not in contradiction with Islamic principles should be framed for the local *jamaat*, the regional council and the national federation. These constitutions should put in written form the consensus of the Muslims regarding the means of handling their affairs. They should be changed with the change of such a consensus.

The third condition is that the organizational set-up should be effective. To be effective an organization should gather all those Muslims who find themselves under similar conditions represented by a given non-Muslim establishment. In other words, this implies the gathering of all the Muslims living within a given non-Muslim political entity.

## Economic Problems

The differential treatment to which the minority is subjected is often of an economic nature. If the Muslim minority considered was part of a Muslim majority, then the differential pressure of the invading power usually tends towards confiscations of *awqaf* property, elimination from positions of influence of members of the Muslim Community, nationalization of businesses from which the minority draws its strength, expropriation of property, especially land, etc. As for the Muslim minority that came into being as a result of the gathering of Muslim immigrants and converts, such a minority should start everything from scratch by resisting such an economic encroachment.

In both cases, the minority should make an effort to resist such an economic deterioration. In order to achieve this, it should increase its solidarity-inducing action and support its organizational set-up.

No organizational set-up can be successful without financial backing. Muslims have been urged in the *Quran* and also by the Prophet to 'spend in the Way of Allah'. Allah in the *Holy Quran* commands the Muslims to 'strive with their properties and their selves'. 'Striving in the Way of Allah' as exemplified by the *sirah* (life-example) of the Prophet implies giving one's money, time, energy, and when necessary even life for the furtherance and defence of Islam and for the protection and advancement of Muslims. For a Muslim minority this implies that it is the duty of Muslims to contribute with money, time, knowledge and experience to the functioning of their organization, the establishment of their mosques, the building of their schools, and in extreme conditions, the support of their *mujahids*. Such financial contributions are over and above the *zakat*, and are limited by the needs of the community. These are indispensable since without them, the very existence of the Muslim minority would be in jeopardy, and the survival of Islam in that part of the world would be endangered.

However, most of the individuals who are Muslims as defined above, are unaware of this duty or are unwilling to know about such matters because of the weakness of their Islamic identity. It becomes, therefore, the duty of those who are the leaders of the community to create this awareness in their members. To do this, the organization should have some financial means to start with. In this respect, the help of Muslims of *dar-ul-Islam* becomes necessary, but such a help should be so geared as to make the community independent of any help in the future as soon as possible. The best help would be the one that is based on co-operation. In such a case, the Muslim countries should take due note of the support needed by the Muslim minorities so as to offset the effects of differential treatment to which these Muslims are usually subjected in such countries. This support should not be limited to the fields of employment, business, exchanges, etc.

To be financially sound, the organization should be sure to protect itself against the danger of corruption and of misuse of Muslim funds. To do this, it is necessary that those elected as office bearers at all levels of the organizational set-up be completely prohibited from receiving payments for their services to the community. The hired staff in the organization, however, should be remunerated but their function should be solely of an executive character and should consist of carrying out the directives of the elected office bearers. In this way, the competition for office would be based on the desire and the ability to serve the community and not the attraction to any financial gain.

A healthy Muslim minority should be able to receive enough contributions from its members to establish all its mosques and schools, to pay the salaries of its teachers and *imams*, etc. This minority should be in a position to provide Islamic education for all its children and to remind the adults of their Islamic duty.

## Social Problems

The most serious problem that can face a minority is social absorption by the majority. Such an absorption is usually the result of a long assimilation process that nibbles at the Islamic characteristics of the minority until it disappears altogether. The process of assimilation is particularly effective and fast when the Muslim community is badly organized, has no special schools for its children and does not have an adequate number of mosques (as community and religious centres) for its adults.

The cases of wilful conversion of Muslims to other religions are usually rare. However, as the community starts to absorb non-Islamic traits which influence its sense of Islamic identity, mixed marriages with non-Muslims conspicuously increase and instead of being a means of growth of the Muslim community as a result of outsiders embracing Islam, they become a strong means of social and cultural assimilation. The most ominous sign of social absorption is the dropping of Muslim first names, a phenomenon quite common among the offspring of such mixed marriages. Many of these become only remotely linked to Islam or even neutral as far as their religious affiliation is concerned. However, if they marry again in the majority community, the chances are that their off-spring would follow the religion of the majority. Therefore, the process of assimilation takes usually the span of three generations.

The process of assimilation becomes more widely diffused when the Muslim minority is deprived of its elite. Most often, the elite deserts the minority by emigration to *dar-ul-Islam*. This emigration is often induced by special and constant persecution by the majority, as it is clear that a leaderless community is much easier to assimilate. Sometimes the elite deserts Islam altogether by following the policy and the way of the majority thus eroding any confidence that the Muslims might have in them. When either of these occurs, the community becomes unable to face the changed circumstances in such a way as to retain the former hegemony of Islam in their lives. This in turn leads to a continuous erosion of its organization with the result that the Muslim Community becomes more and more confined to people who lack influence and social status. Such a community would disappear in the course of time, if it is not helped effectively by *Dar-ul-Islam*.

Islamically, it will not harm the Muslim community to absorb the characteristics that are not contrary to Islamic principles. One of these characteristics is the learning of the language of the majority (which will not be harmful if the Muslims are able to keep on learning Arabic, the language of the *Quran*); the wearing of its dress, provided it does not violate the decency of dress advocated by Islam; and the absorption of minor social habits which are not Islamically objectionable. However, members of a Muslim community should refrain, and teach each other to refrain from absorbing non-Islamic characteristics. These are the dropping of Islamic names, the adoption of promiscuous habits; the absorption of alcoholic beverages, and above everything else, the belief that all religions are equally valid in the sight of the Creator. On the contrary, Muslims should continue to believe that Islam is the only true religion and that all other religions, as stated in the *Holy Quran* will be rejected by the Creator. Believing that all religions are equally valid is the first sign of religious assimilation.

It is the organization of the Muslim minority that can help it resist the different assimilative trends. In order to be able to do so, the community should have, geographically speaking, some area or areas of concentration. For the Muslim schools and mosques to be efficient, they should be able to serve the largest number of Muslims within the shortest possible distance. Moreover, social communication between Muslims should be kept at a maximum all the time, not only in the mosque, but also by exchange of visits by families, mutual co-operation in professional work, in community affairs, at play, etc. This can only be possible when specific areas within the overall country have higher Islamic concentrations so that Muslims can feel at home.

However, Islamically speaking, a Muslim community cannot be enclosed in a ghetto-like mentality. It should be capable of interacting with members of the non-Muslim community so as to fulfil its duty of *dawah*. Therefore, the two requirements of maximum desirable interaction between members of the Muslim community and reasonable interaction between Muslims and members of the non-Muslim communities should lead to the development of areas of high – but not exclusive – Muslim concentration.

A Muslim community should try to move from a position of mere defensive concerns, and try to spread the message of Islam outside the community. If successful, such a community would grow constantly in influence and numbers so as to become in the course of time a majority community. To become a successful community should be the aim of every Muslim minority. This is an ideological necessity without which the very presence of the minority becomes Islamically unacceptable.

## Political Problems

One of the most serious problems facing a Muslim minority is the gradual denial of political rights to the Muslims as a community and the persecution of its members, not to mention the fear of genocide in some cases.

The denial of political rights of the community may take the form of the non-recognition of an Islamic entity for one reason or another. This leads automatically to the application of laws specially made for the non-Muslim majority to use against the Muslim individual. This lends strength to the process of assimilation initiated by the majority which would tend to destroy the Islamic presence. Sweden can serve as an example. The official Church of Sweden is the Lutheran Church; this means that the Government supports financially that Church by taxing 1 per cent of the income of the population and strengthens it by introducing the teaching of the doctrines of that Church in the school curricula. To protect religious minorities the State recognizes some religious bodies such as Roman Catholicism and Judaism. Such recognition means that these religious groups receive collectively their share of the religious revenue and their children receive the teachings of their own religion. Until recently, Islam whose followers number more than 30,000 people, was not recognized, meaning that while the Muslims had to pay taxes to the official Church, their children were exposed in public schools to the proselytism of other religious bodies. In the most extreme cases, the majority might go to the extent of denying the right of citizenship to the members of the Muslim minority and even proceed to obliterate them by expulsion and mass killings as happened in Burma in 1978.

The second case, *viz.* the denial of political rights to Muslims, has the effect of putting tremendous pressure on the most active members of the community. They would sometimes react in one of the three following ways, all of which are harmful to the future of the community: they would emigrate; they would water down their Islamic identity, eventually isolating themselves from the Muslim community; or they would join extremist alientated groups in different walks of life, expressing their complete frustration with the majority as well as with their own community.

Once the community is well organized, its leaders should strive to seek the recognition by the authorities of Muslims as a religious community which has the right to maintain its characteristics. Once recognized, the community should continue to request the same rights as the other religious communities enjoy in the country. Eventually, the community may seek to gain political rights as a constituent community of the nation. Once these rights are obtained, the community should seek to disseminate its characteristics throughout that land.

Many communities succeeded in reaching several levels of these stages. For instance, the Muslim community in Finland is recognized as a religious community. In Yugoslavia, it is recognized as a nationality. The Muslims of Fiji, Trinidad and Guyana were capable of persuading the authorities to recognize Muslim holidays such as *Id Al-Adha* and *Al-Mawlid* as national holidays.

Muslim individuals who are politically ambitious should seek the votes of Muslims so that they can be truly their representatives. The Muslim community should realize this and establish accordingly the mechanics of political Islamic representation. Otherwise, Muslim politicians would be put in office by non-Muslim forces and would consequently be used to the detriment of the interests of the Muslim community.

## Example of an Extinguished Muslim Minority

Christianity, in its European version, has been the chief persecutor of Muslim minorities. This is due to the inherent difference in attitude between Islam and Christianity towards proselytism. Islam wants people to come to its fold of their own free will. The *Quran* categorically states: 'There is no compulsion in religion' (*Holy Quran* 11;256). Hence, Islam often spreads slowly, but having been spread as a result of genuine change of conviction, it endures. There are scarcely any instances of forced conversion to Islam and whenever these occurred they were frowned upon, even strongly opposed by the Muslim *ulama*. In European Christianity, the attitude has been different. People have been expected to follow the religion of their rulers. If they resisted, they were converted forcibly. The only exception has been the attitude of Christianity towards Judaism, because of the historical link between the two religions. Jews, in spite of all forms of discrimination, were allowed to survive as a group all over Europe except Christian Spain. The Muslims were given no such chance. The following Andalusian example is revealing.

Before the arrival of the Muslims, the Iberian Peninsula was overrun by Germanic overlords, the descendants of the Vandals. They persecuted the local population to the extreme. After a call for help by the Iberians, Musa Ibn Nusayr, the Arab Muslim General of the North African armies, sent his lieutenant, the Berber Tariq ibn Ziyad at the head of an army of 30,000 people, mostly Muslim Berbers. The liberation of the Peninsula was accomplished quite speedily, between the years 711–713 C.E.

The territory opened up for Islam included almost the whole of present-day Portugal and Spain, as well as the south-eastern corner of France. It did not include, however, the extreme north-western strip of Iberia. These territories were organized in a sub-province and were placed administratively under the Province of Al-Maghrib which had its capital at Qayrawan (in Tunisia today). A small stream of Muslim immigrants kept moving to al-Andalus and a much bigger population movement set on from Northern Morocco. But most of the strength of Islam was in the conversion *en masse* of the Iberian population.

When Abd al-Rahman (al-Dakhil), the Umayyad prince came to al-Andalus, the Muslims constituted already a sizeable percentage of the population of the Peninsula. The year was 756 C.E. (six years after the fall of the Umayyads of Damascus). Abd al-Rahman founded the Umayyad state of the West, and with it al-Andalus became an independent Muslim state with its capital at Qurtubah (Cordoba). During the Umayyad era, the Muslim population became an overwhelming majority in the Peninsula, and al-Andalus reached the highest levels of refinement and civilization in the world. The Christians became a tiny minority which gradually lost a great many of its cultural characteristics and became thoroughly arabized, even in names. But they were never to develop any sense of loyalty to the Muslim state and were ready to strike at its roots as soon as any opportunity presented itself. Most of the Christian resistance was organized in the mountainous territories of the north west which had been overlooked by the Muslims.

The Umayyad State reached its height of power and influence under Abd al-Rahman III (al-Nasir) during his long reign 912–961 C.E. However, the dynasty lost much of its hold during the regency of al-Mansur ibn abi Amir over the grandson of al-Nasir. Al-Mansur was himself a great statesman and an able soldier. He once again united the Iberian Peninsula under Islam, but he committed a terrible mistake which eventually did great harm to the future of al-Andalus. He destroyed the Umayyad dynasty without bringing anything to replace it. After his death the collapse seemed to be complete and for all practical purposes Islam would have been

finished in al-Andalus, if it had not been for the holding intervention of the Moroccans. The Muslims of al-Andalus were deeply
divided along racial lines: the Arabs, the Berbers, the Iberian
Muslims forming the mass of the population, and the Sicilian
Muslims forming the officer corps. Because of these divisions the
Umayyad dynasty collapsed, al-Andalus lost its unity and became
divided in a multitude of small states broadly organized along
racial lines and known as the Taifah kingdoms. It became, therefore, easy for the Christian conquest to proceed at a fast rate at
the expense of these tiny states. When the Christians swept over
the Muslim territories, the Andalusians were quick to call for help
from the growing al-Murabit (Almoravid) power of Morocco. The
great Murabit Yusuf ibn Tashfin checked the Christian advance at
his memorable victory of Zallaqah in 1086 C.E. He united what
was left of al-Andalus with North Africa. The same scenario was
repeated by the Moroccan Muwahhidun (Almohades) fifty-nine
years later.

The Muwahhid power collapsed in 1212 C.E. at the battle of Al-
Uqab (Las Novas de Tolosa) where they were defeated by the
Christians. The Marinids intervened again from Morocco, but the
Muslims of al-Andalus were then already a spent force. Most of
the Muslim territories were taken by the Christians including
the great metropolises of Ishbiliyah (Sevilla) and Qurtubah
(Cordoba). The Muslim power survived only in a small territory in
the south eastern corner of Iberia until 1492 C.E. when Gharnatah
(Granada) fell to the enemy after heroic resistance. No help came
from the Muslims abroad this time, whereas the whole of Christian
Europe was helping the Castillans.

Until 1492 C.E. there remained large Muslim communities in the
territories annexed by the Christians. These were called *al-
Mudajjanin* (the tamed ones!). They lived as Muslims for centuries. They were tolerated as quasi-slaves. They were subjected
to continuous pressure. Slowly they started losing their majority,
first by a continuous stream of Muslim emigration to territories left
in Muslim hands, then by continuous colonization of the conquered Muslim lands by the Christians coming from Galicia in
north western Spain and from southern France.

This policy of continuous annexation and persecution was
changed after the fall of the last Muslim stronghold, Gharnatah
(Granada). By the turn of the century [1502 for Gharnatah and
1525 for Balansiyah (Valencia)] Muslims were forcibly converted
to Christianity in Spain. This act opened an era of Muslim heroism,

unparalleled in Muslim history. For about 120 years, the Muslims of Spain fought to keep their faith against extremely heavy odds. These baptized Muslims, called Moriscos by the Spaniards, were subjected to the Spanish Inquisition. They were ceremoniously burnt alive at the stake or tortured as soon as they were discovered to be Muslims. They fought hard, sometimes militarily as they did in 1568–1571 in the al-Busharat (Alpujaras) mountains south of Gharnatah under their leader Muhammad ibn Ummayyah, who had been baptized by the Christians under the name of Fernando de Valor. Finally they succeeded in winning the right to emigrate to the Muslim lands of North Africa. By a royal decree of 22 September 1609, they were expelled from their beloved land with barely their clothes on their bodies and under most inhuman conditions. The exodus lasted for five years. But they were happy, happy to be free in the land of Islam. Their numbers amounted to somewhere between 600,000 and 2 million people in a country that at that time had no more than 8 million people.

Since 1979, Islam has witnessed a revival in the south of Spain, more specifically in the region of Andalucia. More than 2,000 people have returned to Islam and they have established Islamic societies and centres in Granada, Cordoba, Sevilla, Malaga and Jerez de la Frontera.

## Example of a Nascent Muslim Minority

The best example of a nascent Muslim community in recent times is that of Korea. Indeed, the Korean Muslim community is an integral part of the Korean nation and is not the result of any movement of population.

Until the Korean War in the early 1950s, there were very few scattered Muslims in Korea. The first presence of Islam as a community in modern times in Korea was due to the arrival of the Turkish forces under the banner of the United Nations during the Korean War. With the Turkish soldiers there was an *imam*. The soldiers built a makeshift mosque in their headquarters for their own usage. Many Koreans who established contacts with the Turkish soldiers were impressed by their Islamic lifestyle. Several of these Koreans adopted Islam and became the first elements of a Muslim community which was soon to grow in numbers.

When the Turkish contingent left for home, the first Korean Muslims started an effort of Islamic propagation among their compatriots. They also established contact with Muslims all over the world from Malaysia to Morocco. By 1963, the number of Muslims reached around a thousand, all converts. Then they felt ready to organize into a community. They did so in 1963, by establishing the Korea Muslim Federation, whose first chairman was Haji Sabri Su Jung-Kil.

The work of organization continued all through the 1960s with a reorganization of the Federation in 1966, the creation of the Korea Islamic Foundation (corresponding to *awqaf* in Muslim countries) in 1967 and the establishment of the Korea Muslim Students Association. Apart from the regular religious and social functions, the federation also takes special interest in providing Islamic education of youth so as to strengthen the Islamic faith of the community, and concerns itself with the establishment of the Islamic institutions. By December 1976, about fifty-three young Muslim Koreans were receiving Islamic education in Indonesia, Malaysia, Pakistan, Saudi Arabia, Egypt, Libya and Morocco.

Since the early 1960s, Korean Muslims have been trying to build their first mosque. Their efforts with the Korean Government started in 1961 and culminated in 1969 when President Park Chung Hee formally donated 5,000 square metres of land in the city of Seoul for the construction of the mosque and Islamic community centre. The planning for the construction of the complex started in October 1972 and construction was completed in May 1976. It cost about US$400,000 a good part of which was borne by the local Muslims and the rest was covered by donations from Muslims overseas. The mosque and the community centre have a total floor space of 2,900 square metres. This includes the main prayer hall, two conference rooms, two office rooms, an Arabic Language Institute, the office of the Korea Islamic Foundation, the missionary workers' room, etc. Another mosque, the Fellagh Mosque, was opened in 1980 in Pusan. In 1980, the entire village of Sang Yong, near the town of Kwangju, converted to Islam. They built the third mosque of Korea in 1981. The Korea Islamic University was launched in 1980 and may be completed soon.

The construction of these institutions and the education of the young in the Islamic faith gave new impetus to the community. By May 1976, the number of Muslims reached 4,000 people, which rose to 7,050 in July 1977, 11,000 in January 1980 and 22,000 in 1982. The imbalance between the male (5,141 Muslims in 1977) and female (1,909 Muslims in 1977) ratio shows that the Muslim population is in a state of dynamic growth, mainly by conversion. Indeed, most of the Muslim males are young and will certainly increase the numbers of the community by conversion through marriage.

The dynamism of the community shows in its initiation of triennial master plans of growth. During the first plan (1974–1976), the Federation launched an Islamic propagation programme through the mass media, started its own publications, intensified Muslim students' activities, increased Arabic language diffusion, established a scholarship foundation, arranged student exchanges between Korea and Muslim countries, founded a Muslim Institute, achieved the translation of the meaning of the *Holy Quran* into the Korean language, etc. The second plan (1977–1982) established Muslim communities around the three mosques as well as the launching of an Islamic university, an Islamic library, a Muslim orphanage and medical facilities. The third plan will see the establishment of local mosques in other areas of Muslim concentration in the country.

The birth of this Muslim community seems to be well accepted by the Korean population. The Muslim community is treated by the Government on an equal footing with other religious groups. Korea itself became closer to the Muslim world by the existence of this community. The latter seems, under the circumstances, guaranteed sustained growth.

In a country where there were no Muslims thirty years ago, we see now in existence a fully-fledged well-organized Muslim community which has the optimism and the dynamism of the young.

## Overall View of Muslim Minorities in the World Today

It would be more appropriate to list the number of Muslims by country after we finish the study of the different communities around the world. To know the importance of the subject, however, it seems appropriate now to estimate the number of Muslims making up these minorities. Based on the censuses of 1982, and the estimates of the minorities themselves, we reach the totals shown in Table 1.1.

Thus, in 1982, there were about 382 million Muslims in the world living as minorities. In 1971 this number was 290 million people. The increase is due to three factors: natural increase; emigration from Muslim countries; and conversion to Islam by non-Muslims. This figure represents more than one third of the entire Muslim community (*ummah*) of the world, which is estimated at about 1 billion people. This third of the Muslim *ummah* often lives in the most tragic circumstances under direct or indirect efforts of assimilation by the majority communities.

*Table 1.1*   Muslims in minority communities, 1982

|  | thousands |
|---|---|
| Asia | 228,000 |
| Africa | 116,000 |
| Europe | 34,000 |
| America | 4,000 |
| Oceania | 300 |
| Total | 382,300 |

## Conclusion

In general, the future of a Muslim minority depends on two important factors. First of all, it depends on the quality of the founding fathers of that community in terms of their attachment to Islam, their enthusiasm and capacity to propagate it, their social influence, etc. In the second place it depends on the conditions under which they have to live. It is perhaps not enough for the Muslims constituting a minority to be just 'good' Muslims, in the narrow sense of the term, to ensure the survival of the community. If those Muslims do not have the means and the desire to transmit their religion to the forthcoming generations, the community is likely to stagnate, then dissipate and ultimately disappear altogether.

Maintenance of ties with the main body of Islam (*dar-al-Islam*) is a very potent factor in the efforts to counteract these developments. Historically speaking, the *Hajj* played a major role in the maintenance of these ties and in the nourishment among Muslims all over the world of a sense of mutual belonging, as well as strengthening and activating their faith in Islam. In addition to that, education of the Muslim children, both religious and cultural (i.e. Arabic, Muslim history, geography of Muslim lands, etc.) should be the first priority of the Muslim community.

Practically, one can see that the odds against the survival of a minority are numerous. Many communities fail in their struggle to survive and only a few do become successful minorities. The chances of survival for a minority would be greatly enhanced, however, if Muslims in minority countries behaved as true members of the Muslim *ummah* by keeping Muslim solidarity working. Muslim countries in dealing with the non-Muslims of the world should never lose sight of the manner in which those countries treat their Muslim minorities. Muslim countries should also consider it a priority to support morally, culturally, politically and otherwise Muslim minorities who are in need of help. Last of all, Islamic solidarity is a necessity for Islamic survival in general. Without it the future of Islam as a whole is endangered.

In summary, if Muslim minorities are allowed to disappear, Muslim majorities would sooner or later follow suit. Supporting Muslim minorities is, therefore, not a matter of opinion for a Muslim; it is an Islamic duty and a necessity for the survival of the entire Muslim *ummah*.

## References

1. M. Ali Kettani, *Muslims in Europe & America*, two volumes (Beirut, Lebanon, 1976) Arabic.
2. Constitution of the Australian Federation of Islamic Councils; 1977.
3. Constitutions of the Islamic Councils of New South Wales, West Australia, New England, Northern California, etc.
4. E. Levi-Provencal, *Histoire de L'Espagne Musulmane*, three volumes (Paris, France).

# 2  Muslims in Europe

## Introduction

In the past, Europe has seen Muslims establish themselves and flourish. The three most important areas where they prospered were Al-Andalus (Muslim Spain and Portugal), Sicily and Crete.

The Andalusian Muslim community began its eventful existence in 711 C.E. when the Muslim General Tariq ibn Ziyad crossed the Strait of Jabal Tariq (Gibraltar: Mountain of Tariq) at the head of his army. This community, after nine centuries of its existence altogether disappeared in 1614 when the last of the Moriscos (forcibly baptized Spanish Muslims) left Spain under the order of expulsion of 1609 which was decreed by the King of Spain. Thus, the Andalusian part of the *ummah* had a life span of 903 years. In Al-Andalus Islamic civilization flourished in one of its most resplendent forms. This land also remained a brilliant seat of Islamic learning that served as the point of radiation for all Europe. Today, only several hundred of these original Muslims have returned to Islam in Al-Andalus, forming burgeoning new Muslim communities. However, descendants of the Andalusians are scattered by the millions in the Mediterranean Muslim countries, especially in North Africa, and keep the memory of their origin and their culture (music, cooking, dialect, last names, etc.) very much alive.

The Muslim community of Sicily which had a history of several hundred years owes its beginning to the efforts of Qadi Asad Ibn Al-Furat in the year 827 during the rule of the Aghlabid dynasty of Tunisia. First, Sicily became part of the Tunisian State. It then became an independent Muslim state under the Kalbid dynasty. The island was finally seized by the Normans with the assistance of the European Christian forces (1061–1091 C.E.). The Muslims who formed the greatest majority of the population even after the Norman conquest, were mainly of Sicilian origin, and remained a tolerated community during the Norman period. With the fall of the Normans and the conquest of the island by the German Emperor Henry VI in 1194, a hostile policy was pursued against the Muslims. This policy sought to obliterate Islam altogether which resulted in forced conversion, expulsion, enslavement, mass murder, etc. A Muslim rebellion followed in 1219 and was crushed in 1224. Muslims were then banished and many of them were sent into exile in Lucera (in the mainland of Italy). It was in 1246 that the Muslim community of Sicily seems to have been completely extinguished after a new rebellion of its members was put down. Thus, the Sicilian Muslim community lasted for a total of 419 years.

Another important centre of Islam in Europe was Crete. A Muslim state was established there in 827 C.E. by Andalusian refugees under the Balluti dynasty. This state lasted until 961 C.E.. The Ottoman Turks reconquered the Island for the Muslims between 1645 and 1669 C.E., but they lost it in 1898 C.E. The Muslim population, which was Greek-speaking, was then subjected to continuous persecution and expulsion that led to a decrease in their percentage of the population from 26.4 per cent in 1881 to 11 per cent in 1900. The entire Muslim population was finally expelled to Turkey in 1923 after an agreement between Greece and Turkey on population exchange.

The Muslim communities which live today in Europe can be divided into two categories: the communities which survived the fall of the Ottoman Empire, concentrated in Eastern Europe; and the communities resulting from immigration due to the colonial past of Europe in Muslim countries. These are concentrated mostly in Western Europe.

Islam started its spread in Eastern Europe long before the Ottoman advance. The Muslim community of Hungary, for instance, was active and prosperous during the tenth and eleventh centuries, until its destruction by Catholic fanaticism in the thirteenth century. The movement of conversion to Islam in Eastern Europe was mainly due to the spread of the Sufi orders which led to the Bogomile heresy within the Christian Churches of Bosnia, Albania and Bulgaria. Bogomiles tended toward the original Christianity which is evident from their rejecting the principles of the trinity, original sin, divinity of Christ, etc. This brought the wrath of the established churches. After the efforts of forcible conversion to the Catholic Church were stepped up by the Kings of Hungary, the Bogomiles requested the intervention of the Muslim forces of the Ottomans in 1463. After the incorporation of the Bogomile lands in the Muslim state, all Bogomiles adopted Islam within about one century. Today the Bosniacs (South-Slav Muslims), Kortesh (Macedonian Muslims), Albanians and Pomaks (Bulgarian Muslims) are descendants of these first Muslims. To them were added immigrants from the two Muslim States of Europe: the Ottoman Empire and the Crimean Khanate.

A majority of the Muslims of Western Europe can be traced to the colonial period. Indeed, the colonial expansion of Europe in the nineteenth and twentieth centuries ended by incorporating most of the Muslim World. This colonization transformed both the

*Table 2.1*   Muslims in Europe, excluding USSR and Turkey, 1982

Source: From official census figures and estimates from different sources, including the Muslim community.

|  | Muslims/percentage of total population | |
| --- | --- | --- |
|  | *thousands* | |
| Yugoslavia | 4,825 | 21.5% |
| France | 2,500 | 4.6% |
| Albania | 2,110 | 75.0% |
| West Germany | 1,800 | 2.9% |
| Bulgaria | 1,700 | 19.3% |
| United Kingdom | 1,250 | 2.2% |
| Netherlands | 400 | 2.8% |
| Belgium | 350 | 3.6% |
| Greece | 160 | 1.6% |
| Cyprus | 155 | 24.4% |
| Spain | 120 | 0.3% |
| Italy | 120 | 0.2% |
| Austria | 80 | 1.1% |
| Switzerland | 70 | 1.1% |
| Romania | 65 | 0.3% |
| Denmark | 35 | 0.7% |
| Sweden | 30 | 0.3% |
| Poland | 22 | 0.06% |
| Norway | 12 | 0.4% |
| Other | 31 | |
| Total | 15,835 | 3.2% |

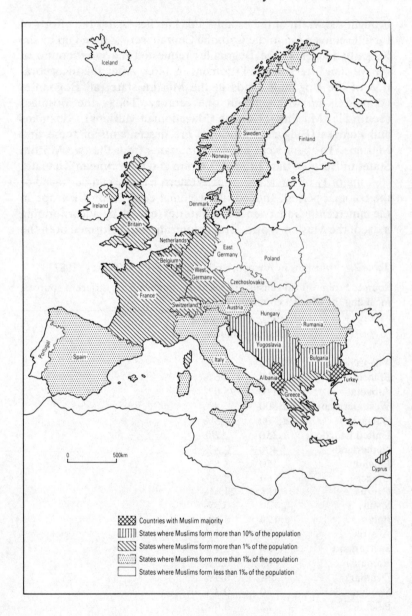

Countries with Muslim majority

States where Muslims form more than 10% of the population

States where Muslims form more than 1% of the population

States where Muslims form more than 1‰ of the population

States where Muslims form less than 1‰ of the population

culture and the economy of Muslim countries, culturally linking each former colony to the colonizing power and converting its economy into an economy of consumption of exported products. The colonial powers ended not only by importing raw materials from their former colonies, but manpower as well when the local manpower could not suffice for the economic expansion of the 1960s.

Figure 1 shows the present distribution of the Muslim minorities in Europe. Excluding the Soviet Union, which will be treated in a separate chapter, and Eastern Thrace, which is part of a Muslim state (Turkey), Muslims in Europe amounted to nearly 11.6 million people in 1971. They could be estimated in 1982 at about 15.8 million. The distribution by states is reported in Table 2.1. The Muslim population exceeds 10 per cent in five countries: Albania (75%), Cyprus (24.4%), Yugoslavia (21.5%), Bulgaria (19.3%) and Gibraltar (10%). It exceeds in numbers the million point in six countries: Albania, Yugoslavia, France, the United Kingdom, West Germany and Bulgaria.

## Albania

Theoretically, this is the only country in Europe with a Muslim majority. Practically, the Albanian Muslims are among the most suppressed communities in the world. Since the government of Albania follows the most fanatical brand of atheism, and since the Muslim majority has no say in its affairs, the Muslims of Albania can be treated as a minority in spite of their numerical majority.

Albania declared its independence from the Ottoman Empire in November 1912. As soon as this was done, the neighbouring Christian powers started invading entire provinces of Albania and incorporating them into their own territories. Serbia acquired Kossovo and Western Macedonia; Montenegro conquered the neighbouring regions and Greece took over Khamiria, including the famous city of Janina. However, while Serbia and Montenegro kept the Albanian population, the Greeks followed a policy of expulsion of Albanian Muslims from the areas they had conquered. The original area of Albania was thus reduced from about 70,000 square kilometres to only 28,748 square kilometres. A conference of European ambassadors then met in London and fixed the boundaries of the new state giving to the conquerors their spoils. Worse, these powers chose a Christian foreigner Prince Wilhem of Weid, to be the King of the new state. The latter remained in Albania only for a few months. A period of about ten years of anarchy followed until Ahmed Beg Zogu declared the state to be a republic with himself as its first president. In 1928, he became the king of the new state. The new kingdom hardly had time to organize itself when it was invaded in 1939 by Italian forces which expelled the king. During World War II, communists organized a guerrilla movement which took over the country at the end of the war. This situation was consolidated on 10 November 1945 when Great Britain, the USSR and the USA recognized the provisional government led by General Enver Hoxha (a communist of Muslim origin) with the condition of holding 'free elections'. The 'free elections' brought into being a parliament controlled by the communists which declared Albania to be a republic in 1946. The group that had come together during World War II is still running the country in accordance with one of the most dogmatic forms of Stalinism.

In 1971, the population of Albania was about 2,220,000 of which 1,580,000 were Muslims. Thus, about 71 per cent of the total population consisted of Muslims. The natural rate of increase of population in Albania is one of the largest in the whole world, with the result that the total population of Albania in 1982 is estimated to be 2,810,000, of which about 2,110,000 or 75 per cent are estimated to be Muslims. Racially, Albanians are the descendants of Illyrians, the ancient inhabitants of the Balkans before the Greek and Slavic invasions. The Muslims are Sunnis and belong to the Hanafi School. The Bektashi Sufi order had a great influence in the country.

Before the communist take-over, Albania was as Muslim a country as any other Muslim country. The laws and customs were deeply rooted in the principles of Islam. The leaders of the country were largely committed to upholding Islamic ideals. There was a Council of Ulema under the chairmanship of a Grand Mufti which managed the mosques and religious schools and supervised the Islamic education of the youth, and had a great influence in legislative matters. In fact, until the country fell a prey to Communist take-over, the Muslim community of Albania had remained religiously organized in the same manner as it had been during the Ottoman period.

After 1946, the Communist establishment began to make attempts to infiltrate the Islamic religious system. Only those religious leaders whose allegiance to the regime was fully assured were allowed to survive. By 1956, the policy of infiltration was followed by a crude policy of repression which culminated in 1967 in the virtual banning of all forms of worship (Muslim and Christian), by closing all mosques and churches in the country, by imprisoning all *imams* and destroying all Muslim literature, and finally by declaring Albania the first atheistic country of the world. In 1976, the government went a step further and banned Muslim names.

At present, the Muslim community of Albania is experiencing one of the darkest moments of its history under a regime which could be compared, by its fanaticism and its oppression, to the Catholic Inquisition established in Spain in the sixteenth century. A vociferous effort is now afoot to destroy all allegiance to Islam in the country. Many mosques have been razed to the ground. People who dare to show religiosity are ridiculed and humiliated, and sometimes have been executed.

However, in spite of this state of affairs, Islam is still very much alive in Albania, albeit in a secret form. This is proved by the accounts of the rare visitors to the country from among the Albanians living abroad. It is also proved by the hysterical campaigns of the government in the press and on the radio against vestiges of Islam.

Albanian Muslims who live outside the present borders of Albania amounted in 1982 to about 2,340,000 people, more than in Albania itself. Of these, 1,810,000 lived in Yugoslavia, 250,000 in Turkey, 70,000 in Arab countries, 40,000 in the USA, 20,000 in Australia and the rest (about 150,000) in other countries, mainly in Canada, Belgium, Italy and New Zealand.

Since 1978, there have been some signs of opening up Albania to its European neighbours. If this trend is continued, there might be some hope of freedom for the population of Albania.

## Yugoslavia

Most of the territories making up today's Yugoslavia, with the exception of Slovenia, formed an integral part of the Muslim Ottoman Empire. Croatia was conquered by Austria in the early seventeenth century, and the Montenegro became independent in 1697. Serbia revolted against the Ottomans and received its independence in 1830. The Muslim populations of these reconquered territories were quickly expelled with the exception of the south west corner of Serbia. In 1878, Austria-Hungary conquered Bosnia-Herzegovina, a region whose population was mainly Slavic and Muslim. Finally, in 1912, Serbia and Montenegro invaded large chunks of the newly formed Albania and added them to their own territories.

The Yugoslav state was established after World War I as a union of Serbia and Montenegro with the Slavic provinces of the defunct Austro-Hungarian Empire. The King of Serbia became King of the newly formed state. The country was invaded by the Germans during World War II. After its liberation by Communist partisans, it was declared a Federal Republic on 13 January 1946. The States of the Federation were reorganized, and in the 1950s Yugoslavia rejected Russian hegemony. Since 1969, the regime has become more and more liberal towards its populations.

The Muslim populations of Yugoslavia were highly persecuted by the Austrian regime in the nineteenth century as well as by the States of Serbia and Montenegro. They gained some degree of freedom between the two World Wars. However, during World War II, they were subjected to the worst atrocities and lost to all kind of partisans more than 200,000 victims in mass executions. The establishment of the Communist regime was first followed by an intense persecution of the Muslim community with confiscation of religious endowments (*awqaf*) and the closing of most of the mosques and religious schools. This situation improved greatly during the last ten years, when Muslims became virtually free to practise their religion.

Indeed, the Government recognized for the first time in 1973 the Bosnian Muslims as a nationality which has its own separate characteristics within the Yugoslav family of nations. At present Yugoslavia consists of six federal states and two autonomous regions. The number of Muslims and their percentages to the total population are shown in Table 2.2. Muslims are in majority in Kossovo, they form 51.6 per cent of the population of Bosnia-Herzegovina, 31.4 per cent of the population of Macedonia, and 25.7 per cent of that of Montenegro. All these percentages have a tendency to increase because of a higher rate of natural increase of Muslims compared to others.

The Muslims of Yugoslavia belong to the Hanafi School of Sunnism. They are well organized under the Muslim Religious Union which has four superiorates in the different Republics: at Sarajevo (Bosnia-Herzegovina), at Skopje (Macedonia), at Titograd (Montenegro) and at Pristina (Kossovo). Mosques and Islamic community centres have been established across the federation including the states of lower Muslim density such as Serbia

*Table 2.2*  Muslims in Yugoslavia

Figures for Muslim populations have been estimated from censuses on nationalities, using some assumptions concerning those Muslims declaring Yugoslav, Croatian or other non-Muslim nationalities. (AO = Autonomous Region.)

| Republic with area in Km² | Population in thousands | | | |
|---|---|---|---|---|
| | 1971 | | 1981 | |
| | Total | Muslim | Total | Muslim |
| Bosnia-Herzegovina 51,129 | 3,746 | 1,541 41.5% | 4,125 | 2,130 51.6% |
| Kossovo (AO) 10,887 | 1,244 | 1,010 81.0% | 1,584 | 1,360 85.6% |
| Macedonia 25,713 | 1,647 | 418 25.0% | 1,912 | 600 31.4% |
| Montenegro 10,275 | 531 | 119 22.4% | 583 | 150 25.7% |
| Serbia (proper) 55,968 | 5,250 | 303 6.0% | 5,687 | 400 7.0% |
| Croatia 56,538 | 4,426 | 124 3.0% | 4,601 | 150 3.3% |
| Slovenia 20,251 | 1,727 | 10 0.5% | 1,891 | 20 1.1% |
| Vojvodina (AO) 21,506 | 1,953 | 12 0.5% | 2,028 | 15 0.7% |
| Total 255,804 | 20,523 | 3,537 17.2% | 22,411 | 4,825 21.5% |

(Belgrad, Nis, etc.), Coatia (Zagreb, Rijeka, etc.) and Slovenia (Ljubliana). The highest religious authority is the Supreme Synod of the Muslim Religious Community which elects a *Reis-Ul-Ulema* (Grand Mufti) and the Muslim Supreme superiorate. The *Reis-Ul-Ulema* today is Imam Naim Hadziabditic and his seat is Sarajevo, capital of Bosnia-Herzegovina. The Muslim community of Yugoslavia has today about two thousand mosques and new ones are always under construction. It has two schools for the training of *imams* (secondary school level) one at Sarajevo (in the Serbo-Croatian language), and the other at Pristina (in Albania). A third one is being reopened in Skopje, capital of Macedonia. In the autumn of 1977, an Islamic faculty of the university level was reopened in renovated buildings after being closed for more than thirty years. (The faculty was established in 1536 C.E. by Gazi Husrewbeg). There are three Islamic reviews in the Croatian language (Glasnik, Zemzem and Preporod) and one in the Albanian language (Educate Islame).

As for the national origin of Muslims of Yugoslavia, the most numerous are the Bosniacs (2,340,000 in 1981) who share with the Serbo-Croatians racial origin as well as language. They are highly sophisticated and well integrated in the political life of the country. The second in number are Albanians (1,730,000 in 1981) who live mainly in the State of Kossovo, but also in neighbouring regions. Their most important political demand is the establishment of a Federal Republic for their Autonomous State. The Turks, only about 120,000 in 1981, are concentrated in Macedonia where they have sixty-five primary schools. Finally, Gypsy Muslims (100,000 in 1981) are among the poorest of all Muslims and live mostly a nomadic life across the Federation. There are also several thousand Muslims who identify themselves as Croatians, Serbians, Macedonian, Circassians, etc. But all the smaller Muslim groups have a tendency to be absorbed by the two larger ones: the Bosniacs and the Albanians.

In conclusion, the situation of Muslim Yugoslavs, which has not yet reached, in many respects, the level of the inter-war period, is improving greatly. The community has all the characteristics of a viable and well integrated community which has a reasonable degree of freedom of worship. Its contact with the Muslim world is increasing; more delegations are sent to Muslim countries, more students are exchanged, and about two thousand pilgrims go to Mecca annually. Because of its treatment of the Muslim community which is not different from its treatment of other religious groups in the country, the Yugoslav government has built up a capital of respect in all Muslim countries.

## Bulgaria

Under continuous pressure from the Russian Empire, the Ottoman State was forced in 1878 to give autonomy to the two principalities of Rumelia and East Rumelia. The two principalities united in 1885 to form one single state which declared its independence in 1908 under the name of the Kingdom of Bulgaria. Since then, the boundaries of the new state have been changed twice, once after World War I and another time after World War II. In 1946, the Communist Party took power, abolished monarchy and declared Bulgaria a Socialist Republic. This same regime is still in power in the country till this day.

In 1850, about one third of the population of the lands which today form Bulgaria was Muslim. About 500,000 persons of these were Pomaks, i.e. Bulgarian-speaking Muslims. Even in 1876, Muslims were in majority in many major cities, such as Varna, Plovdiv (Filipe), Pleven, etc. They were also an important minority in the city of Sofia. After the Crimean War, the Ottoman State installed Muslim refugees from Crimea in the area, or about a total of 350,000 people of whom 100,000 were Tartars and 90,000 were Circassians. But the Turco-Russian War of 1877 was catastrophic to the Muslim population. It led to great dislocation and mass emigration to Anatolia.

Persecution of the Muslim community increased in intensity after independence in 1908, which led to a new wave of emigration towards Turkey. In fact, the Royal Government of Bulgaria was consistent in following a policy of elimination of the Muslim population with a zeal tainted with religious fanaticism. This led to the reduction of the Muslim population from about 50 per cent in 1876 to a mere 13 per cent in 1939 with only 858,000 Muslims in a total population of 6,600,000.

The policy of expulsion of Muslims continued during the first years of the Communist regime. Indeed, in 1951 alone about 160,000 Bulgarian Muslims were expelled towards Turkey. But as the natural rate of increase of Bulgarian Christians was too low, the Communist government of Bulgaria started to worry about the economic dangers resulting from the depopulation of entire regions. It thus replaced its policy of expulsion by one of forced assimilation, i.e. Christianization. Nevertheless, in the 1970s, both expulsion and assimilation were pursued against the Muslims. About 115,140 Muslims (ethnic Turks) were expelled to Turkey in the decade 1968–1978 under an agreement on the reunion of divided families which was signed in March 1968 and which expired in December 1978.

At present, Bulgaria has an area of 110,912 square kilometres and it had a population of 8,814,000 people in 1982. The same year the Muslim population was about 1,700,000 strong. Muslims of Bulgaria are Sunnis of the Hanafi School. Ethnically, they are divided into three groups: the Turks, including Tartars (about 1,050,000 people in 1982); the Pomaks, or Bulgarian Muslims (370,000 people in 1982); and the Gypsies (of whom about 280,000 people were Muslims in 1982). Thus, in spite of continuous expulsions, the proportion of Muslims in the entire population increased from 13 per cent in 1939 to about 17 per cent in 1971, and 19.3 per cent in 1982.

Geographically, Muslims are concentrated in two separate regions, in the north-east near the Rumanian border, and in the south-west, near the Greek border. They form the majority in seven provinces. Five of these are in the northeast (Silistra, Tulbuhin, Razgrad, Shumen and Turgovi) where Muslims are Turkish-speaking; the other two provinces are in the south (Smolyan and Kurzali) and are strongholds of the Pomaks. About 900,000 Muslims live in the northeast; 500,000 Muslims live in the south-east and the remaining 300,000 are scattered about the entire country.

There do not seem to be many mosques still open in Bulgaria today. In 1966, there were 1,300 mosques, of which 1,180 were Turkish-speaking and 120 Bulgarian-speaking. In 1956, there were about 2,715 *imams* serving the Muslim community. The Muslims were religiously organized under a Grand Mufti. Bulgaria was divided into six religious regions, each region having a *Majlis-Ul-Ulema*. The Mufti for the Turkish speakers had Burgaz as a seat (Imam Hasan Adamov) and the Mufti for the Bulgarian speakers had Smolyan as a seat (Imam Husayn Seferkov).

This organization exists only in name today. In fact Bulgarian Muslims are experiencing a period of intense persecution and cultural genocide. There are no schools for *imams* and no religious Islamic literature (the Christian counterparts are, on the other hand, thriving). Most of the mosques of the country have been closed down, including the single remaining mosque of Sofia. Muslims are forced to change their names to Christian names under the cover of Bulgarization; Christian names are considered Bulgarian, Muslim names are 'of course' foreign. All Islamic holidays have been abolished and any outside appearance of Islam severely suppressed. Many mosques have been razed to the ground. Muslims have been pushed down to the lower classes of the social order. Publication and purchase of Muslim books including the Quran have been forbidden. No contact with the Muslim *ummah* is allowed and no pilgrims have reached Mecca for decades.

The difference between the Albanian and the Bulgarian persecutions of Muslims is that in the first case, persecution is against all forms of religion, whereas in the second case it is against Muslims alone. The Bulgarian Government supports intensely the Bulgarian Orthodox Church and respects the religious practices of Jews and other Christian denominations. New churches and synagogues are under construction, whereas mosques are demolished.

The situation of the Muslim community of Bulgaria is as serious as that of Albania. The Muslim World worries intensely about the efforts of destruction against such an important community.

## Cyprus

Cyprus was part of the Ottoman Empire until 1878 when the Sultan was forced to accept the British presence on the island with the condition of keeping Ottoman sovereignty over it. In 1914, Britain abolished unilaterally the 1878 agreement and declared the island Crown Colony. The young Turkish Republic (inheritor of the Ottoman State) recognized this state of affairs in 1925. In 1955, the Greeks of the island started a terrorist campaign against the British in an effort to unite the island with Greece (Enosis). The Muslim community, keeping a fresh memory of what happened in nearby Crete just half a century earlier, opposed Enosis which they felt would have led to their expulsion from their homeland. The Muslims (Turkish-speaking) and the Greeks (Greek Orthodox by religion), the former supported by Turkey and the latter by Greece, finally agreed to the formation of an independent Cypriot State on 19 February 1959 in Zurich. This agreement was signed by Turkey, Greece, Great Britain and the representatives of both Greek-Cypriot and Turkish-Cypriot communities. This agreement was implemented on 16 August 1960. It guaranteed the independence of Cyprus and safeguarded the vital interests of both communities.

When the Cypriot President (Greek) repudiated unilaterally the Zurich agreement in December 1963, a civil war broke out which nearly ended in the destruction of the Cypriot Muslim community. This community found itself blockaded inside seventy-five enclaves which were scattered across the island and subjected to intolerable economic pressure. It was also completely removed from all political and economic activity in the country. Without intense financial support from Turkey the resistance of the community for survival would have collapsed. During this period, negotiations between the two communities dragged on as the Greek-Cypriots seemed uninterested in changing the status quo. When on 15 July 1974 a Greek-Cypriot military coup took place and was followed by the mass murders of Muslims, Turkey found itself obliged to intervene to fulfil its obligations under the Zurich Agreement. The Turkish intervention saved the Muslim community of the island from the annihilation which had seemed imminent. Thus began a completely new era for the Turkish-Cypriot community.

The area of Cyprus is 9,251 square kilometres. In 1973, it had a total population of 632,000 people of which 116,000 were Muslims, all Turkish speaking and of the Hanafi School. The percentage of Muslims in the entire population amounted to 18.3 per cent. This figure compares poorly with the census of 1790 which showed a total population of 80,000 people of which 60,000 were Muslims, i.e. a Muslim proportion of 75 per cent. After British colonization, Muslim emigration (more or less induced) and Greek (Christian) immigration reduced the proportion of Muslims to 19.7 per cent in 1921 (61,339 people). Because of continuous discrimination and often outright persecution from 1878 up to 1974, there was a continuous flow of Muslim emigration from the island. The number of Cypriot Muslims forming the Turkish-Cypriot diaspora amounted to about 700,000 people in 1982, of which 550,000 were in Turkey, about 60,000 in Britain, and 40,000 in Australia, etc.

The Turkish intervention of 1974 revitalized the Cypriot Muslim community and gave it new hope. Of the six provinces which form the state of Cyprus, this intervention gave the Muslim community the entire Province of Kyrenia, half the Province of Nicosia, 90 per cent of the Province of Famagousta and about 10 per cent of the Province of Larnaca, i.e. about 3,354 square kilometres or 36 per cent of the area of the island. In fact, this resulted in a great movement of Muslim and Christian populations. Indeed, in 1960, Muslim presence was more dense in the provinces of Paphos (23%), Larnaca, Nicosia and Famagousta (20% each) and less in the provinces of Kyrenia (13%) and Limassol (11%). Thus, about 60,000 Muslims have been uprooted from their homes in the southern part of the island and about 120,000 Christians were uprooted from the northern part. This led to a polarization of the population of the island with few Greeks left in the Turkish part and few Turks in the Greek part. The total Cypriot Muslim population reached about 155,000 people in 1982 due to the return of some Turkish-Cypriot expatriates to their homeland. The new Muslim percentage is about 24.4 per cent, about the same as that of 1881.

On 13 February 1975, the Turkish-Cypriot community declared the establishment of the Turkish-Cypriot Federal State. The efforts of this state are directed toward finding a solution to the constitutional problem of the Cypriot State and a new relationship between the Greek and the Turkish parts of the country. The

Muslim community refuses to go back to the status quo ante because this status had almost led to its doom. They are feeling that the Greek-Cypriots could not accept them as equals in their midst and respect them for what they are: Turkish by language and Muslim by religion. They seek a guarantee for their future in a bi-state federal system. Unfortunately, the negotiations drag on and the Turkish-Cypriot Federal State finds itself under a new economic boycott by the world community. Indeed, while the so-called Cypriot Government represents in fact only the Greek-Cypriot community, it is considered by most countries of the world, including Muslim countries (out of ignorance or big power pressure?) as the legitimate representative of the Turkish-Cypriots as well. All economic co-operation, exchange, services, etc. with Cyprus is done with the Greek side and the only outlet to the outside world of the Turkish side is through Turkey. There is, however, no comparison between this situation and that of the 1970s. In its state, the Muslim community lives its religious and cultural life without any outside interference. Its hope for a better future is based on solid foundations and it tries to reach some arrangement with the Greek-Cypriot state that will give both of them the right to live as equals on their island. On 15 November 1983, the Turkish side, tired of waiting for the Greek side to solve their common problem, declared its independence as the Turkish Republic of North Cyprus.

## France

France has an area of 547,026 square kilometres and, in 1971, a population of 54,350,000 people. It is administratively divided into twenty-two regions. The majority of its Muslim population is of colonial origin. By 1900, the French Empire included a multitude of Muslim countries, the most important of them being Algeria. But until then, Muslim emigration to France had remained negligible. Indeed in 1900, there were only 1,000 Muslims in France. They became 6,000 in 1912.

After World War I, a severe manpower shortage was felt in France and to make up for this Algerian immigration was encouraged. In 1924, the Muslim population reached 120,000 people falling to 70,000 in 1936 due to the economic recession. Muslim immigration into France took a new upward trend after World War II, with the Muslim population reaching 240,000 people in 1950.

The greatest emigration toward France of Muslim populations started, however, after the independence of the colonies, especially Algeria. By 1971, the Muslim population surpassed two million people making it the second religion of the country after Roman Catholicism. By 1982, this figure had reached about 2.5 million people (or about 4.6 per cent of the population) making it, in number, the second largest Muslim population of Europe after Yugoslavia. At present, immigration has become considerably less important, and the Muslim population grows mostly by natural increase and conversion.

Although the Muslim community of France is only second to that of Yugoslavia in Europe, it is much less rooted in the country and far less organized. Of the 2.5 million Muslims in France in 1982, about 1,960,000 were of North African origin. The others came from Black Africa, Yugoslavia, the Arab East, Turkey and Iran. There were about 70,000 Muslims of French ethnic origin. Indeed, the trend of conversion to Islam had already started at the turn of the century, and many French have been Muslim for two or three generations. Most Muslims of France are of the Maliki School.

Among the Muslim immigrants, about 600,000 are French citizens. Their majority, about 450,000, consists of the Harkis of Algeria and their descendants (Harkis were Muslim soldiers in the French army who fought against the Algerian revolution). Consequently, in spite of the fact that French is understood by most Muslims in France, these are however in their majority, Arabic speakers. Geographically, Muslims are found in all parts of France, with a higher concentration in the regions of Paris (Region Parisienne), Marseilles (Provence Côte-d'Azur) and Lyons (Rhônes-Alpes).

Most of the Muslims of France occupy the less attractive occupations and make up the 'proletariate' of the French cities. A small minority are professional, especially in the Paris region. In principle and in appearance, the rights of Muslims as individuals are respected by the French law. However, as a community, the Muslims are suffering in France from an anti-Islamic attitude which may be traced back to the time of the Crusades, and by a racism reminiscent of the colonial period. The influence of the Muslim community in France is negligible in practically all fields, especially if one were to compare it to the much smaller Jewish and Protestant communities.

Until 1968, there was practically no religious organization of the

Muslim community, and Muslims practised their religion privately. True, there has been a large mosque in Paris since 1930, but this was never controlled by the Muslim community of France. The recent efforts at organization started on a local scale as an increasing number of Muslims settled in the country and became concerned about the religious future of their children. Spontaneous religious associations were formed, establishing mosques and Quranic schools for children. The buildings of mosques and schools were often very modest, but the effort was sincere and the results were encouraging. The number of such makeshift mosques reached 410 in 1982. There were only ten about fifteen years ago. One single mosque, the Jami Mosque of Paris, has all the facilities necessary for a Muslim Community Centre. It also manages thirty mosques in the Paris region. However, the Paris Jami Mosque is managed now by Algeria and not by the Muslim Community of France. There are 150 mosques in the Paris region (of which twenty-three are in Paris city), sixteen mosques in Lyons, fifteen in Marseilles, etc.

For instance, if Auvergne is taken as an example, one sees that Clermont-Ferrand, the capital of the region, has four mosques, each in a room no larger than 30 square metres. In each mosque, weekly meetings and friday prayers are held, and religious instruction for children and adults is carried out. The Mayor's office donated to the community a piece of land to be used as a cemetery for Muslims. The town of Vichy has also a mosque in a rented building, and a mosque is planned for Thiers. The Muslims of Auvergne formed in 1976 the Council of the Muslims of Clermont-Ferrand, thus increasing the organizational scale from the local to the regional level.

There is no national organization for the Muslims of France, no schools for *imams* or for the Muslim children, and no Council of *Imams*. However, it seems that the Muslims of French origin are well organized. There are also several national organizations for Muslims which belong to the same country called Amicales (Algerian, Moroccan, Tunisian, etc.), but their effect on the survival of the Muslims as a community is small.

The Muslim population of France is not organized. Therefore, its chances of survival as a community are minimal if no changes take place in this situation. However, it is heartening to note that the community is moving through a normal phase of organization. If this trend continues, the Muslim community of France would eventually establish some form of national organization that would enable the growth of the necessary Islamic institutions. This community is however handicapped in its efforts by a lack of acceptance by the French authorities and population and the strong attraction of the countries of origin which are too close to allow the community to build its independent Islamic culture. Muslims as a community are not treated on the same footing by the French authorities with the other religious groups. But this discrimination is certainly due to the inertia in the laws and the present weak organization of the Muslims, rather than to a deliberate policy.

## West Germany

Among the western nations, Germany had colonized only a few Muslim areas (Tanganyika and Cameroun) and for a limited period of time. This German colonial period had no effect on the growth of the Muslim community of Germany. On the other hand, no part of the present day West Germany was ever part of any Muslim state. Consequently, the origins of the Muslim population of West Germany are different from that of France as well as from that of Yugoslavia.

The first modern traces of Muslim presence in Germany date from the eighteenth century when Prussia and the Ottoman State decided to exchange embassies. During the same period a mosque was built in Schwatzingen (near Stuttgart) by a German nobleman convert to Islam. This was the first mosque in Germany. During the nineteenth century many Germans embraced Islam. But their number remained limited.

A stronger link was established between Germany and the Muslim World during World War I, when Germany and the Ottoman State were fighting as allies a war which both were to lose. After the war, many Muslim prisoners of war freed by the Allied forces preferred to settle in Germany, especially in Berlin. Immigrants from Afghanistan and Iran later joined this first nucleus.

Between the world wars, the number of Muslims in Germany did not exceed a few thousand. However, after World War II, a new wave of Muslims settled in Germany. These were Muslim prisoners of war originally from Communist countries, especially the Soviet Union, who requested asylum in that part of Germany which was under Western control (later to become the Federal Republic of Germany, i.e. West Germany). In 1951, there were in West Germany about 20,000 Muslims.

It was only after 1966 that the number of Muslims started to increase dramatically in West Germany. This was due mainly to the immigration of guest workers from Muslim countries, especially Turkey.

In 1971 the number of Muslims was about 1,150,000 people (1.9 per cent of the total population) of which 900,000 were Turks, 150,000 Yugoslavs and Albanians, 50,000 North Africans, and 50,000 Muslims of different ethnic origins of whom about 20,000 were from Soviet Central Asia and several thousand were of German origin (many for several generations). Among this large number of Muslims, about 50,000 were German citizens, either by origin or by naturalization. Consequently, most of West German Muslims are still foreigners who have not put down any roots in the country. Since 1971, the number of Muslims has continued to increase to about 1,800,000 Muslims in 1982 (2.9 per cent of the population) in spite of the end of Muslim immigration and the return of many guest workers to their countries of origin. This is due mainly to natural increase as those who remained behind are raising new families and are striking deeper roots in the country. Of the total of 1.7 million Muslims in 1982, about 1.5 million were of Turkish origin.

Of this total, about 1,650,000 were of the Hanafi School, 80,000 of Maliki School, 20,000 of the Shafi School and 20,000 of the Jafari School (especially in Hamburg).

Geographically, Muslims are present in all German states, with higher concentration in Bayern (about 250,000 Muslims) and Rhenania-Westphalia (about 400,000 Muslims). There are 600,000 children in the community and 40,000 students (from foreign-countries) in the universities and professional schools. Aside from students and several thousand professionals, most of the Muslims of West Germany are blue-collar workers occupying the least desirable occupations. Politically, the influence of the community is negligible, even that part of the community which is made up of German citizens.

The Muslims of West Germany are at the beginning of their organizational effort. The first local Islamic organizations were established after World War I. The first mosque, that of Schwatzingen, became a museum, and was reconverted for Islamic worship only in March 1977. The mosque of Potsdam near Berlin, built in 1720, disappeared, but a new mosque was built in 1926. This mosque survived World War II, but it is no more in Muslim hands for it has been taken over by Qadianis. There are four other mosques in West Germany with Muslim architectural designs: The Hamburg Mosque, the Aachen Mosque (opened in 1967), the Munich Mosque (opened in 1973) and the Stadt Allendorf (Hessen) Mosque. But a multitude of makeshift mosques totalling about 600 play a big role in keeping Islam alive in the country. These are houses, apartments, rooms, halls owned or rented by Muslim religious groups. In these makeshift mosques as well as in the more sophisticated big centres, prayers are held, including Friday prayers, Islamic education is imparted to children and adults, community services are administered, etc. Some cities have many of these mosques, for instance, Cologne has forty-two mosques for a Muslim population of 80,000. The most important of these mosques are those of Cologne, Frankfurt, Stuttgart, Nurenberg, Saarbruck, Hanover, Hamburg, Munster (Westphalia), Bielefeld, Hamm (Westphalia), Munich, Lubeck and West Berlin. Each of these 600 mosques is organized and maintained by a local Muslim organization. There are about 350 Turkish *imams* in the country and about fifty *imams* of other origins, but their number is much less than needed. There are about thirty-five Quranic schools and only one full-time Muslim primary school. Islam is not taught to Muslim children in German schools. There are no Muslim regional organizations yet, nor are there national ones. The large Islamic centres developed on a very inefficient organizational pattern in which each centre is run by a closed Muslim organization which is not limited territorially. They have consequently been only slightly effective in their Islamic missions.

Legally, the Muslim community of West Germany is handicapped by the fact that most of its members are foreigners. The rights of individual Muslims are, however, more and more respected. But the Muslim community as a whole is not recognized by the Federal Republic as a religious community with the result that Muslims as a community have no rights. For more than thirty years, the community has been pleading for recognition (*koperschaft*) but to no avail. German converts are subject to indirect discrimination and many of them feel forced to keep their religious convictions secret.

Thus, as in France, the basic problem of the Muslim community of West Germany is one of organization. But this is a normal transitional process, and the community seems to be heading toward a national organization. Maybe it is only then that enough pressure could be put on the German authorities for the rights of the Muslim community to be recognized and thus stand on an equal footing with the other religious communities of the country. Unless this is done the future of Islam in West Germany will remain unpredictable.

## The United Kingdom

The history of the growth of the Muslim community of Great Britain is similar to that of France. The community has its roots in the colonial past of the country.

The first Muslim immigrants to Britain were Yamanis from Aden, who established themselves in Cardiff and built there in 1870 one of the first mosques of the country. Before the turn of the century other Muslims came from India and settled near London where they built Shah Jehan Mosque in Woking. During the first half of this century Muslims arrived in Britain from Cyprus, Egypt and Iraq. On the eve of World War II, the Muslim population of the UK already numbered 50,000 people.

Immigration increased dramatically after the War doubling the number of Muslims to 100,000 by 1950. This immigration reached new peaks in the 1960s, especially from India, Pakistan and Bangladesh. In the 1970s, however, the British Government became more strict about foreign immigration from former colonies, with the result that the inflow of Muslims from outside has recently slowed down.

By 1971, there were about one million Muslims in the UK, or 1.8 per cent of the total population. This figure rose in 1982 to 1,250,000 Muslims (2.2 per cent of the population). The Muslim community of the UK is better organized than that of France, or even West Germany, but less than that of Yugoslavia. At least 700,000 of the total number of Muslims were British citizens in 1982. They are originally from lands where Muslims have been either preponderant or at least had large communities for a long time. The converts from Britain and the West Indies number several thousand. A great majority of them are originally from the Indian sub-continent (about 900,000 people). Others come from about ten other countries most important of which are Cyprus, Yemen, Iraq and Palestine. There are also about 30,000 Muslim students in British Universities. The majority of the Muslims are of the Hanafi School, the rest are Shafi, Jafari or Ismaili.

On the whole, the Muslims of Britain are at a slightly higher level, in terms of social status, than the Muslims of France and West Germany. They comprise professionals, physicians, engineers and other white collar workers. The majority, however, consist of factory workers or small business employees. Geographically, about 40 per cent of all Muslims of Britain are in the Greater London Region. The others are in great majority in Lancashire, Yorkshire and Midlands. Politically, the influence of the Muslim community is meagre but not altogether negligible. At present the Muslim population increases mostly by natural excess of births over deaths.

The efforts of organization of the Muslim community are in their first stages. Most of the Muslims of the country are already organized on a local scale within about two hundred local religious organizations. Usually, each one of these organizations has its own mosque, and covers the Muslims of one city or one district of a city. Most of these mosques are makeshift ones, but several are large community centres as well. Of these one can cite Shah Jehan Mosque (Woking, 1870), Nour-Al-Islam Mosque (Cardiff); the mosques of Coventry, Liverpool, Preston, Birmingham, Manchester and Nottingham. Many abandoned churches have been bought by local Muslim groups and converted into mosques such as in Manchester, Bristol and Sheffield. There are about one hundred mosques in the Greater London area, fifty in Lancashire, forty in Yorkshire and thirty in the Midlands. There are three mosques in Scotland, two in Wales and one in Northern Ireland (Belfast). The Central Mosque of London was opened for worship in 1977. It is not administered, however, by the Muslim community of Britain. It was established by the Muslim diplomatic corps representing different Muslim countries. It is an institution for, though not of, the Muslim community of Britain. The establishment of this mosque goes back to 1940. It is at present administered by a Council of Ambassadors.

The local Muslim religious organizations have already started an organizational effort among themselves on a national scale. But this effort is still weak and not very effective. The 'Union of Muslim Organisations' (UMO) formed in 1970 had a membership of about 200 Muslim organizations in 1982. It is the most serious organizational effort at a national level in Britain, but the institutional relationship between the different organizations in the Union is very weak and therefore the efficacy of UMO as the representative of the Muslims of Britain has yet to be proved. Its most important activity is an annual convention. The services that it should have rendered to the community are rendered however by service organizations whose activity encompasses all Great

Britain. For instance, the Islamic Foundation, established in Leicester in 1968, specializes in the publication of Islamic literature in English; the Muslim Womens' Association, established in 1962, concerns itself with the problems of Muslim women and orphans; and the 'Muslim Educational Trust' established in 1966, specializes in the Islamic education of Muslim children. The latter was able to obtain from the British Government the right to teach Islam to Muslim children in public schools. They now have about twenty teachers (paid by the organization) who teach about 2,500 children in fifty-six schools in eight British cities. Arrangements for Islamic education exist in several mosques.

There is no separation of Church and State in the UK. The recognized religions, such as Roman Catholicism, Judaism, etc., receive the support of the state at the same level as the official Anglican Church. Islam is not recognized, and consequently Muslims find themselves religiously quite handicapped, financially and otherwise. Even the marriage celebrated by an *imam* is not recognized as is done in some other countries, whereas marriages celebrated by priests and rabbis are.

Thus, in the UK again, the basic problem of the Muslim community is the lack of a strong organizational set-up on the national level. This leads to a lack of recognition by the authorities and a weakness in the services offered, especially in the area of education of the children. The Muslims of Britain suffer also from racial discrimination to as great an extent as their brothers in West Germany and France. In general, however, the condition of the Muslim community seems to be improving.

## Other Countries

There are Muslims in all the other countries of Europe and they are organized in most of these countries. Their situation varies from one country to another in terms of number, origin, organization and acceptability. In the following pages, the situation of the Muslim communities in each of these countries will be considered briefly, in order of numerical importance.

In 1971, about 1 per cent of the population of the Netherlands, or about 132,000 was Muslim. By 1982, this number rose to about 400,000 (2.8 per cent of the total population). The first Muslim immigrants arrived between the two world wars from the former colonies of Indonesia and Surinam. Their number was very limited and barely reached 5,000 in 1950. In 1982, there were among the

Muslims of the Netherlands about 220,000 Turks, 100,000 North Africans, 40,000 Malays (Indonesians and Malaysians) and 40,000 Muslims of various origins including about 2,000 Dutch converts. About 40,000 Muslims are Dutch citizens. Most of the Muslims of the Netherlands are blue collar workers and are concentrated in the large cities. About 60,000 Muslims live in Amsterdam alone. The first Muslim organizations which attempted to bring together Muslims of the same national origin were established in the 1960s. In 1974, these organizations united to form the Union of the Islamic Organizations of the Netherlands. There are about 300 makeshift mosques in the country. The Muslim embassies are planning an Islamic Centre in Amsterdam. The Dutch Government recognizes Islamic marriage, but in spite of the continuous request of Muslims, Islam is not recognized in the Netherlands on the same footing with other religious bodies. There are no Islamic schools, but some Islamic education is imparted to some Muslim children in public schools by teachers sent by Turkey and Morocco.

In 1971, there were 121,000 Muslims in Belgium (or about 1.3 per cent of the population). The first Muslim immigrants arrived in Belgium after World War I from eastern Europe, especially Albania. Immigration in sizeable numbers started, however, in the 1960s. By 1982, there were about 350,000 Muslims in Belgium (or about 3.6 per cent of the total population) of whom 220,000 were North Africans, 80,000 Turks, 15,000 Albanians and 35,000 Muslims of various origins, including about 2,000 converts. There are about 2,000 Muslim students in the universities and about 80,000 children in the community. Most of the Muslims are foreign workers; only about 20,000 are Belgian citizens. There are about 200 makeshift mosques in Belgium, each administered by the local Muslim community. The Mosques of Liege and Gant are converted churches. In 1977, the remodelled old mosques of the Place du Cinquantenaire in Brussels, built in 1883 was renovated by donations from Saudi Arabia and opened for worship. This mosque is administered by a Council of Ambassadors from Muslim countries and not by the Muslim community itself. There is no national organization of the Muslims of the country. Nevertheless, Islam was recognized officially in July 1974 by the Government, thus treating the Muslim community on the same footing as the other religious communities of Belgium.

The Muslim community of Greece was very important in numbers until recently. Many of these Muslims were Greek by origin and language. The Greek State has been extremely unkind to Muslims: massacres and expulsions in the nineteenth century reduced the Muslim community to only a fraction of what it used to be (30 per cent of the population in 1828). The 1923 Treaty of Lausanne, stipulating the exchange of populations between Turkey and Greece brought the extinction of the Muslim community in most parts of Greece, excepting Western Thrace (in exchange for Greeks in Istanbul) and Rhodes and Chios (which was an Italian colony). Massacres in Epyrus after World War II eliminated the Muslim community of Epyrus (Albanian). In 1920, there were 285,000 Muslims in Western Thrace, or 75 per cent of the population. Slow persecution reduced this number to 120,000 by 1982 or 31.4 per cent of the population. In 1982, there were also about 15,000 Muslims in Rhodes and Chios and 35,000 Muslims in Athens, thus a total of 160,000 Muslims or 1.6 per cent of the population of Greece. The core of the Muslim community of Greece is in Western Thrace where Muslims were divided into two ethnic groups: Pomaks, (Bulgarian-speaking, 40,000 in 1982) along the border with Bulgaria, who are shepherds; and the Turks, who are farmers. Muslims have been organized under the Association of Islamic Union since 1932. They have 200 primary schools, four secondary schools and 300 mosques. The community is subject to considerable persecution: economically, the Muslims are squeezed out of their land (they owned 94 per cent of land in 1923, only 30 per cent today) and their institutions are destroyed. For instance, in Komotini the Greek Government took over the Gazi Evranos Religious Foundation and Imaret Mosque; it destroyed the Jami Mosque of Xanthi as well as the Tabakhane Mosque; at Dimetoka twelve mosques, five mausoleums, four Islamic schools and two *waqf* buildings have been taken over or demolished, all this since the 1960s; even Muslim cemeteries are desecrated. The schools are being suffocated by stopping the immigration of qualified teachers etc. In short, the attitude of the Government of Greece toward its Muslim citizens is almost as unfriendly as that of the Bulgarian Government.

There were about 90,000 Muslims in Spain in 1971, of whom about 13,000 were Spanish citizens. There were about 120,000 in 1982. Most of these Muslims are foreign workers especially from North Africa. The Spanish Inquisition against Islam in the sixteenth century which destroyed the Muslim community actually lasted until 1967 when for the first time in Spain freedom of religion was allowed. Complete religious freedom was established after the death of General Franco in 1975. However, centuries of misinformation by the Spanish Catholic Church against Islam had a bad effect on the population forcing many Spanish Muslims to keep their religious convictions secret for fear of persecution. Nevertheless, Muslims, among whom there are students in universities and workers in factories, succeeded in establishing Muslim associations in most major cities as well as about forty makeshift mosques across the country. Since 1980, a great number of Andalucians returned to Islam, especially in the Region of Andalucia. They formed organizations, the most important of which are the Comunidad Islamica en Al-Andalus with sections in Seville, Granada, Malaga, and Jerez and Comunidad Islamica en Espana in Granada. The Muslim embassies are planning to build a mosque in Madrid on land offered by the municipality. The Union of Muslim Students' Associations, attracting mostly foreign students, has its headquarters in Madrid and sections in major Spanish cities.

There were about 50,000 Muslims in Italy in 1971. In 1982, there were about 120,000, mostly immigrants from eastern Europe, Northern Africa and Somalia. They are concentrated in Milan, Rome and Sicily. The Muslims of Italy are not well organized. After World War II, a Union of the Muslims of the West was established by the Muslim refugees from eastern Europe. This organization was unfortunately eclipsed by the Islamic Centre of Rome, established by Muslim embassies. This centre is planning to build a large mosque in the city. At present the mosque is located, however, in an apartment in Rome where prayers are held, education imparted and Islamic literature disseminated.

There were about 35,000 Muslims in Austria in 1971, and about 80,000 in 1982 of whom about 8,000 are Austrian citizens. The rest are mostly workers from Yugoslavia and Turkey. Muslims are well organized in Austria under the Muslim Social Service established in 1962. This organization established a mosque and a community centre in downtown Vienna and caters for the religious needs of the Muslims of Klagenfurt and Salzburg as well. They are holding discussions with the Austrian authorities for the recognition of Islam in the country on the same footing as other religious groups. Muslim embassies established a large mosque and Islamic community centre in the outskirts of the city of Vienna. This project was started in 1967.

There were 30,000 Muslims in Switzerland in 1971 and about 70,000 in 1982. There are many foreign workers and students among them, and at least 4,000 Swiss converts, many of whom keep their religion a secret. There were about 10,000 Swiss citizens among the Muslims in 1982. The first Muslim organization was established in Geneva in the 1960s, but it was not based on the community. Muslim enbassies established the Islamic Institute in Geneva in 1972 and a large mosque and Islamic community centre was built in 1978. There are Muslim organizations in Zurich and Lausanne as well.

The Muslim population of Rumania (260,000 people), was prosperous and well organized before World War II, but was greatly reduced in numbers after the war due to the redemarcation of boundaries. It could be estimated at about 50,000 in 1971 and about 65,000 in 1982. These Muslims are of Turco-Tartar origin and are based in the Dobrudja Region near the Black Sea with their centre at Constanta. Most of the Muslims are farmers and employees. These Muslims are subjected to more or less the same degree of persecution as the Muslims of Bulgaria. Out of hundreds of mosques in pre-war times only one dozen mosques are presently open for worship. The Muslims are organized religiously under the leadership of a mufti in Constanta, but their religious freedom is tampered with, their religious literature suppressed and their *imam* schools have been closed. Turkish is not taught and the new generation finds language a serious barrier between itself and the elders.

In Denmark, the Muslim population was about 16,000 in 1971. This number reached 35,000 in 1982. Of these, there were about 16,000 Turks, 6,000 Pakistanis, 5,000 Yugoslavs, 4,000 Arabs and about 4,000 Danish citizens. Most of the Muslims are technicians, workers and small businessmen. The Muslim community of Denmark is well organized under a Muslim Union with six branches, two in Copenhagen and one each in Arhus, Vognmandsmarken, Gladsaxe, Ishog and Albertslund. Muslim children in public schools receive Islamic education from teachers chosen by the Muslim community who are paid by the State. Islamic education is also given in the local mosques. As in Sweden, Denmark is tending toward the recognition of Islam.

There were 17,000 Muslims in Sweden in 1971 and about 30,000 in 1982. Of these about 15,000 were Turks and Tartars, 4,000 Arabs, 7,000 Yugoslavs, and about 4,000 Swedish citizens. The Muslim community of Sweden was organized in 1948 under the Islamic Union of Sweden. It was reorganized in 1973 and then in 1975 to form the United Muslim Community of Sweden with

branches in Stockholm, Malmo, Goteborg, Eskilstuna, Jonkop-
ing, Vasteras, Mariestad and Trollhattan. There are makeshift
mosques in all these cities and about twelve Quranic schools, of
which six are in Stockholm alone. Negotiations between the community and the Government led in 1979 to the recognition of Islam
on the same footing as all other religions.

Poland has a very old Muslim community of Tartar origin. This
community was very prosperous before World War II. It was also
well organized under a mufti whose seat was Vilnius (now in the
USSR). World War II caused great damage to the Polish Muslim
community. Their number totalling about 100,000 just before the
war was reduced to about 15,000 in 1971 due to changes of borders
and deaths during the war. By 1982 there were about 22,000
Muslims. They are well organized under the Muslim Organization
of Poland whose seat is Warsaw. Two Muslim villages with their
mosques survived the War: Bhoniki and Kruziani in the district
of Byaltok in the north-east. Since 1973, a Muslim review has
been appearing in the Polish language. There is no persecution
of Muslims in Poland, but the community lacks young Muslim
*imams*, and the arrangements for religious education are
quite inadequate. The dangers of assimilation are consequently
real.

There were about 12,000 Muslims in Norway in 1982, many of
them of Pakistani or Turkish origin (8,000 and 3,000 respectively).
There are two Muslim organizations in Oslo with modest facilities
used as mosques and community centres: the Anjuman-e-Hanifia
and the Islamic Cultural Centre.

The Muslim community of Hungary, very important in the past,
was reduced to about 5,000 between the two world wars. But they
were well organized under the leadership of their *imam*. After
World War II the number of Muslims was further reduced to about
3,300 in 1949 and their organization withered away. Their number
today is about 6,000 and they are trying to reorganize.

The Muslim population of Portugal of about 6,000 in 1982 is
originally from the former Portuguese colonies of Mozambique,
Guinea-Bissau, Timor and Macao. They were organized for the
first time in 1968, establishing an Islamic Centre in a rented apartment. The community has an Islamic publication in Portuguese
and is planning to build a mosque in Lisbon.

There were about 4,000 Muslims in Ireland in 1982, many
of them were students, and half of them were in Dublin. There
are two organized communities, one in Dublin, the other in

Galway. The Dublin Islamic Society has a Community Centre and a mosque facility.

The Muslim population of Finland is of Tartar origin. It was organized in 1925 and was recognized fully by the Finnish Government. Their number is, however, small: no more than 3,000 in 1982 including foreign workers. The Finnish Muslims are prosperous (businessmen and bankers). They established community centres, mosques and schools in Helsinki and Tampere, and organized groups in Yarvenka, Turku and Kotka.

There were about 3,000 Muslims in Gibraltar in 1982, or 10 per cent of the population. These are almost exclusively Moroccan workers. However, their stay is temporary for they have no right to settle down. They have one makeshift mosque.

Muslims are not yet organized in the five other countries of Europe. But efforts at organization are being made at present in each of the following: Luxemburg (about 3,000 Muslims); East Germany (3,000 Muslims); Czechoslovakia (2,000 Muslims); Iceland (about 500 Muslims); and Malta (about 500 Muslims).

## Conclusions

The Muslim communities of Europe are in a dynamic state of change and no definite predictions about their chances of survival can be made at present. Among the relatively large Muslim communities (Yugoslavia, France, Albania, West Germany, Bulgaria and the United Kingdom), the Muslim communities of Eastern Europe (Yugoslavia, Bulgaria, Albania) are the result of a prolonged Muslim presence. Their Muslim populations are indigenous; they are religiously well organized and deeply rooted in the land. In these three countries, only the Muslims of Yugoslavia seem to be in a reasonably good and improving situation. In the other countries, the situation is much worse than it was in pre-World War II days. The existence of the Muslim community of Bulgaria is seriously threatened. In Albania, however, the fact that Muslims form the mass of the population and that Islam is fully integrated with the Albanian nationality, gives rise to the hope that in the course of time the perilous state through which they are passing now will be over and will be remembered as a nightmare which leaves no damaging effect behind it.

The Muslim communities of Western Europe (France, West Germany, UK) are of recent origin, and their presence was negligible before World War II. These populations are directly (UK and France) or indirectly (West Germany), a result of the colonial era. These communities are still in the process of getting themselves organized. They are most advanced organizationally in the UK, and least in France. These communities are also still struggling for acceptability in the host countries.

The financing of the establishment of Muslim institutions is overwhelmingly through contributions from Muslim individuals in these communities. The old *awqaf* in Eastern Europe have all been confiscated by the authorities. The support of Muslim countries is still of a very limited nature compared with the needs of the communities and compared to the European Christian missionary activity across the world. Moreover, this support is often directed towards establishing Islamic centres which are not run by the communities. These centres, in the present state of affairs, have a very limited impact on the future of these communities.

With the exception of Yugoslavia and France, knowledge of the Arabic language is not widespread. However, Islamic literature has been translated into Serbo-Croatian, English, Albanian, French and German in this order of importance. There is no well developed Islamic literature in Bulgarian.

As for the other countries of Europe, the Muslim community is recognized on an equal footing with other religious communities only in Finland, Belgium and Sweden. It is hoped that the same recognition will be accorded to the Muslims in Denmark and Austria. In general, Muslim communities of Eastern Europe have greatly suffered since World War II, especially those of Rumania, Poland and Hungary who are facing a serious danger of extinction. On the other hand, the Muslim communities of Western Europe have gained greatly since World War II, by a flow of immigrants who brought a new awareness of the Islamic identity.

To summarize, the modern attitude of Europe toward Islam is on the whole considerably better than in the past. This improved position is certainly still at variance in the Western democracies, with the principle of freedom of belief they claim. Indeed, Muslims in these countries are still handicapped by the actual bias of non-Muslims. The state of continuous rejection, persecution, or non-recognition is widespread, with the rare exceptions mentioned above, and is independent of the political system prevalent. For instance, Islam is practically free in Yugoslavia and Poland, but highly persecuted in Bulgaria and Rumania, in the communist bloc countries. For Western countries, Islam is not recognized in

France, West Germany and the UK, whereas it is recognized in Finland and Belgium. However, given the modern means of communication, no community can be completely cut off from the rest of the Muslim *ummah*. For this reason alone, it seems that Islam has already put down sufficient roots in Europe to give rise to the hope that it has come to stay and to thrive, in spite of the difficulties and the hardships that the Muslims might be facing. This would certainly be for the benefit of both Europe and the Muslim World.

## References and Further Reading

GENERAL

1. E. Levi-Provencal, *Histoire de l'Espagne Musulmane*, three volumes (Paris, France).
2. M. Amari, *History of the Muslims of Sicily*, five volumes (Italy, 1939) (Italian).
3. Aziz Ahmad, *A History of Islamic Sicily* (Edinburgh, 1975).
4. M. A. Kettani, *Muslims in Europe & America* (Beirut, 1976) I.

ALBANIA

1. K. Frasheri, *History of Albania* (Tirana, Albania, 1964).
2. K. Lavrencic, 'Albania' *Impact International* (London, April 9–22, 1976).

YUGOSLAVIA

1. Abdul-Salam Balagija, *Les Musulmans Yugoslaves* (Algiers, 1940).
2. A. Lopashich, 'A Negro Community in Yugoslavia' No. 231. (Nov. 1958).
3. Abu-Nureddin, 'Twenty Days in Yugoslavia' *Al-Shihab* (Lebanon, April 4, 1975 and May 1, 1975) (Arabic).
4. Ahmed Smajlovic, 'Muslims in Yugoslavia' *Institute of Muslim Minority Affairs Journal* (Winter 1979 and Summer 1980) (pp. 132–145).

BULGARIA

1. Anonymous, 'The Situation of Muslims in Bulgaria' *Al-Mujtama* 308 and 309 (Kuwait, July 1976) (Arabic).
2. K. Lavrencic, 'Bulgaria' *Impact International* (April 9–22, 1976)

CYPRUS

1. S. N. Bukingham, 'Muslims in Cyprus' *The Islamic Quarterly, II* 2 (July 1905).
2. Public Information Office, Turkish Federated State of Cyprus *The Tragedy of Zyyi* (April 1977).
3. R. R. Denktash, *The Cyprus Triangle* (London, 1982).
4. P. O. Oberling, *The Road to Bellapais* (Colombia, 1982).
5. N. M. Ertekun, *The Cyprus Dispute* (Oxford, 1984).

FRANCE

1. M. J. J. Roger, *Algerian Muslims in France and Muslim Countries* (France, 1950) (French)
2. J. C. Guilleband, 'Harkis Forgotten by History' *Le Monde* (France, 3, 4, 5 and 6 July 1973) (French)
3. G. Menant, 'The Harkis: Are They French?' *Paris-Match* (23 February 1974) (French)
4. J. M. Durand-Souffland, 'Musulmans en France' *Le Monde* (12, 13, 14 and 15 July 1983).

WEST GERMANY

1. H. H. Hawt, 'Muslims in West Germany' *Muslim World News*, No. 527, 21 Jumada I, 1397 (1977) (Arabic).
2. M. S. Abdullah, 'Islam in West Germany' *Muslim World Journal* (Oct. 1976).
3. M. S. Abdullah, 'Germany: Old Relations, New Community' *Impact International* (April 9–22, 1976).
4. F. M. Bhatti, 'Muslims as Migrants: The Turks in West Germany' *Institute of Muslim Minority Affairs Journal*, (Winter 1979 & Summer 1980). (pp. 47–63).

THE UNITED KINGDOM

1. G. Sarwar, 'The Muslim Educational Trust' *Rabitah Journal* (Mecca, July 1975) II, No. 9.
2. Anonymous, 'The U.K. Islamic Mission' *Impact International* (London, April 9–22, 1976).
3. Anonymous, 'London's Anxious East End' *The Economist* (July 15, 1978).

OTHER COUNTRIES

1. M. Konopacki, 'The Muslims of Poland' *Review of Islamic Studies* (1968), p. 124 (French).

2. R. Pike, 'An Urban Minority: The Moriscos of Seville' *International Journal of Middle East Studies* (1971) II, p. 368.
3. M. Degirmenci, *Meet the Muslims of Finland* (Helsinki, 1975) (Arabic).
4. S. V. Mamede, 'Islamic Community of Lisbon' *Islamic Culture Forum* (Islamic Cultural Society, Japan, Feb. 1976).
5. West Thrace Turks, *How West Thrace Muslim Turks are Annihilated* (1976) (Turkish & English).
6. R. Mantran, 'Crete' in *Islamic Encyclopedia* (Leiden, 1976) (pp. 1082–1087) (English).
7. M. Anwar, 'Muslims as Migrants: The Scandinavian Case' paper presented at the Muslim Minorities Seminar London (August 1978).
8. S. Balic, 'Muslims in Eastern Europe' paper presented at the Muslim Minorities Seminar (London, August 1978).
9. M. A. Kettani, 'Muslims in Greece' *Journal of Institute of Muslim Minority Affairs* – 82 (Winter 1979, Summer 1980) (pp. 145–158).

# 3 Muslims in the Soviet Union

## Introduction

Islam in the Soviet Union has had to endure one of the worst cases of persecution in history since the October revolution of 1917. The communist heirs of the Tsars, who came to power as a result of the revolution, saw Islam as incompatible with the ideas of militant atheism propagated by them, and also perceived in Islam a major threat to the consolidation of their rule in the Muslim lands of the disintegrating Empire. As a result, the bolshevic leaders went back on their promises of self-determination for the Muslims of the Russian Empire given earlier when they were not in power and resorted to physical extermination of Muslim leaders. Consolidation of Soviet rule in Muslim territories occupied during and after the Civil War was accompanied by a reign of terror against Muslims, the destruction or closure of mosques and the suppression of all Islamic activities by the regime.

This policy was reversed during the difficult years of World War II, when Stalin found it expedient to harness even the religious feelings of his subjects for the promulgation of victory over the foreign enemy. The regime renewed its onslaught on Islam after the war was over, albeit with less vigor and bloodshed. During the post-Stalin era, a new, more sophisticated approach towards Islam has been gradually developed by the Soviet leadership. The officially sanctioned administrative infrastructure of four muftiats on the territory of the USSR created during the war years was allowed to evolve into a so-called 'official Islam' in the USSR, serving occasionally as a mouth-piece of the regime in its relations with Muslims abroad, and at the same time, despite its submissiveness to the regime, providing an institutional framework for Islamic activities on a limited scale at home.

In terms of territorial distribution, 47,330,000 Soviet Muslims inhabited vast territorial expanses of Central Asia, Siberia and the Volga-Ural region in 1982, thus forming 17.8 per cent of the total Soviet population. Nine-tenths of these are Sunni Muslims belonging to the Hanafi school, and speak a number of mutually intelligible Turkic dialects. The most prominent group among them prior to and immediately after the October revolution, were the Volga Tartars. It was among them that an unprecedented Islamic renaissance took place at the turn of the century gaining momentum especially after the revolution of 1905. This Islamic renaissance was spear-headed by the jadidist (new method) movement aimed at the modernization of the Muslim schools, and the adaptation of a dynamic, flexible approach to the changing economic and industrial environment of the time. The main proponents of this movement were the Tartar Muslim scholars such as Kursavi, Marjani, Kultasi, Gasparali and many others who understood the importance of taking up the challenge of the approaching industrial era and resorted to the inherent dynamism of Islam in order to adapt to new conditions. For instance, Marjani created an uproar among the conservation ulema of the time when he, instead of joining in the denunciations of newly discovered photography as shaitan's (satan's) work, allowed himself to be photographed and declared that the Prophet banned the depiction of human images so as to keep his followers away from the folly of paganism. And as no such danger existed any more, photography was not forbidden.

Tartar leaders and intellectuals like Mirsaid Sultangali, Chelebi Cihan, Veli Ibrahim, Ismail Gabit and many others who played prominent roles in the revolutionary period before being killed by the Soviets, were the typical products of jadidism.

As the most determined and articulate group to voice opposition to the new-colonial policies of the Soviet regime, and to wage a determined struggle for national independence, the Volga Tartars had to suffer the heaviest blow of the Soviet terror machine. Not only their intelligentsia were to a great degree exterminated during the years of the Civil War and Stalin's purges, but also their future national development had been handicapped by relegating them to a second degree status of an autonomous republic within the Russian Federation in contrast to some of their far less numerous co-religionists in Central Asia, such as the Tajiks or the Turkmens who were granted the status of Union Republics. At present, Tartars endure far less autonomy within the Soviet system than their Central Asian brethren despite the fact that numerically they are the third Muslim people of the USSR after the Uzbeks and the Kazakhs, and are known as the most advanced group socially and culturally.

Muslims suffered the worst form of persecution during the Stalinist era. Things reached such a point that their present situation in the Soviet Union, despite the extremely harsh attitude of the Government toward them, appears to be an improvement. Muslim institutions have been eliminated progressively: of the 26,000 mosques in 1917, all but 1,000 had been done away with by 1978. Out of the hundreds of Muslim schools which functioned in 1917 only two were in existence in 1982. The Communist regime carries on a thorough campaign against Islamic culture and religion. It cut the Chagatai Turkic language, the lingua franca of the Muslim population, into pieces by converting every local dialect into a fully-fledged language. It waged and still wages a ruthless war against the teaching of the Arabic language and the usage of the Arabic script by the Muslims.

The Muslim religious organization is kept under close surveillance. This organization is subdivided into four directorates: Russia, Caucasus, Transcaucasus, and Central Asia. The Muslim *ulama* were, however, able to organize some international Islamic activities such as the commemoration of the 1,200th anniversary of Imam Al-Bukhari in 1974.

The Tsarist regime used to hold censuses which required an indication of the religious and ethnic affiliations of the citizens. Thus in 1897, there were sixteen million Muslims in the Russian Empire. The Communist regime does not take into account the religion of the citizens for the census, pretending it to be irrelevant. The nationality of the citizens, however, is recorded. Thus, the number of Muslims could be deduced from the Muslim nationalities, and was estimated to be 35,943,000 in 1970 and about 44,600,000 Muslims (or about 17 per cent of the population of the USSR) in 1979, about 47,330,000 Muslims (17.8 per cent of the population) in 1982.

## Historical Background

Islam reached Central Asia and won a large number of converts in the very first century of *Hijrah* (seventh century A.D.). Central Asia became an important centre of intellectual activity of the Muslim world in the fourteenth century.

The Muslim *ummah* in these areas has been represented by the

Turkic peoples the majority of whom gradually embraced Islam between the first and the sixth centuries of *Hijrah*. Among the earliest to become Muslims were the Bulgars of Idel (Volga), who formed in the middle ages a succession of the most advanced Muslim states. The first of them was the Khanate of Bulgar. The capital city of this state, Bilar, impressed foreign visitors by the architectural sophistication of its main stone and brick buildings which were in sharp contrast to other wooden structures, and had underground central heating systems.

According to Ibn Rushd, mosques and schools existed in the cities and villages of the kingdom at the beginning of the fourth century *Hijrah* (tenth C.E.). By then Arabic script was already displacing ancient runic scriptures of the Bulgars and other Turkic peoples.

Ahmed Ibn Fadlan, one of the envoys of the Abbasid Khalif Jafar Al-Muqtadir, visited the Bulgars in 922 C.E., witnessing the embracing of Islam by their King Almush (Almas), who took the name of Jafar after Khalif al-Muqtadir. This remarkable event occurred on the 16th of Muharram 310 *Hijrah* (Thursday, 15 May 922 C.E.), and must be viewed as the culmination of the gradual process of voluntary Islamization of the region.

In 986 C.E., the Bulgars despatched Muslim scholars to Grand Prince Vladimir of Kievan Russia in an effort to persuade him to accept Islam rather than Orthodox Christianity.

In 1236 C.E., Tartar armies of Batu Khan invaded the Kingdom of Bulgar and conquered it after a series of hard-fought battles. Subsequently, the seat of the new Empire of Golden Horde was established in Sarai. The superior Islamic civilization of the Bulgars, however, was to absorb the invading pagan Tartars in the following decades. Islam flourished again under the great-grandson of Batu, Uzbek, who was instrumental in convincing the pagan elements of his Kingdom to embrace Islam. By then the conquering Tartars were undergoing the process of cultural and linguistic assimilation by the Bulgars, although their name was being uniformly applied to the subjects of the Golden Horde.

When the Moroccan traveller Ibn Battutah crossed the lands which form today the Soviet Union in the fourteenth century, he noted that the people lived in Muslim states, had Turkish as main language and belonged to the Hanafi school of law. The largest of these states was the State of Sultan Uzbek whose capital As-Sara (Sarai, now ruined) was on the River Idel (Volga). As for the Russians, they were weak and primitive tribes about whom Ibn

Battutah says: 'they were Christians with blond hair, blue eyes, ugly faces, and great deceit'.

During the reign of Toktamysh Khan at the end of the fourteenth century, the Golden Horde suffered a devastating blow from the armies of Timur the Lame. Its main cities, including the capital city, Sarai, were destroyed and the population substantially reduced in numbers as a result of indiscriminate mass-slaughters by the victorious armies of Timur.

In the autumn of 1395 C.E., Timur started his advance on Muscovy and actually devastated the region of Riazan, but decided not to proceed with the sacking of Muscovy, and returned to Central Asia.

The fact that Timur the Lame turned his armies back after the destruction of the Golden Horde resulted in the emergence of Muscovy as the major military power in the region ripe for imperial expansion. The remnants of the Golden Horde gradually evolved into four khanates: those of Kazan, Astrakhan (Nogay), Siberia and the Crimea.

Under Ulu Muhammed Khan, the khanate of Kazan emerged as one of the most advanced Muslim states of the time. The artisans of Kazan were the first in Europe to produce cast iron, long before it was done in Britain. Their jewellery, leather goods and ceramics were famous far beyond the borders of the Kingdom. The architects of Kazan erected magnificent mosques and palaces. International trade fairs were held annually in Kazan, attracting thousands of merchants from Russia and distant lands of the Orient.

The Russian conquest of Kazan in 1552 after a number of earlier unsuccessful attempts ended economic prosperity of the Khanate. Marauding armies of Ivan the Terrible massacred the survivors of the siege of Kazan and floated their bodies down the Volga river to frighten into submission the population of the Khanate of Al-Haj Turkhan (Astrakhan).

Ivan the Terrible initiated forcible conversion of the Volga Muslims into Christianity by methods similar to those employed by the Spanish Inquisition against the Muslims of Spain. After the fall of Kazan in 1552, the Khanate of Astrakhan suffered the same fate in 1556, followed by the conquest of the Khanate of Siberia in 1598.

All these conquests were consolidated through the expulsion of surviving Muslims from their cities, confiscation of all their belongings and above all forced mass-scale conversion to Christianity. But the Tartars resisted, and like their Morisco brethren in Spain were able to maintain their faith for generations in secrecy until they declared it openly in their great majority during the reign of Catherine the Second, when Muslims were persecuted less vigorously. By the end of the nineteenth century Muslims managed to restore and re-build their mosques and schools. For instance, in the region of Oufa alone there were 1,555 mosques and 6,220 Muslim schools by 1897.

After the above Khanates, the next major Muslim State to fall to Russian expansionism was the Giray Khanate of Crimea (Crimea Tartars). Its capital was Baghche Saray, and it enclosed much of the southern part of the Ukraine and the lower Don-Kuban region. It had borders with Russia, Poland and the Ottoman State. In its struggle against Russian encroachment, the Crimean State was supported by the Ottoman Empire. But when the Ottoman State itself weakened, the Crimean State could not resist alone. It was defeated by Russia and invaded in 1783. Then followed the fall to Russia of one Muslim State after another in quick succession in Central Asia and the Caucasus. Kazakhstan and the Daghestan were conquered in the eighteenth century; the State of Bokhara in 1850; the State of Ferghana in 1873; the State of Khiva in 1876. Both Khiva and Bokhara remained protectorates until 1920 when they were incorporated in the Soviet system. Other Muslim lands were taken away from Afghanistan, Persia, and Turkey around the turn of the century. The main centres of Islamic civilization for twelve centuries in Central Asia thus fell to Russian colonialism while other such centres fell to English, French, Italian, Dutch, Spanish and Portuguese colonialisms.

Just before the Communist Revolution, the mass of Muslims subjugated to the Russian Empire concentrated their efforts on Islamic education. Kazan itself was the seat of a university having 7,000 students, a Muslim press which printed 2.5 million copies of 250 different books in 1902 alone, and a Muslim library visited yearly by more than 20,000 readers. Mosques and schools were built on such a scale that the ratio was one Mosque for every 150 Muslims. All this happened in spite of Russian discrimination and persecution. As the Russian State weakened, Muslims started to think about gaining their freedom.

The October 1917 Revolution brought in its wake a new situation. Muslims rose in rebellion, asking for independence in many areas. These popular movements of liberation took place in Bashkiria, in Khiva (1918–1920) and Ferghana (1918–1926) under the leadership of Mohammed Amin Beg; in Bokhara under the leadership of Akram Khan, and in Crimea under the leadership of Tchalabi. Sayyid Sultan Ali-Oglu who put forth the idea of a bi-national Muslim–Russian Federation under the communist system, was imprisoned and then executed in 1937.

The Communist Government followed a policy of dividing the Muslim Community into linguistic groups which totalled about forty-two entities, many of them sharing no more than dialects of the same language. They put an end to the teaching of the Arabic language, to the usage of the Arabic script, and followed this up by a continuous propaganda war against Islam, its beliefs, culture and civilization.

## Numerical Strength and National Distribution

Demographically speaking, the Muslims passed through very severe conditions between 1897 and 1939 which had a highly negative effect on their numbers. Russians killed hundreds of thousands of Muslims when they rebelled in Bashkiria and Kirghizia in 1917. At least one million Kazakh and Khirgiz Muslims died in artificial famines in 1921. Another one million Kazakh Muslims died of hunger in 1929 (25 per cent of the remaining Kazakhs of the time) as a result of communist confiscation of their herds. Then the Russians brought in Russian colonizers to take the lands of the dead nomads.

In the census of 1897, a total of sixteen million Muslims were reported in the Russian Empire, or about 12.6 per cent of the total population. The census taken by Tsarist Russia requested the religious affiliation, and we thus knew the number of Muslims. But in the censuses of the Soviet State, this question was never asked. Given the intense official propaganda against religion in general, and Islam in particular, it is not easy to know who is Muslim in the Soviet Union. But the Soviet census gives information about the nationality of the person, and since the Muslim nationalities are well known, it is possible to deduce the number of Muslims from the official Soviet censuses, just by adding the numbers of the Muslim nationalities. Past experience has shown that the generations of Muslims subjected to persecution always see their beliefs strengthened, and thus it is assumed that those belonging to a Muslim nationality still consider themselves (even secretly sometimes) to be Muslims.

The Muslim populations of the Soviet Union can be divided into two categories: the Turkish-speaking Muslims, who are the most numerous; and the rest. Most of these Muslims belong to the Hanafi school, and some, especially in the South East Caucasus, are of the Imami school. The nationalities which are members of the Turkic group are in the descending order of their numerical strength: the Uzbek; the Tartars; the Kazakhs; the Azeris; the Kirghiz; the Turcoman; the Bashkir; the Kara Calpak; the Balkar; the Karatchay; the Kara Nogai and other groups of smaller numbers. As for those who speak other languages than Turkish they are: the Tajik; the Tchechen; the Ingush; the Kabards; the Ajars; the Abkhaz; the Adighians; the Circassians; the Daghestanis; the Udmurts; the Mary; the Ossets; the Tchuvash and others of smaller numbers. In all, there are forty-two Muslim nationalities with 'nationality' as defined by the Soviet State. Some Muslim nationalities are not listed as such in the Soviet census. The most important are the Adjar of Georgia who are Georgian Muslims. Their number has been estimated as 80 per cent of the population of the Adjar ASSR. We also estimated that 80 per cent of Kurds are Muslims, so are 50 per cent of the Abkhaz, 30 per cent of the Ossets and 20 per cent of the Chuvash, Mary, Mordvins and Udmurts. The Meskhetians, Talysh, Karapapakh, Ingiloy (Georgia Shias) and Hemshins (Armenian Muslims) have not been counted, since they most probably are counted with other Muslim nationalities. Table 3.1 represents the number of Muslims belonging to the most important nationalities in the 1959, 1970 and 1979 censuses.

From Table 3.1, it becomes clear that the demographic situation of the Muslim community improved greatly since 1959. This statement is true for all Muslim nationalities, with the relative exception of the Tartars and the Bashkirs. The highest rate of increase in the period 1959–1979 was among the Tajiks (107.4 per cent) followed closely by the most numerous single Muslim nationality, the Uzbek (107.1 per cent). The smallest rate of growth was among the Tartars (27.2 per cent) and the Bashkirs (38.6 per cent) who came much earlier than the others under Russian occupation. However, the rate of increase of these two nationalities was still higher than that of the non-Muslim nationalities of the Soviet Union during the same period (18.6 per cent). The overall growth of the Muslim population was more than four times this rate (75.9 per cent).

This demographic fact created a new situation for the Muslims of the Soviet Union. Indeed, their percentage in the total population of the Soviet Union increased from 11.3 per cent in 1939 to

17.0 per cent in 1979 and an estimated 17.8 per cent in 1982. In other words, their percentage exceeded largely that of 1897 in spite of the incorporation of many new non-Muslim areas in the Soviet Union after World War II.

Table 3.1    Muslims in the Soviet Union by nationality

| People | Population in thousands | | | | | | Increase |
|--------|------|------|------|------|------|------|----------|
| | 1959 | | 1970 | | 1979 | | 1959–79 |
| Uzbek | 6,015 | 23.7% | 9,195 | 25.6% | 12,456 | 27.9% | 107.1% |
| Kazakhs | 3,622 | 14.3% | 5,299 | 14.8% | 6,556 | 14.7% | 81.0% |
| Tartars | 4,968 | 19.6% | 5,931 | 16.5% | 6,317 | 14.2% | 27.2% |
| Azeris | 2,940 | 11.6% | 4,380 | 12.2% | 5,477 | 12.3% | 86.3% |
| Tajiks | 1,397 | 5.5% | 2,136 | 6.0% | 2,898 | 6.5% | 107.4% |
| Turkmen | 1,002 | 4.0% | 1,525 | 4.2% | 2,028 | 4.5% | 102.4% |
| Kirghiz | 969 | 3.8% | 1,452 | 4.0% | 1,906 | 4.3% | 96.7% |
| Bashkirs | 989 | 3.9% | 1,240 | 3.4% | 1,371 | 3.1% | 38.6% |
| Others | 3,456 | 13.6% | 4,785 | 13.2% | 5,591 | 12.5% | 61.8% |
| Total | 25,358 | 100 % | 35,943 | 100 % | 44,600 | 100 % | 75.9% |
| Turkic | 21,398 | 84.4% | 30,263 | 84.2% | 37,553 | 84.2% | 75.5% |
| Non-Turkic | 3,960 | 15.6% | 5,680 | 15.8% | 7,047 | 15.8% | 78.0% |

## Geographical Distribution and Political Organization

The Soviet establishment divided the Muslim community into a multitude of nationalities. Of the most important of these nationalities a Federal Soviet Republic was established. There are 15 such republics in the Soviet Union, six of which belong to Muslim nationalities. To fourteen of the remaining nationalities twelve autonomous republics were constituted: ten are in the Russian Soviet Republic (Bashkiria, Tataria, Daghestan, Udmurtia, Tchuvachia, Mordvia, Tchechen-Ingush, Mary, Kabard-Balkar and Northern Ossets) and two are in the Georgian Soviet Republic (Abkhazia and Adjaria). Three autonomous regions were established of four more Muslim nationalities: two in Russia (Adighia, and Karachai — Tcherkess) and one in Georgia (Southern Ossets). Five of the Muslim Soviet Republics are in Central Asia (Kazakhstan, Uzbekistan, Tukmenistan, Tadjikistan and Kirghizia) and one is in the Caucasus (Azerbaidjan).

As for the Crimean Autonomous Republic it has been abolished as we shall see later. There are other Muslim regions whose Muslim communities have not been incorporated in any special

*Table 3.2* The administrative units in the Soviet Union set for Muslim nationalities

FR, Federal Republic; AR, Autonomous Republic; AO, Autonomous Region

| Administrative Unit (Type) *Capital* | Area Km$^2$ | Population 1979 *thousands* | Year of conquest | Year of establishment |
|---|---|---|---|---|
| Uzbekistan (FR) | | | | |
| Tashkent | 450,000 | 15,380 | 1873 | 1924 |
| Kazakhstan (FR) | | | | |
| Alma-Ata | 2,750,000 | 14,684 | 1866 | 1936 |
| Tadjikistan | | | | |
| Dushanbe | 143,000 | 3,806 | 1873 | 1929 |
| Kirghizia (FR) *Frunze* | 198,000 | 3,529 | 1886 | 1936 |
| Turkmenistan (FR) | | | | |
| Ashkhabad | 487,790 | 2,765 | 1873 | 1925 |
| Total Central Asia | 4,028,790 | 40,164 | | |
| Azerbaijan (FR) *Bakou* | 87,000 | 6,027 | 1920 | 1936 |
| Daghestan (AR) | | | | |
| Machackala | 50,300 | 1,627 | 1723 | 1921 |
| Tchechen-Ingush (AR) | | | | |
| Groznyj | 19,300 | 1,155 | 1850 | 1957 |
| Kabard-Balkar (AR) | | | | |
| Nalcik | 12,500 | 675 | 1557 | 1936 |
| Northern Ossets (AR) | | | | |
| Ordzonikidze | 8,000 | 597 | 1784 | 1936 |
| Abkhazia (AR) *Sukhumi* | 8,600 | 505 | 1810 | 1930 |
| Adyghya (AO) *Majkop* | 7,600 | 404 | 1878 | 1922 |
| Karachai-Tcherkess (AO) *Cerkessk* | 14,100 | 369 | 1878 | 1957 |
| Adjaria (AR) *Batumi* | 3,000 | 354 | 1878 | 1921 |
| Southern Ossets (AO) | | | | |
| Chinvali | 3,900 | 98 | 1878 | 1922 |
| Total Caucasus | 214,300 | 11,811 | | |
| Bashkiria (AR) *Oufa* | 143,000 | 3,849 | 1557 | 1919 |
| Tataria (AR) *Kazan* | 68,000 | 3,806 | 1552 | 1920 |
| Udmurtia (AR) *Izevsk* | 42,100 | 1,490 | 1560 | 1934 |
| Tchuvachia (AR) | | | | |
| Ceboksary | 18,300 | 1,293 | 1552 | 1925 |
| Mordvia (AR) *Saransk* | 26,200 | 990 | 1552 | 1936 |
| Mary (AR) *Joskar-Ola* | 23,800 | 703 | 1552 | 1936 |
| Total Volga | 322,000 | 12,131 | | |
| Grand total | 4,562,100 | 63,736 | | |

entity. The most important among these are the cities of Astrakhan (Al-Haj Turkhan) and Kasimov (Qasimi). But large Muslim groups are found in these territories as well as in all other parts of the Soviet Union, most notably in Moscow and Leningrad, as well as in all the other large cities of the Soviet Union.

All the above political divisions are, however, of only a super-ficial nature and are no more than administrative divisions. Russian is actually the official language in all the republics and national languages always have a secondary value, often of only a folkloric nature. As for the federal republics, Russian ministers are put in key ministries in all of them. Table 3.2 indicates the different Muslim administrative units and some of their characteristics.

It can be deduced from Table 3.2 that, if we take into account Muslim lands incorporated into non-Muslim nationality terri-tories, the lands taken by the Soviet Union (Russian Empire) from the Muslim World amount to about one third of the total territory of the Soviet Union. The territories left to Muslim nationalities constitute about 20 per cent of the area of the Soviet Union and are among the richest and more valuable lands in the Union.

It can also be noticed that the total population in these terri-tories was 63.732 million in 1979 whereas the entire Muslim popu-lation of the Soviet Union amounted to 44.6 million only. If we estimate the number of Muslims outside these territories at about three million, there would be a Muslim percentage of only 65 per cent in their own lands. This low percentage is a result of a long period of colonization of Muslim lands by Slavic immigrants throughout the nineteenth century and first half of this century. This trend is being reversed after 1959 as will be seen in the following section.

## Colonization of Muslim Areas

Before making any deductions on the scale of Russian colonization of Muslim lands, consider first table 3.3 which provides compara-tive figures for the percentage of Muslims in the different Soviet Republics between the three censuses of 1959, 1970 and 1979.

Table 3.3 shows that the percentage of Muslims increased stead-ily and steeply in all the six Muslim Republics between 1959 and 1979, thus reversing a dangerous trend in the period between the beginning of colonization and 1959. The percentage of Muslims in Russia and Georgia increased as well, but decreased in the other

Table 3.3   Population increases in the Soviet Republics

Population in thousands

| Republic | 1959 Total | 1959 Muslim | 1959 % | 1970 Total | 1970 Muslim | 1970 % | 1979 Total | 1979 Muslim | 1979 % |
|---|---|---|---|---|---|---|---|---|---|
| Uzbekistan | 8,119 | 6,535 | 80.5 | 11,799 | 9,787 | 82.9 | 15,380 | 13,099 | 85.2 |
| Kazakhstan | 9,295 | 3,278 | 35.3 | 13,009 | 5,018 | 38.6 | 14,684 | 6,241 | 42.5 |
| Azerbaijan | 3,698 | 2,685 | 72.6 | 5,117 | 4,016 | 78.5 | 6,027 | 5,013 | 83.2 |
| Takjikistan | 1,982 | 1,624 | 81.9 | 2,900 | 2,468 | 85.1 | 3,806 | 3,285 | 86.3 |
| Kirghizia | 2,066 | 1,179 | 57.1 | 2,933 | 1,781 | 60.7 | 3,529 | 2,305 | 65.3 |
| Turkmenistan | 1,516 | 1,169 | 77.1 | 2,159 | 1,728 | 80.0 | 2,765 | 2,283 | 82.6 |
| Sub-total | 26,676 | 16,470 | 61.7 | 37,917 | 24,798 | 65.4 | 46,191 | 32,226 | 69.8 |
|  | 12.8% | 64.9% |  | 15.7% | 69.0% |  | 17.6% | 72.3% |  |
| Russia | 117,534 | 8,092 | 6.9 | 130,079 | 10,133 | 7.8 | 137,552 | 11,137 | 8.1 |
| Georgia | 4,044 | 549 | 13.6 | 4,686 | 680 | 14.5 | 5,015 | 843 | 16.8 |
| Armenia | 1,763 | 135 | 7.7 | 2,492 | 186 | 7.5 | 3,031 | 214 | 7.1 |
| Ukrainia | 41,869 | 89 | 0.2 | 47,127 | 117 | 0.2 | 49,609 | 150 | 0.3 |
| Other | 16,941 | 23 | 0.1 | 19,419 | 29 | 0.1 | 20,868 | 30 | 0.1 |
| Sub-total | 182,151 | 8,888 | 4.9 | 203,803 | 11,145 | 5.5 | 216,075 | 12,374 | 5.7 |
|  | 87.2% | 35.1% |  | 84.3% | 31.0% |  | 82.4% | 27.7% |  |
| Total | 208,827 | 25,358 | 12.1 | 241,720 | 35,943 | 14.9 | 262,266 | 44,600 | 17.0 |
|  | 100.0% | 100.0% |  | 100.0% | 100.0% |  | 100.0% | 100.0% |  |

Republics which are devoid of any Muslim Autonomous Republic or Autonomous Region.

In 1959, the total number of Muslims in the six Muslim Republics was 16,470,000 or 64.9 per cent of the total Muslim population of the Soviet Union and 61.7 per cent of the total population of these republics. This population amounted to 26,676,000 of whom a total of 10,206,000 were non-Muslims.

In 1979, the total number of Muslims in the six republics was 32,226,000 or 72.3 per cent of the total Muslim population of the Soviet Union. This shows that there was, during the period 1959–1979, an increase in Muslim concentration, rather than a dispersion. This is due mostly to a higher natural growth rate of Muslims in these republics compared to Muslims in other republics. In 1979, the total population of the six republics amounted to 46,191,000 people of whom 13,965,000 people were non-Muslims. The Muslim percentage in these republics also increased to 69.8 per cent in 1979.

The percentage increase of the non-Muslim population in the six Muslim republics amounted to 36.8 per cent in the twenty years under consideration. This figure is to be compared to a percentage increase of 95.7 per cent for the Muslim population of the six Muslim republics.

Table 3.4 shows the national origin of the non-Muslim population of the six Muslim republics. Assuming a natural increase of the Russian and Ukrainian growth rate outside the Muslim area, one can estimate readily the rate of immigration. Thus, the net increase in the non-Muslim population of the six Muslim republics amounts to 3,759,000 people in the period 1959–1979. Of these 2,244,000 people are due to natural growth and 1,515,000 people to net immigration (1,370,000 Russians and 145,000 Ukrainians).

*Table 3.4*  National origin of the non-Muslim population of the six Muslim republics

| Nationality | Population in thousands | | | | Increase |
|---|---|---|---|---|---|
| | 1959 | | 1979 | | |
| Russians | 6,714 | 65.8% | 9,788 | 70.1% | 45.8% |
| Ukrainians | 1,060 | 10.4% | 1,221 | 8.7% | 15.2% |
| Others | 2,432 | 23.8% | 2,956 | 21.2% | 21.5% |
| Total | 10,206 | 100.0% | 13,965 | 100.0% | 36.8% |

Thus, in the six Muslim republics, in spite of continuing non-Muslim immigration, the percentage of Muslims with respect to non-Muslims increased dramatically, due to a much higher natural growth in the Muslim population compared to others. Furthermore, it is obvious from the above figures that Muslims refuse to leave Muslim areas, as the percentage of Muslims in the six Muslim republics with respect to the total Muslim population of the Soviet Union increased dramatically during the same period (1959–1979).

Because of higher natural growth rates among Muslims compared to others, Muslim percentages increased also in the two republics where Muslims exist in substantial numbers: Russia (from 6.9 to 8.1 per cent) and Georgia (13.6 to 16.8 per cent). Muslim percentages decreased in the same period in Armenia from 7.7 to 7.1 per cent. In Armenia, Muslim percentages dropped slightly in the same period due mainly to immigration of Armenians estimated to amount to about 413,000 people, and emigration of Muslim Azeris out of Armenia, estimated to be about 40,000 people during the same period.

From the above, it appears clearly that there is a tendency of Muslims to emigrate back to their areas of concentration, thus enabling them to protect themselves better from the dangers of cultural assimilation. Furthermore, the higher natural growth rate of Muslims is bound to give their republics more weight in the future, as their percentages in these republics increases continuously, giving these republics a stronger Islamic identity.

## Official Assault on Muslim Identity

The religious organization of the Muslim community is divided into four directorates: European Russia and Siberia (seat Oufa in Bashkiria); Northern Caucasus and Daghestan (seat Bujnaksh in Daghestan); Transcaucasia (seat Bakou in Azerbaijan); and Central Asia and Kazakhstan (seat Tashkent in Uzbekistan). The latter is headed by Imam Babakhanov. It has become the most active since it was founded in 1946.

The apparent policy of the Soviet authorities with this organization of the community is tolerance and control. In fact, however, the policy of the Soviet Government seems to be to try all possible means to frustrate the efforts of the Muslims to live as an organized community. Article 124 of the 1936 Soviet Constitution stipulates 'the freedom of religious practices and anti-religious activities as well'. What this has meant in practice is that the state has waged a continuous war against religion in general, and Islam in particular, and denied the people the means by which they could preserve their religious identity and defend it against the state-sponsored onslaughts.

The article of M.S.I. Umahanov, the First Secretary of the Community Party in the Daghestan Autonomous Region which appeared in the official Communist Party journal *Party Life* in September 1975, shed some light on the efforts of the Communists to undermine Islam. Umahanov states that work against religion has been stepped up considerably: that fifty-four theoretical seminars had been held for more than 2000 educators specialized in anti-Islamic activity. He also mentioned that 980 older students in high schools have joined atheistic clubs to propagate anti-religious ideas among fellow students. Special adult education classes for women have also been introduced in order to fight effectively against religion. The 'educated' class, according to Umahanov, had been mobilized to 'enlighten' the population regarding the need to reject religious practices such as alms-giving during funerals, circumcision, sacrifice of sheep in Eid-ul-Adha and religious weddings. Just as during the Spanish Inquisition, once a group of people has been won over for atheism they are immediately called upon to convey the benefits of their 'conversion' to those who are still religious. Umahanov also points out that much of the cultural and artistic life of the Republic was also geared to anti-Islamic propaganda. Festivals of anti-religious films were held every year. In the Daghestan Autonomous Republic alone, according to Umahanov, there were 200 centres for anti-Islamic lectures accompanied by films and slides. Radio and TV were also used for this purpose and anti-Islamic broadcoasts were made in the seven main languages of the Autonomous Republic.

In his article, Umahanov also appeals for mixed marriages between people of different nationalities (so they can all be Russianized) and urges people to become more 'internationally' minded (i.e. forget about their own nationality). He also mentions that religious festivals have been replaced by State-invented ones. Umahanov, naturally, is not only highly pleased with all this, but also feels strongly that these efforts need to be strengthened.

The above is illustrative of the Soviet State policy toward Islam. The methods used by the Soviet Government and the Communist Party constitute an educational/motivational approach that is not much different from that of the former Russian Greek-Orthodox Church against Islam during the Tsarist era. The effort is carried out with an intense zeal inherited directly from the Tsarist times. At the same time the Soviet information media paints a rosy picture of Islam in the Soviet Union so as to deceive the outside world, especially the Muslims, as regards the real situation of the Muslims.

In its war against Islam, the Soviet propaganda resorts to sheer lies, fabrications, distortions, and concealment of facts. The media ascribe the survival of many social evils and inequities to Islam, which is reminiscent of the propaganda of the European colonial powers in Africa and Asia. Islam is decried as harmful for industrial discipline, and as an enemy of growth and progress as such. It is seen as a major obstacle in the efforts to make the USSR the exclusive centre of devotion and loyalty. Above all, Islam is considered a stumbling block which prevents the assimilation of all races within the Russian system.

The result of this continuous war has been catastrophic to Islamic institutions. There were 26,000 mosques in the Russian Empire at the time of the October 1917 Revolution. Just before the revolution the number of religious functionaries amounted to 45,000. There were thousands of Islamic schools and enough *awqaf* to run the Islamic institutions. Today (1982) none of the *awqaf* (religious endowments) are run by Muslims, for they were confiscated by the government long ago. The number of mosques is estimated now to be somewhere around 450 in the whole of the Soviet Union. Even a historical Muslim metropolis like Tashkent which today has a total population of two million (of whom 1.4 million are Muslims), has no more than twelve mosques (and six churches and two synaguogues). Construction of new mosques or rehabilitation of old ones are rarely permitted. The number of religious functionaries dropped to 8,000 in 1955 and stood at a much lower figure in 1982. Only two *madrasahs* (religious seminaries) survived today in the Soviet Union; the one in Bokhara, Mir-Arab School, is the largest. It is forced to accept every year twenty-five candidates and reject more than 400 applicants. The last two *madrasahs* of Samarkand were closed down as far back as 1921. Religious education in public is banned. Muslim youth are openly persecuted and rejected from the Konsomol movement. Only thirty Muslims are allowed to perform the *Hajj* to Mecca every year. Religious literature is practically non-existent. The *Holy Quran* has been printed six times since 1956, but no interpretation of its meaning in any Muslim language has been permitted since the October 1917 Revolution.

## Inner Resistance of the Muslim community

What is, then, the reaction of the Muslims to this onslaught on their religion? In their struggle for survival, Muslims have the choice between: cleverly contrived and discreet effort designed to ensure the continued survival of Islam; and open conflict and resistance in order to secure freedom to live according to the teachings of Islam. They tried the second method up to World War II. It brought few results and did considerable damage to the community. The discouraging results seem to have induced the Muslims to resort to the first method. This is done by following up efforts in three directions: asserting the Islamic identity, strengthening the cohesion of the Muslim community, and increasing its contacts with the Muslim world; trying to avoid provoking the Soviet regime by pointing out its positive achievements, and stressing the common ground there is between the regime and Islam; and abandoning customs and practices which were not an inalienable part of Islam in the first place, and stresssing that the Muslims ought to stay within the teachings of the *Quran* and the *Sunnah*.

Illustrative of this attitude is the article written by the late Mufti Dhiauddin Babakhanov in the January 1975 issue of the Tashkent Magazine entitled '*Muslims of the Soviet East*' that there was 'full freedom of religion' in the Soviet Union. His statement about religious freedom makes sense if we take it in a relative sense and consider it to mean religious freedom as compared to what it was in the Stalinist era, or in comparison to such countries as Communist Albania and Maoist China. Muslims also often thank the Soviet regime for delivering them from the 'persecutions of the Tsarist era and of the Greek Orthodox establishment', which is technically true. The fact that they became victims of another type of persecution is certainly understood by the mass of Muslims. Mufti Babakhanov again declared to Alain Woodrow (*Le Monde*, 8 September 1978) that 'believers accomplish freely and without persecution their religious obligations. To believe or not to believe is a personal matter of each citizen'. Imam Yusufkhan Shakir, the assistant to Mufti Babakhanov declared to the same correspondent: 'The Muslims of the Soviet Union can participate in the building of the new society. Their faith in God Almighty does not prevent them nor does it forbid them from being the carriers of the Socialist Culture'. In a book published in Moscow recently on Muslims in the Soviet Union Abdul-Wahhab, a Soviet Muslim, writes: 'The participation in the building of the new society does not prevent the faithful from following the right path shown by the *Quran* and the *Sunnah* of Prophet Muhammad. Indeed the teachings of Islam as expressed by the *Qadis* stress that: love of one's homeland is an integral part of faith in God.'

In another way of appeasing the Soviet regime, Imam Shakir told the correspondent of *Le Monde* that 'we have relations with all the countries of the Muslim world, even with Saudi Arabia, whose capitalist regime does not entertain any relations with the Government of the Soviet Union. As for us, our organism does not get involved in politics'. He was, in a way, right.

This policy of avoiding conflict with the Soviet Government, coupled with other factors, brought some advantages to the Muslim community. In October 1970, the *Muslim Ulama* of the Soviet Union sponsored a conference in Tashkent 'For unity and solidarity of Muslims in the struggle against imperialist aggression'. This was followed a year later by a conference in the same city which was devoted to the 'struggle against Zionist intrigues'. Another conference, held in August 1974 in Samarkand, was of great importance in view of the eminence of the personality in whose honour it was held. The conference was termed 'Scientific Conference of the USSR Muslims' and marked the 1200th anniversary of Imam Bukhari, the most important compiler of *hadith* and a native of the region. The meeting of more than one hundred *imams* from the Soviet Union and hundreds of distinguished Muslim guests from twenty-seven countries around the world was a kind of reunion and get-together of the Muslims of the Soviet Union with their brothers from the rest of the world. The meeting had certainly lasting effects on both and was charged with an air of brotherly emotion. The then pro-rector and present rector of Al-Azhar University (Cairo), Sheikh Muhammad Bisar was not only talking to his Muslim audience when he said in the meeting: 'Imam Bukhari may have lived twelve centuries ago, but he was well ahead of his time, and his work for the advancement of science and technology provided excellent evidence to show that Islam has been suited to all times and all historical stages'. In October 1976, another conference was convened in Tashkent by the Muslim Religious Body to which delegations from all the Muslim world were invited. The occasion was the thirtieth anniversary of the establishment of the Islamic Religious Body in the Soviet Union. Seeing the sorry state of the mosques in the capital of Islam in the Soviet Union and comparing it with all the stadiums, operas and play-houses on the construction of which the regime had spent lavishly the late Sheikh Abdul-Rahman Kettani, the Assistant-Chairman of the Board of Moroccan *Ulama* declared to the Soviet Press: 'I wish you could put the same effort in letting the Muslims establish their mosques as you are putting in taking care of their need for sport and culture'.

These meetings, notwithstanding the propaganda purposes underlying them and despite the limitations on individual freedom in the Soviet Union, have played some part in opening the way for communication with the entire Muslim *ummah*. This communication has also been possible by the fact that some Muslim students were allowed by the Soviet Government to go to Egypt and Morocco for higher studies. There are also some signs of a relaxing attitude toward the Muslims. During the last few years it has been noticed that some new mosques were built in USSR with official approval. Such 'liberties' would have been impossible just a decade ago.

The mass of Muslims in the USSR is presently witnessing an Islamic revival. It seems far too strong to be crushed by force. Even the large mosques of Moscow and Leningrad are overflowing with the faithful on friday. Official propaganda is often ignored by Muslims as boring and ridiculous. Muslims of the Soviet Union are gaining in self-respect and self-confidence, making the job of their atheistic prosylitizers increasingly difficult. For instance, Mr Gapurov, the Communist leader of Turkmenistan wrote in the issue of April 1973 in the journal *'Turkmenskaya Iskra'*: 'The number of people observing religious rites is not decreasing in our Republic. An insistent and stubborn struggle is needed against the carriers of religious infection which stems from the past. Muslim religion causes particular concern in that it frequently acts as a depository of reactionary national customs and traditions and encourages national exclusiveness'. The resistance against atheism is evident from the behaviour of young people, boys and girls, which are often inclined to make a point of saying that they were fasting during Ramadan. They do so in spite of the risks to which such a statement exposes them. It is also evident from the visits, in great numbers, to the tombs of famous religious leaders and national Muslim heroes whose memory they wish to honour. It is also evident from the network of Muslim *imams* which is parallel to the official one. Private study groups which hold prayers and classes in homes, in spite of the risks of heavy penalities, are also indicative of the same trend. Finally, it seems to be gleaming through the eyes of the Muslims of the Soviet Union whenever and wherever they happen to meet Muslim brothers from abroad.

## The Case of the Crimean Tartars

The Crimean Tartars have been among the biggest losers of Russian colonization. Their case is treated here with some detail since it is an extreme case which still awaits a just solution. It is, however, not a unique case, for several other Muslim nationalities in the Soviet Union have fared as badly.

The Crimean Muslim state was established in the fifteenth century under the Giray dynasty. It expanded in the following centuries to cover much of what is now Ukrainia. In 1571, they besieged Moscow and burned it to the ground. The Crimean State had borders with the the Ottoman Empire, the Russian Empire and the Polish Empire. It was the natural ally of the Ottoman Empire against Russian expansionism. In its apogee the Crimean State had a Muslim population of about seven million. From the second half of the seventeenth century, Russia began to gain the upper hand over Crimea. Although Crimean Tartars defeated Peter the Great in 1711, Russians invaded and ravaged Crimea during the Russo-Turkish wars of 1735–39 and 1768–74. In the middle of the eighteenth century, the population of the Crimean State was about one million persons, 80 per cent of whom were Crimean Tartar Muslims. The remaining were mostly Greeks. There were no Russians among them. By then the Crimean State was reduced to the Crimean Peninsula with an area of about 27,000 square kilometres. The capital was Baghche Saray.

After the Russian conquest of Crimea in 1783, a large number of Muslims fleeing Russian onslaught emigrated to Turkey, bringing the number of Crimean Tartars in their land to about 500,000. Many of these died of poverty and disease, the remainder became greatly impoverished. They however still constituted about 75 per cent of the total population. Indeed, the Russian conquest was followed by intense persecution of the Muslims and their forced conversion to Christianity. Their conquest of Crimea was followed by a continuous trickle of emigration of Crimean Tartars to the lands that were still within the Ottoman Empire. On the other hand, from 1784, the Russians sponsored a policy of territorial colonization of Muslim lands.

The recognition of the Ottoman Empire of the Russian annexation of Crimea in 1792, deprived the Crimean Muslims of their last hope to ever free themselves from Russian domination. This led to the second major Tartar emigration, reducing the population of Crimea to about 610,000 people in 1851. The Crimean War (1854–1856) was fought between Russia on the one hand, and by the Ottoman Empire, Britain and France on the other, on the Crimean territory. It was extremely costly for all its participants in terms of human life. But for the Crimean Tartars, the war was not only a loss but a catastrophe. Most of the Crimean Tartar population was forcibly expelled out of their homeland to other parts of Russia and about 200,000 of them were expelled to the Ottoman Empire, of whom 100,000 were settled by the Ottoman authorities in Bulgaria (Rumelia).

More waves of Muslim emigration, with the encouragement of the Russian State, occurred in the 1860s and 1870s. By 1897, there were left only 188,000 Tartars in Crimea, constituting about 35 per cent of a total population of 540,000 people. The number of Russians and Ukrainians increased meanwhile to 240,000 people (or 45 per cent of the total population). A new wave of emigration occurred in the period 1891–1902. By the October 1917 Revolution, the Crimean Tartar population of the Crimean Peninsula was further reduced, bringing their number down to 102,000 people or 25 per cent of a total population of 410,000 people.

The Bolshevic authorities decided to establish an Autonomous Republic in the Crimean Peninsula in 1921. They recognized the Crimean Tartar nationality, and at last the Crimean Tartars felt that their miseries were coming to an end. However, they still formed a minority in their own state. In the census of 1926, there was 624,000 people living in the Crimean Autonomous Republic of whom 162,000 were Crimean Tartars (26%); 318,000 Russians (51%); 50,000 Germans (8%) and 94,000 (15%) of other nationalities. In that year, there was a total of 300,000 Crimean Tartars in the Soviet Union; i.e., about 138,000 Crimean Tartars still lived outside their Republic. By 1939, the Crimean Autonomous Republic increased to 200,000 or 28 per cent of the total population, in spite of the deportation of 30,000 to 40,000 Crimean Tartars in the late 1920s and early 1930s to the Urals and Siberia, during the Soviet collectivization drive. During this same period a violent anti-religious drive led to the assassination or the deportation of most Tartar Muslim *ulemas*. The state terror then turned to the Muslim masses in the 1936–38 period.

World War II brought on the Crimean Tartars a catastrophe similar to that of the Crimean War. During the war, Germany invaded the Crimean Republic. When the Soviet Union reconquered the lost territories, it falsely accused the Muslim population of collaboration with the Germans. Stalin decided to punish the entire Crimean Tartar population in a manner reminiscent of the most barbaric periods of the middle ages. On 18 May 1944 the entire Crimean Tartar population was exiled to Central Asia (mainly Uzbekistan) and Siberia. Two years later, on 15 June 1946 the Crimean Autonomous Republic was abolished. The Crimean Tartars were also deprived of their civil rights, including the right to foster their language and culture. The Crimean Peninsula was then made a Region of the Russian Federal Republic. It was transferred in 1954 to the Ukrainian Federal Republic.

A total of 238,000 Muslims were thus deported in the most horrible circumstances, leading to the death through starvation, hunger, cold, illness and sorrow of 110,000 people mostly women and children (or 46 per cent of the total). After their departure Soviet authorities bulldozed their mosques, their *madrasahs*, their cemeteries. They burned their books and they destroyed their museums, removing any memory of their existence in Crimea. The Crimean Tartar language was abolished, and the Crimean Tartar nationality was declared nonexistent.

During his de-Stalinization programme, Premier Nikita Khruschev of the Soviet Union absolved the Crimean Tartar Community of the accusations made against them. The exiled Crimean Tartars regained their civil rights in Uzbekistan in 1956. They were, however, not only denied any compensation for the harm that they had unjustly suffered, they were not even permitted to return to their homeland. The Crimean Tartars have been agitating for return to their country ever since. Protest demonstrations in the 1960s and 1970s in Uzbekistan were suppressed and the leaders of the community were tried as dissidents. But the Crimean Tartars have shown extraordinary persistence. On 22 August 1978 five thousand members of the community sent a petition to the Central Committee of the Soviet Communist Party requesting authorization to leave Uzbekistan and settle in Crimea. They demanded the re-establishment of the Autonomous Republic of Crimea and the right to return to their homeland.

In 1970, the population of the Crimean Peninsula was 1,623,000 people of whom 1,136,000 were Russians (70 %); 406,000 Ukrainians (25 %); and 81,000 were members of other nationalities (5 %). As for the Crimean Tartars, only 1,600 families were permitted to return to their homes between the years 1967 and 1978. Thus, in 1982 there were only about 10,000 Crimean Tartars in Crimea, which constitutes less than 1 per cent of the total population, while many thousands were evicted by force whenever they dared come back to Crimea.

In 1982, one can estimate the total number of Crimean Tartars in the Soviet Union at about 400,000 people, of whom at least 250,000 lived in Uzbekistan and the rest were scattered across the Soviet Union. However, these figures are only estimates, since the Soviet census does not count Crimean Tartars separately, but counts them with the Kazan Tartars.

## Endangered Nationalities

The other Muslim national group that suffered most from Russian annihilation tactics are the Cherkess. They are to be found today in great numbers in Turkey, Syria, Lebanon, Jordan, Palestine and Egypt. By the time of the establishment of the Soviet State in 1917 only a tiny fraction of them remained in their homeland. There were 30,000 in the Soviet Union in 1959 and they became 46,000 in 1979.

Under the Soviet Regime, the other Muslim national groups which were deported en masse to Siberia, and whose republics were abolished after World War II are the Chechens and the Ingushs (about 500,000 in all) and the Karatchay and the Balkars (about 120,000). Thus, after World War II, two Muslim Autonomous Republics (Crimea and Chechen-Ingush) as well as an Autonomous Region (Karatchay) were abolished. Moreover, Muslims in other districts have been removed from their homes and dispersed across the Soviet Union. Among these are the Nogay people of the Kizliar district in Eastern Caucasus; the Tartars and the Cherkess of the Taman Peninsula, the Cherkess of the Adigh Autonomous Region and the Meskhetians of Georgia. Thus, a total of more than two million Muslims have been condemned to cultural death by the Soviet authorities since World War II.

It was during Premier Khruschev's tenure that the Chechen-Ingush territory was re-established first as an Autonomous Region in 1957, and then as an Autonomous Republic. Under the same decree, the Kabard Autonomous Republic became the Kabard-Balkar Autonomous Republic; and the Cherkess Autonomous Region became the Karachai-Cherkess Autonomous Region, all within the Federal Republic of Russia. A. F. Gorkine, the Secretary of the Presidium of the Supreme Soviet characterized the deportation of these populations as 'a gross violation of the

Leninist policy toward nationalities' in declaring the re-establishment of the above mentioned territories. Yet, he did not say a word about the Crimean Tartars.

The operation of repatriation of the exiled Muslims lasted until 1960. For instance, in 1970, of a total of 1,084,000 people in the Chechen-Ingush Autonomous Republic, 635,000 people were Chechen-Ingush, or 58.5 per cent of the population. The number of Chechens in the Soviet Union rose from 419,000 in 1959 to 756,000 in 1979; that of the Ingush, from 106,000 to 186,000; that of the Karachai, from 81,000 to 131,000; and that of the Balkar, from 42,000 to 66,000. Thus, these nationalities have regained their territories and their demographic vitality.

But those who suffered most from the Russian campaign of physical and cultural elimination as well as dispersion are the Tartars in general, of whom the Crimean Tartars are one important section. In numbers, Tartars were second among the Muslim nationalities only to the Uzbeks. They became third in 1979 census after the Uzbecks and the Kazakhs. But while the Uzbeks and the Kazakhs are well concentrated in their republics, the Tartars found themselves dispersed in a diaspora that encompasses most of the Soviet Union owing to the five centuries of Russian persecution and deportations. The Tartar communities are found outside the Soviet Union as well: in Poland, Rumania, Bulgaria, Turkey, Saudi Arabia, China, Japan, Australia, and the US (especially California and New York).

Christianization was imposed on the Volga Tartars at least four times without much success. First, in the sixteenth century under Ivan IV. Then, in 1740, when a decree from the Tzar imposed taxes and military service on the Kazan Tartars who refused to be baptized. Then, in 1742, when the Russian Senate decided to destroy all mosques, except those of villages and towns where there are no Christians. Thus, 418 mosques out of a total of 536 were razed to the ground. Finally, in 1864, when Ilminsky baptized by force about 160,000 Muslim Tartars. Most of their descendants returned to Islam in 1905 when a new constitution allowed them to do so. Tartars were continuously transferred from one region to another under a variety of pretexts.

Today, the Tartar communities are found in most large cities of European Soviet Union, specifically in Kasimov, Vilnius, Astrakhan, Leningrad and Moscow, as well as in Siberia and Uzbekistan. The low rate of growth of the Tartars with respect to other nationalities is a result of low birth rates and continuous assimilation due to this dispersion. In 1920, a Tartar Autonomous Republic was established with Kazan as capital. But the population of this Republic was made up mostly by Russian settlers. However, since World War II the percentage of the Tartar population in the Tartar Republic tended to increase. For instance, in 1959, there were 1,345,000 Tartars in their Republic out of a total population of 2,850,000 and a total Tartar population of 4,968,000 in the Soviet Union. Thus their percentage in the Republic was 47.2 per cent and the percentage of those Tartars who lived in their own Republic with respect to the total Tartar population of the Soviet Union was 27.1 per cent. In 1970, there were 1,536,000 Tartars in their Republic out of a total population of 3,131,000 and a total Tartar population of 5,930,000 in the Soviet Union. Thus, the percentages became respectively 49.1 and 25.9. The 1979 census shows a trend of stabilization in both the dispersion of the Tartar population and in their dilution in their own Republic. Indeed, there were 1,642,000 Tartars in their republic compared to 6,556,000 Tartars in the Soviet Union. Thus, the above percentages became respectively 47.6 and 26 per cent.

It was on 15 November 1944 that all Meskhetians were deported from Georgia along with other Muslims near the Turkish border. There were about 200,000 Muslims, thus punished for the simple reason that they were Muslims. They were transported to Kazakhstan and Uzbekistan under the most terrible circumstances, leading to the death of 25 per cent of them. On 28 April 1956, they were freed from the 'special settler' regime. Since then, they agitated unsuccessfully for the right to return to their homes in Georgia or to emigrate to Turkey. To this day, their efforts brought no results.

## Conclusions

After this overview of the situation of Muslims in the Soviet Union, the questions to be posed are, what are their chances of surviving and thriving as Muslims? What are the future trends in general in the Soviet Union?

To answer these questions a comparison between the situation before and after World War II is necessary. Between the censuses of 1926 and 1939, the Russian population of the Soviet Union increased by 27 per cent whereas that of the total population of the Union (including the Muslims) increased by only 16 per cent Demographically, the period was a catastrophe for the Muslim population: the Muslim nationality which suffered most were the Kazakhs and the effect of the catastrophe is felt to this day. From 1939 to 1970, the situation reversed itself, and the trend is becoming more pronounced after 1970. The Muslim populations increased at a faster rate than the other populations. This in effect halted the efforts of Russification, even in Kazakhstan, where Muslims became a minority. While some regions, such as Crimea were purged entirely of their Muslim populations, one can nevertheless say that demographically the situation improved greatly for the Muslims.

In terms of their distribution, the Muslims occupy a compact area making up about 20 per cent of the area of the Soviet Union. While the Muslim republics and autonomous regions seem to be split into three main areas: the Caucasus, the Volga and Central Asia, the territories lying between these areas are also regions of Muslim concentration, although excluded from the Muslim nationality regions. Since 1939 there was no further dispersion of the Muslim population. Today about 93 per cent of Soviet Muslims live in areas where they form the majority or near majority of the population.

Religiously, there is official segregation against those who practice Islam openly. However, public prayers are not forbidden, Islamic festivals are celebrated and the Muslim religious organization is in existence and functioning. Even smaller groups of Muslims such as those of Leningrad and Moscow get together to pray. Thus, even in this respect, the situation is improving. The Muslim religious leadership has lately showed great wisdom and tact to induce improvement without antagonizing the Soviet authorities. For acting wisely they deserve the respect of the Muslims both inside and outside the Soviet Union. The religious organization is paid by the Soviet State in exchange for the confiscated *waqf*. It is also recognized by the Soviet authorities as a civil entity.

The number of existing Muslim institutions decreased greatly. But the existing ones are fully used to the point that the construction of new mosques has been tolerated here and there. Thus, the lowest point in the downward trend in this respect seems to be already over and slow improvement is expected.

Modern communications media, the freeing of the colonies elsewhere in the world, the spread of Islam in the American continent, the revolutionary movements of suppressed Muslim populations in Africa and Asia inspired by Islam, the heroic struggle of the Afghan people against Soviet imperialism, all these had the most impressive effects on Islam in the Soviet Union. Muslim youth are getting greater awareness of their Islamic heritage, and are less inclined to hide positive feelings towards Islam. Their adherence to Islam is a kind of super-national feeling that binds together all Muslims of the Soviet Union. When in 1978, the Muslim American heavy-weight champion, Muhammad Ali, visited the USSR and met the highest authorities, he made a point to visit Tashkent (in fact the Muslim capital of the Soviet Union) and pray in its Mosque. This act was received with wild excitement, and the champion was received more like a Muslim champion than just a heavy-weight champion.

Economically, the Muslim areas have the greatest impact on Soviet economy: most of the Soviet cotton is produced in Uzbekistan, Kazakhstan and Azerbaijan. Muslim areas produce 75 per cent of electricity, over 50 per cent of oil, 75 per cent of lead, 50 per cent of zinc, etc. The importance of these regions is expected to increase rather than decrease.

Thus, in spite of all the miseries of the past, Islam in the Soviet Union has retained a good deal that is necessary for its survival. It has been pushed outside the political, economical and social life of the country, but could not be obliterated from the hearts of its followers. As the atrocities of the Tsars, Lenin and Stalin become more and more impossible to repeat, Islam is bound to come back to the surface again.

Once Muslims are given back their religious freedom of expression and their political rights as Muslims, they will certainly respond by collaborating in building up the Soviet society as a multicultural society where Islam will have the important and increasing role it deserves. Materialism alone as developed by the Communist theories brought only human and spiritual misery. Many see that this spiritual void can only be filled by Islam. In this lies the challenge presented to the Muslims of the Soviet Union. Among a people who were able to survive centuries of atrocious persecution and colonization a growing confidence is noticeable: that the Islam which they had tried to retain is not only the remedy for their own ailments but also for the ailments of the country in which they live, and the people with whom their destiny seems inextricably linked and to whom they can still bring salvation through Islam.

## References

1. F. de Romainville, *Islam en Union Sovietique* (Paris, 1947).
2. R. Pipes, *The Formation of the Soviet Union* (Mass., USA, 1954).
3. V. Monteil, *The Soviet Muslims* (Paris, 1957).
4. J. P. Roux, *Islam in Asia* (Paris, 1958).
5. A. Hetmatek, *Islam under the Soviets* Ph.D. thesis (Georgetown University, Washington, D.C., 1965).
6. A. Benningson & C. Lemercier Quelquejay, *Islam in the Soviet Union*, (London, 1967).
7. M. A. Kettani, *Muslims in Communist States* (Mecca, Saudi Arabia, 1974).
8. K. Lavencic, 'Muslims in USSR' *Impact International* (London, 9–22 April 1976).
9. M. Abdul-Wahhab, *Muslims in the Soviet Union* (Moscow, Soviet Union, 1977) (in Russian).
10. S. Maslouh, 'Muslims in the Soviet Union' paper presented at the International Seminar on Muslim Communities in non-Muslim State (London, July 1978).
11. A. Woodrow, 'La Vie Religieuse en USSR' *Le Monde* (Paris, 7 and 8 September 1978).
12 H. Carrere d'Encausse, *L'Empire Eclaté* (Paris, 1978).
13. Radio Liberty, 'The All-Union Census of 1979 in the USSR' *Research Bulletin* (Munich, September 1980).
14. A. Sheehy and B. Nahaylo, *The Crimean Tartars, Volga Germans and Meskhetians* (Minority Rights Group 1981).
15. A. Seytmuratova, *The Plight of the Crimean Tartars*. International Conference of the 15th Century Hijra, Kuala Lumpur, Malaysia (24 November – 4 December 1981).
16. S. Akiner, *Islamic People of the Soviet Union* (England, 1983).

# 4 Muslims in China

## Introduction

Islam arrived in China by two commercial routes: the earlier, maritime and the more recent, terrestrial. The Muslim community of China has increased constantly throughout the years by immigration, conversion, and mixed marriages.

With the exception of Eastern Turkestan (Sinkiang–Uighur), which is actually a part of the Turkic rather than the Chinese world, Islam was never able to establish an enduring independent political entity in China. True, under the Mongol regime (1279–1368), the Muslims of China were extremely influential, to the point that many historians considered the Yuan dynasty a Muslim one. This influence did not decline under the Ming dynasty (1368–1644) during which the Muslims became well integrated within the Chinese culture without any loss to their Muslim identity.

The Muslims of China went through a period of atrocious and continuous persecution which lasted about three centuries under the Manchu dynasty (1644–1911). This led in the nineteenth century to Muslim revolutions and to the establishment of short-lived Muslim states in Yunnan, Khansu and Eastern Turkestan. All these states were destroyed at an enormous cost of Muslim lives.

Coming to the present century, the Chinese Nationalist Revolution of 1911 was supported by the Muslim masses which were exceedingly eager to destroy the Manchu regime. From 1911 to 1948, Islam witnessed a true Renaissance in China and the Muslims began to retrieve some of their erstwhile influence. Since the establishment of the Communist regime in 1948, a new type of persecution was perpetrated against Muslims. All contacts between Muslims in different parts of China and the rest of the world ceased. Mosques and Muslim schools were closed, *imams* were killed or imprisoned. The Muslim family structure was assaulted and its members dispersed.

A large majority of the Muslims of China follows the Hanafi school of law. 90 per cent of Muslims are Chinese in almost every sense of the term. Their names are Chinese, their facial features are Chinese and so is their culture. These are often called Huis by the other Chinese. The remaining 10 per cent are Turks and Mongols. Muslims are more numerous in the northern than in the southern provinces.

The Communist regime does not require the religious identification in the census. However, the number of Muslims who are not of Chinese ethnic origin can be assessed from the census on nationalities. For those who are ethnically Chinese, their numbers can be calculated on the basis of the 1936 census. This census indicates the number of Muslims in each province as well as the total Muslim population. The total was assessed then at 47,437,000 persons or 10.5 per cent of the total population. Assuming that this percentage has remained unchanged, we arrive at the figure of 107 million in 1982.

Muslims are in majority in two territories: the Sinkiang–Uighur Autonomous Region and the Chinghai Province. Muslims form also near-majorities in two other territories the Ninghsia-Hui (47%) and the Khansu (40%). However, territories with high Muslim percentages are subject to intense non-Muslim immigration which tends to dilute their Islamic character.

For the Muslims of China the period 1952–68 was similar to the Stalinist era in the Soviet Union. Artificial famines were created, Muslim populations were dispersed, mosques were burnt, copies of the Holy *Quran* were torn apart, and Muslim leaders were persecuted and humiliated. It is only recently, that some improvements in the lot of Muslims seem to have taken place. Hopes have increased after the death of Mao-Tse-Tung and the elimination of the 'Gang of Four'.

The Muslim communities of Hong Kong, Taiwan and Macao will be considered in Chapter 6, since they live under different circumstances.

## Historical Background

Old Chinese sources report that an Arab delegation arrived in China in the year II of the reign of Emperor Yung Way of the

Tang dynasty; ie, in the year 31 A.H. (651 C.E.) during the tenure of Caliph Uthman. Chinese Muslims believe that the members of this delegation, who were 15 in number, were the first Muslims to enter China. They believe that they were under Saad Ibn Abi Waqqas, one of the companions of the Prophet. The delegation came to China by sea, landed at Canton, then went by land to the capital Shang-An (today's Sian) where they were well received by the Emperor and permitted to build a mosque. This mosque, believed to be the first in China, exists to this day. There is also a mosque in Canton on the tomb of Saad, the head of this delegation. However, this story has not been verified in Arab sources, and it is certain that Saad Ibn Abi Waqqas died in Medina. This means that the head of the delegation must have been another Saad.

Muslim armies reached the borders of China for the first time by land during the time of the Umayyad Caliph Al-Walid. Al-Hajjaj Ibn Yusuf Al-Thaqafi, the governer of Iraq at that time sent a Muslim army under the leadership of Qutaybah Ibn Muslim Al-Bahili to the borders of China. The army left Samarkand (Uzbekistan) in 93 A.H. (711 C.E.) and entered Kashgar (Sinkiang) in 96 A.H. (714 C.E.). The Chinese Emperor then agreed to pay tribute to the Muslims as a sign of allegiance to the Muslim State.

Commercial ties increased greatly between the Muslim State and China. Commerce was carried on first by the sea route, and then when Kashgar became part of the Muslim State, by the land route. Most of the merchants were Muslims, and were generally from Arabia and Persia. Relations between China and the Muslim State during the Umayyad and Abbasid dynasties remained continuously cordial and embassies and delegations were exchanged. In 138 A.H. (755 C.E.) the Chinese Emperor requested help from the Muslim State to quell the rebellion of An-Lu-Chan. The Caliph complied by sending an army of 4,000 Muslim soldiers who defeated the rebels and settled in the land. They married Chinese women and raised Muslim families, thus giving a strong demographic support to the first communities of Muslims in China.

The numbers of Muslim merchants from Arabia and Persia who settled in Canton increased significantly until they formed an important proportion of the city's population. In 141 A.H. (758 C.E.), they rebelled against the Emperor because of heavy taxes, which were then removed. In 145 A.H. (762 C.E.), Muslims once more helped the Emperor quell the rebellion of another rebel, Shei-Chu-Bei.

Canton became the focus of expansion of Muslim communities toward Hang-Chu on the northern shorelines. They built mosques and schools wherever they went. In 259 A.H. (872 C.E.), the Arab traveller Ibn Wahb visited Canton and met the Muslims there as he met the Emperor. However, seven years later, catastrophe befell the Muslims as rebels burnt the city and killed more than 100,000 Muslims. The Tang dynasty did not survive these events and fell in 295 A.H. (907 C.E.).

During the Tang dynasty, Muslims were prosperous and were respected in China. But, in spite of widespread mixed marriages, they remained a foreign element, in terms of language, ethnic origin and physical features. However, many emperors accorded them preferential treatment. This privileged situation increased under the following Siung dynasty. There were eighty-six delegations from the Muslim State to China between 31 A.H. (651 C.E.) and 604 A.H. (1207 C.E.). There was continuous flow of Muslim immigrants who built entire satellite Muslim cities near the largest Chinese ports. They built mosques and schools and established their own institutions. They nominated their own governors who were usually accepted by the Emperor.

The Muslims of China formed the rich mercantile class with international connections. They were needed for Chinese commerce and were held in high esteem. During the Siung dynasty the newly created post of Director General of the Sea in Canton was always held by a Muslim. During the same period, the Muslim population increased both as a result of immigration through the Kashgar route, and by conversion of local populations, the most spectacular of which was the mass conversion of Hsiung Nu tribes.

Mongols under Chingis Khan invaded China and brought down the Siung dynasty. Kubilay Khan, son of Chingis, established the Yuan dynasty. By that time the Mongol armies conquered most of the Asian parts of the Muslim world and destroyed the Abbassid Caliphate and the Muslim capital Baghdad. But, the side effect was a Pax Mongolica which enclosed parts of the Muslim world and China in one single unit. This situation encouraged movement of people and ideas which in turn, contributed to mass conversion to Islam, especially among the Mongol overlords. Eventually, Muslims became the leading class in all Mongol states including China. It is around this period that for the first time Persian replaced Arabic as the language of the Chinese Muslim community. Most of the high officials of the army, the government and the administration in the Yuan dynasty were Muslims. The Persian historian Rashid-Din Fadlullah reports in the first volume of his *Encyclopedia of Histories* that 'in the era of the Mongol state of Kubilay Khan, China was divided in fourteen provinces. At the head of each province there was a governor and a vice-governor. Eight of the governors were Muslims and the four vice-governors of the other provinces were Muslims as well.' Among the most famous Muslim statesmen of China in that period was Al-Sayyid Al-Ajall Shamsuddin Umar. He was most remembered as governor of Yunnan province between 1278 and 1279 C.E. His son Al-Sayyid Bayin became the prime minister of the Emperor of China between 1333 and 1340 C.E.

The Moroccan traveller Ibn Battutah visited China during this period. He reports that 'each city of China had a Muslim city in which lived only Muslims. In these cities there were mosques and other institutions. Muslims are very respected'.

The Mongol (Yuan) dynasty collapsed in 1368 C.E. It was replaced by the Ming dynasty which lasted three centuries until 1644 C.E. During this period, Muslims reached the zenith of their prosperity and influence. This period is also characterized by an end of Muslim immigration and a marked increase of Chinese conversion to Islam. The effect was a complete change of the characteristics of the Muslim community, from an alien one, in spite of seven centuries of presence, to a completely indigenous community, without any loss in its Islamic identity. The most spectacular result of this indigenization is the replacement of Persian as the lingua franca of the Muslim community by Mandarin Chinese in which an extensive body of Muslim literature came to be developed. Another effect was the spread of Chinese names among Muslims: Muhammed became 'Ma', Mustapha became 'Mu', Masud 'Si', Dawud and Tahir 'Ta', Hasan 'Ha', Husayn 'Hu', Badruddin, Jalaluddin, etc, became 'Ning'; Najib and Nasir became 'Na'; Salim, Salih became 'Sha', Ali became 'Ay', etc. Muslims absorbed also Chinese habits which did not interfere with Islamic teachings. They intermarried with the Chinese converts so extensively that it became impossible to recognize a Muslim Chinese from non-Muslim Chinese.

The Muslim influence during the Ming dynasty was even bigger than in the Mongol dynasty. The first Emperor of the dynasty, Ming Tsai Tsu, and the Empress are thought to have been Muslims. The Emperor's love for Prophet Muhammed was well known and quite undisguised. He wrote a poem in praise of the Prophet and sculpted it on marble in the Jami Mosque of the city of Nankin (it exists to this day). Emperor Yung Lu (1405–32 C.E.) used the *Hijrah* Calendar as the official calendar of China and sent his Muslim ambassador, Chang Hu, to several Muslim states to establish cordial relations with them. Most of the high officials of the Ming dynasty were also Muslims.

## Modern Islamic Renaissance in China

The Ming dynasty was brought down by Manchu invaders who established the Ching dynasty. This was a foreign occupation which based itself on 'divide and rule'. From the beginning, they showed an intense dislike for Muslims and considered them as supporters of the former dynasty. Under the Ching regime from 1644 to 1911 C.E. Muslims were subjected to the worst atrocities. They reacted by rebelling continuously against the regime which resulted in heavy loss of life, influence and property.

The Ching concentrated their anti-Islamic efforts on regions of high Islamic density such as Eastern Turkestan, Khansu and Yunnan. There was then a string of unsuccessful Muslim revolutions: those led by Su Sei-San (1758 C.E.) and by Ma Man-Sein (1768 C.E.) in Khansu; the revolt led by Gingah in Eastern Turkestan (1825–27 C.E.); the revolt of Sulayman Dwo-Nasyn in Yunnan (1837–55 C.E.), and the revolt of Yaqub in Shau-Si, in Khansu and Eastern Turkestan (1855–75 C.E.).

The most important of these revolutions is that of Yunnan during which, the Muslims were able to free the cities of Dali and Yunnan (the capital of the province). They were also able to establish a Muslim state. However, this state was infiltrated and after eighteen years of independence it was destroyed from within by civil war. This was followed by widespread mass killings of Muslims which reduced their numbers greatly. The revolution of Yaqub in Khansu lasted for twenty-five years. In the beginning the Muslims seemed to have won the war, but in the end they were destroyed just as in Yunnan.

Thus, the nineteenth century in China was a century of continuous Muslim rebellion against oppression. It can be summarized in the words of the well-known Chinese Imam Ibrahim Shiong: 'The history of the Muslim struggle for life during more than three centuries of oppression and despotism is the best proof of their (Muslims') unity and their fantastic will to stand up to any one who dares to threaten their belief and their Islamic way of life for whatever length of time this has been done'.

No wonder then that Muslims were among the staunchest supporters of the Republican Revolution of 1911. The first president of the republic Dr Sun Yat Sen, responded by freeing the Muslims from all persecution. He declared that the Chinese were a nation of five equal components: the Han (Buddhist Chinese); the Hui (Muslim Chinese); the Ming (Mongol); the Man (Manchu); and Tsang (Tibetans).

The three centuries of Manchu persecution left, however, the Muslims poorer, reduced in number, and cut off from the rest of the Muslim world. Although their Islamic adherence was strong, their Islamic practice required much to be improved. After 1911, the Chinese Muslims re-established contacts with the Muslims of the world, made efforts at organization and education and brought back the Muslim masses to the orthodox line. Most prominent was the establishment in 1913 of the Progressive Chinese Muslim Organization in Peking headed by Al-Hadj Ahound Wang Haonan whose activity concentrated on spreading Islamic education, teaching the Arabic language and building of mosques and schools. In 1938, a new Pan-Chinese Muslim organization was established under the chairmanship of a Muslim general in the army. The latter organized a Muslim militia to defend their country against Japanese invasion. The same organization translated the meaning of the *Quran* into the Chinese language, and sent hundreds of young students to Turkish and Egyptian universities for Islamic studies. In 1926, the Chinese Muslim Cultural Organization was established in Shanghai. It was headed by Al-Hadj Jalaluddeen Hat-Hshing. The role of the organization was to arrange for the establishment of Quranic studies (*tafsir*) and *Hadith* of the Holy Prophet. The organization started a great number of schools and libraries and gave scholarships to many students.

Culturally, there took place a genuine Muslim renaissance in China in the period 1911–48. During this period the Muslims built more than a thousand primary schools and scores of secondary ones. They succeeded in introducing Arabic and Islamic studies in Chinese universities such as Peking University, the Central University, Tchung San University, etc . . . They produced a large amount of Islamic literature in the Chinese language through such Islamic magazines as: *Chinese Islamic Studies Magazine*; *the Islamic Gazette*; *the Journal*; *the Light of Islam*; *Sunset*; *the Muslim*

*Youth*; *A-Islah*; *Humanity*; *Tu-Chee Magazine*; *Bang-Tou Magazine, the Borders*; *Al-Awqaf,* etc.

Politically, the Muslims made a spectacular comeback. A great many of them joined the Nationalist revolution and fought with great courage. They responded to the call of Dr Sun Yat Sen when he said in one of his famous speeches: 'The Muslims have strong revolutionary aims. They resisted oppression in the bygone centuries. For this reason we request them to join our revolutionary movement. The Chinese National Movement would not succeed without the help of the Muslims, and the job of vanquishing colonialism would not be done without a complete unity in efforts between the Chinese and Muslim *ummah*'.

By 1946, there were more than one hundred Muslim deputies in the Chinese parliament. The governors of Muslim majority areas were all Muslim: Eastern Turkestan; Tsinghai and Ningsia; and Khansu. There were many Muslim ministers in the government such as Mr Ma Fu Sian, and General Omar Bay who was Minister of Defence after World War II. Muslims joined the army in great numbers and many of them, such as generals Husayn Bufan Ma, Bushin Ma and Jee-Yuan Ma, became prominent.

Efforts at organizing all Muslims of China under one single umbrella were started by the Muslims of Mongolia, who in 1938, sponsored the formation of the 'League of the Five Ma'.

*Table 4.1*   Muslims in China as estimated by Broomhall, 1850 C.E.

| Province | Number of Muslims *thousands* |
|---|---|
| Eastern Turkestan | 2,400 |
| Khansu | 3,000 |
| Hopeh and Peking | 1,000 |
| Shan-Si | 1,000 |
| Yunnan | 1,000 |
| Manchuria | 200 |
| Shan-Toung | 200 |
| Honan | 200 |
| Kiang-Su | 250 |
| Sichuan | 250 |
| Other regions | 141 |
| Total | 9,641 |

## Numerical Strength and National Distribution

The number of Muslims in China was not known with any accuracy
in the nineteenth century. It was actually estimated between five
million and sixty million. But it is certain that their number decreased during that century because of continuous warfare and
persecution. This is attested by the statements of many European
eye-witnesses. They mentioned the existence of a large number
of mosques and schools in towns and cities out of proportion with
the number of Muslims as well as the fact that entire regions in
Khansu and Yunnan were cleared of their Muslim populations.
The nearest estimate to the probable reality is the one given by
Broomhall. Broomhall based his estimates on a survey he made by
questioning two hundred Muslim Chinese from different parts of
China. Table 4.1 reports his results.

The Broomhall estimates give an idea of where the Muslims are
concentrated, but the figures given are certainly lower than reality.
The number of Muslims was most probably around twenty million
by 1850. The situation has been clarified by the 1936 census in
which people were required to mention their religious affiliation.
The results of this census are given in Table 4.2.

The Communist regime made a census in 1953 in China. But this
regime did not give any importance to the religious affiliation
of the populations. In the same manner as in the USSR, it recognized the principle of nationalities in the outlying regions. The
regime recognized six Muslim 'nationalities' in the Sinkiang–Uighur
autonomous region; two in the Khansu Province, and one in
Chinghai.

The census of 1953 estimated the number of Muslims to be ten
million. This figure is completely unrealistic in view of the less
biased census of nineteen years earlier. Muslims could not have
been reduced from 47,437,000 in 1936 to 10,000,000 in 1953, while
the population of China as a whole increased from 452,460,000 to
573,269,000 during the same period, ie by 26.7 per cent. To estimate the true number of Muslims in 1953, let us first explain the
figure presented by the 1953 census.

The Muslims of China can be divided into three main national
groups: The Turks: Uighur, Kazakh, Kirghiz, Uzbek, Tartars
and those who are Muslims among the Salars, Hichus; etc ...
the Uighur forming the core of the Muslim population of Eastern Turkestan; The Chinese Muslims, often called Huis by non-
Muslims; and others who are Tajik (Persian-speaking Muslims)

Table 4.2   Muslims in China, 1936 official census

| Territory | Muslim Population thousands |
|---|---|
| Eastern Turkestan | 3,351 |
| Kuang-Si | 287 |
| Ninghsia | 453 |
| Tibet | 100 |
| Inner Mongolia | 2,359 |
| Chinghai | 786 |
| Khansu | 2,511 |
| Manchuria | 5,534 |
| Shantung | 3,890 |
| Shansi | 2,129 |
| Hopei & Peking | 4,359 |
| Shensi | 1,530 |
| Honan | 6,095 |
| Hupei | 1,587 |
| Szechwan | 2,615 |
| Yunnan | 2,508 |
| Kweichow | 519 |
| Hunan | 1,321 |
| Canton | 558 |
| Kiangsi | 280 |
| Fukien | 7 |
| Taiwan | 70 |
| Chekiang | 357 |
| Anhwei | 2,289 |
| Kiangsu | 1,963 |
| Total Muslim population | 47,437 |
| Total population of China | 452,460 |
| Muslim Percentage | 10.5% |

and minority Muslim representation among the Lolos, Mongols, Sihia, Tibetans, Taosan, etc. ... Actually, the Turks form about 10 per cent of the total number of Muslims, whereas the Chinese Muslims form about 85 per cent of the Muslims population. The result of the 1953 census by nationality and the official estimates of 1978 are given in Table 4.3

It seems that the Communist regime of 1953 took into account only those Muslims who lived in the autonomous regions. They seem to have ignored the mass of Chinese Muslims living in the different provinces. Another possibility is that while 'Hui' is considered as nationality by the Chinese non-Muslims, it is not

*Table 4.3*   Muslims in China, 1953 census and official estimates of 1978

| National Group | 1953 | 1978 |
|---|---|---|
| | *thousands* | *thousands* |
| Uighur | 3,640 | 5,480 |
| Huis | 3,560 | 6,500 |
| Kazakh | 470 | 800 |
| Others | 2,330 | 4,000 |
| Total | 10,000 | 16,780 |

*Table 4.4*   Muslims in the autonomous regions

| | Muslims 1936 | Population 1953 | | |
|---|---|---|---|---|
| | | Total | Muslim, est. | |
| | *thousands* | *thousands* | *thousands* | |
| Sinkiang-Uighur | 3,351 | 4,874 | 4,420 | 90.7% |
| Ninghsia-Khansu | 1,239 | 12,928 | 1,740 | 13.5% |
| Tibet | 100 | 1,273 | 140 | 11.0% |
| Kwangsi-Chuang | 287 | 19,561 | 400 | 2.0% |
| Inner Mongolia | 2,359 | 6,100 | 3,300 | 54.0% |
| Total | 7,331 | 44,736 | 10,000 | |

considered so by the Muslims themselves who consider themselves Chinese by nationality and Muslim by religion. In fact, a similar situation exists in Yugoslavia where only Bosnians consider themselves as 'Muslim' by nationality; and others would declare themselves 'Albanian' or 'Macedonian', or 'Turk' or even 'Croatian' or 'Serbian' without, for that matter, feeling any less allegiance to Islam. Consider, for the sake of argument, the number of Muslims in the autonomous regions given in 1936 and the estimated figures for 1953. This last figure is reached by estimating an increase of 40 per cent of the Muslim population in the 1936–1953 period in the autonomous regions.

Now it becomes possible to deduce the approximate number of Muslims in the whole of China based on figures published by the government in 1968. We will base our calculation on the conservative assumption that the percentage of the Muslim population remained constant between the years 1936 and 1968. However, it is almost certain, at least among non-ethnic Chinese Muslims that the rate of increase has been higher than the national average as assessed in Table 4.4.

Table 4.5 shows that there were seventy-seven million Muslims in China in 1968. However, Muslims were in the majority in only

*Table 4.5*   Estimated Muslim populations in the different territories of China, 1968

T, Autonomous Region; M, Municipality; P, Province

| Territory (Status) | Capital | Population in thousands | | |
|---|---|---|---|---|
| | | Total | Muslim | |
| Sinkiang-Uighur (T) | *Urumchi* | 8,000 | 5,700 | 71.2% |
| Chinghai (P) | *Sining* | 2,000 | 1,300 | 65.0% |
| Ninghsia-Hui (T) | *Yinchuan* | 2,300 | 800 | 35.2% |
| Khansu (P) | *Lanchow* | 12,700 | 4,000 | 31.6% |
| Inner Mongolia (T) | *Huhehot* | 13,000 | 3,800 | 29.2% |
| Tibet (T) | *Lhasa* | 1,000 | 200 | 20.0% |
| Honan (P) | *Chengchow* | 50,000 | 9,900 | 19.8% |
| Yunnan (P) | *Kuming* | 23,000 | 4,100 | 17.8% |
| Shausi (P) | *Taiyuan* | 20,000 | 3,500 | 17.5% |
| Hopei (P) | *Shihchiachuang* | 43,000 | 5,700 | 13.2% |
| Lianing (P) | *Shenyang* ⎫ | | | |
| Kirin (P) | *Changchun* ⎬ | 73,000 | 9,000 | 12.3% |
| Heilungkiang (P) | *Harbin* ⎭ | | | |
| Shensi (P) | *Sian* | 21,000 | 2,500 | 11.9% |
| Shantung (P) | *Tsinan* | 57,000 | 6,300 | 11.0% |
| Anhwei (P) | *Hofei* | 35,000 | 3,700 | 10.6% |
| Peking (M) | | 7,000 | 700 | 10.0% |
| Kiangsu (P) | *Nanking* | 47,000 | 3,200 | 6.8% |
| Hupei (P) | *Wuhan* | 38,000 | 2,600 | 6.8% |
| Szechuan (P) | *Chengtu* | 70,000 | 4,200 | 6.0% |
| Hunan (P) | *Changsha* | 38,000 | 2,100 | 5.5% |
| Kweichow (P) | *Kweiyang* | 20,000 | 800 | 4.0% |
| Shanghai (M) | — | 10,000 | 300 | 3.0% |
| Canton (P) | *Canton* | 43,000 | 900 | 2.1% |
| Kuangsi-Chuang (T) | *Nanning* | 24,000 | 500 | 2.1% |
| Kiangsi (P) | *Nanchang* | 25,000 | 500 | 2.0% |
| Chekiang (P) | *Hangchow* | 31,000 | 600 | 1.9% |
| Fukien (P) | *Fuchow* | 18,000 | 100 | 0.5% |
| Total | | 732,000 | 77,000 | 10.5% |

two territories: Sinkiang–Uighur Autonomous Region and the Chinghai Province. These are neighbouring territories with a total surface area of 2,367,800 square kilometres, or 25 per cent of the total area of China. However, most of this territory is desert area and its total Muslim population does not exceed seven million people, or about 9.1 per cent of the total Muslim population of China. In addition, Muslims form more than 25 per cent of the total population of three more territories: Ninghsia–Hui Autonomous Region, Khansu Province, and Inner Mongolia Autonomous Region. These three territories have a Muslim population of 8.6 million people out of a total of 28 million. About 54.2 million Muslims live in territories where they form more than 10 per cent of the population but less than 50 per cent; i.e. 70.4 per cent of the Muslim population. These territories are concentrated in the northern part of China. About 20.5 per cent of the Muslims live in areas where they form less than 10 per cent of the population; i.e., about 15.8 million in South-West China. The Honan Province has the highest number of Muslims with respect to any single province and is as such the core of the Muslim community of China. In the light of the above, it would be safe to estimate the Muslim population of China in 1982 to be at least 107 million out of a total population of 1,019 million.

## Geographical Distribution and Political Organization

It seems obvious from the above that the land route had a more lasting effect of Muslim influence than the sea route of immigration. Indeed, one can go all the way from Peking to Mecca by land, moving all the time, without any break, through areas of high Muslim density. In fact, one can cross Asia from Khansu to Mecca across Chinghai, Eastern Turkestan, and the Soviet Union without leaving Muslim majority areas.

However, the last two centuries have seen a dilution and dispersion of the Muslim population in China. Indeed Khansu Province had an extremely important place in the Muslim history of China. Muslims were in the majority there before the revolutions of the nineteenth century. Furthermore, the territories that have been grouped by the Communist regime into the Autonomous Region of Inner Mongolia had a Muslim majority during the Nationalist Regime. Non-Muslim Chinese immigration to these areas was so intense that the Muslim majority changed into a minority. In Yunnan Province, Muslims were also in majority in the nineteenth century. After the fall of the Muslim state there, great numbers of Muslims left the province, others were mercilessly killed by the Manchu regime and due to the immigration of non-Muslims into the area, the Muslim majority has been reduced to a minority of less than 20 per cent of the total population.

Thus, we can say that roughly one tenth of the Muslim population of China lives in the north-west Region in areas where they are in majority. Another tenth of the Muslims lives in other areas of the north-west and the north regions where they form more than a quarter, but less than one half of the population. Three fifths of the Muslim population lives in the provinces of the north, the north-east, the south-west and the central-south where they form more than one tenth of the population but less than one quarter. The last fifth lives in areas where they form less than one tenth of the population, and this is mostly in the eastern regions.

There seems to have been a deliberate effort under the Communist regime to dilute the Muslim majorities. Indeed, more than two million non-Muslim Chinese have been settled between 1950 and 1960 in Eastern Turkestan, Ninghsia–Hui, and Inner Mongolia; and several more millions have been settled after 1960. The effect of these efforts might soon lead to an end to any Muslim-majority area in China.

In January 1975 the Fourth National People's Congress approved a new Constitution under which China is considered to be a 'Socialist State of the dictatorship of the proletariat'. There are three types of administrative units: autonomous regions, provinces and municipalities directly administered by the government. There are twenty-two provinces, three municipalities (Peking, Shanghai, and Tientsin) and five autonomous regions: Inner Mongolia, Sinkiang–Uighur, Kwangsi–Chuang, Ninghsia–Hui and Tibet. Each autonomous region is established for a given nationality. Two of these territories have been established for Muslim nationalities, the Sinkiang for the Uighur and Ninghsia for the Hui. There are also a large number of Muslims who are Mongol as well as some Muslims among the Tibetans. These territories, however, have no more autonomy than their parallel ones in the Soviet Union. Nevertheless, they imply a degree of recognition of the national separateness of a given minority. There is also one province with Muslim majority, the Chinghai.

Consequently, the situation of Muslims in China is different from that of the Soviet Union since most of the Muslims of China share with the majority the culture (language) and national affiliation, whereas in the Soviet Union there are no Russian Muslims.

## The Situation of Muslims after the Maoist Revolution

It was seen that Muslims regained some of their freedom after the Chinese Nationalist Revolution of 1911. For this reason they were the best supporters, in general, of the Nationalist Government.

Most of the Muslims fought from the beginning against the Communist Party since they knew very well what happened to their brothers in the neighbouring USSR. The Muslims were more determined in their support to the Nationalists, especially after the Communist Party of China expressed in its constitution of 1931 'the freedom to fight religion'.

However, because of their intense nationalism, the Nationalist Government antagonized those Muslims who are not members of the Chinese nationality, especially in the western parts of the empire. Muslims felt also discriminated against in the areas of the south where they were few in numbers. Thus, many Muslims joined the forces of Mao-Tse-Tung and were organized in separate regiments even before 1949.

The Maoist period could be divided into three sub-periods as far as the attitude of the regime towards the Muslims was considered. The first period is from the establishment of the People's Republic on 21 September 1949 to the beginning of the Cultural Revolution in 1966. The second period is that of the Cultural Revolution and covers the years 1966–1969. Finally, there is the third period which extends from 1969 to the death of Mao-Tse-Tung in 1976.

At the beginning of the first period, Muslims tried to resist. They revolted in Eastern Turkestan in 1949 under the leadership of Yul Pars Khan, Othman Batour and Kalin Khan. They revolted also in Khansu in 1952 under Ma Hin Tao and Yang Gee Youn.

The first period was characterized by a lenient attitude towards Islam compounded with a definite trend towards its atrophy and controlling its religious hierarchy. The leaders of the old 'Chinese Muslim Association' moved to Taiwan. The other Muslim organizations were disbanded one after the other. The cultural and religious freedoms of the Muslim community were limited. However, the oppression during this period was not continuous. Two important Muslim organizations were established in 1953 in Peking: the 'China Muslims Organization' and the 'Hui Cultural Association', grouping together all the Muslims of China. The president of the latter was no less than the president of the Provincial Government of Sin-Kiang himself. The first was led by distinguished Chinese Muslim leaders who were respected all over the Muslim world. It produced a large quantity of Muslim literature for Chinese Muslims. The leader was Haji Burhan Shahidi assisted by two deputies Ahung (*Imam*) Sha Meng-pi and Ahung Tan Tung. Ahung Ma Chien, a graduate of Al-Azhar University was also prominent. A Central Institute of Nationalities was established to 'protect' Islamic culture among other minority cultures. Mosques remained open and well attended. *Wakf* property was not touched. In Sin-Kiang it has even been tax-exempted since 1952. Special schools for Muslims were functioning in Peking and elsewhere, famous among them being the Islamic College. In 1954, the Muslim religion was declared protected after 70,000 Muslims sent telegrams requesting such protection. As for the Central Committee of the Government, it had two Muslim members out of a total of fifty-six (there should have been six if their proportion in the population had been respected). Three-quarters of the members of the Sin-Kiang Government were Muslims. Pilgrimage to Mecca was however stopped from 1949 to 1953 and then stopped again in 1958, and remains so to this date (1982). In 1950, Islamic law was abolished, and the *Qadis* were dispensed with. In 1955, the Institute of Islamic Theology was established to prepare *imams*. The position of the Communist Party was that 'it was necessary for the Muslims themselves to carry on their own revolutionary organizations with a base in the Muslim masses'.

By 1957, a full-blast campaign against Islam was started. Most of the mosques were closed, the call for prayers (*adhan*) and public prayers were forbidden. Islamic teachings were much suppressed and the *imams* imprisoned. Propaganda against Islam was stepped up. By 1958, an organized effort was made to settle non-Muslims in Muslim majority areas, especially in Eastern Turkestan, Khansu and Inner Mongolia. The economic life of the Muslims was also disrupted and famines threatened Muslim territories. Most of the Muslim schools were also closed and were replaced in 1964 by the 'College of Minority Nationalities' and the 'Chinese Islamic Institute' in order to put Islamic education under stricter control and even to suppress it.

During the Cultural Revolution the situation of Muslims deteriorated further reaching its lowest ebb in modern history. Mosques were burnt, *imams* were killed, Islamic literature was thrown away, Islamic leaders were persecuted and insulted, Muslim families were dispersed, etc. This led to violent protest on the part of Muslims. There were Muslim riots in Peking in February 1967, protesting the imprisonment of one of their leaders. Their slogan was 'Muslims of the world unite'. They rebelled elsewhere as well, especially in Eastern Turkestan. This resistance was brutally suppressed, causing considerable damage to Muslim life.

The situation, however, relaxed somewhat after 1969. The

closed mosques, however, were not reopened. Even in Peking out of scores of mosques only Tungzu Mosque remained open as a piece of exhibition to be shown to foreign dignitaries. The mosque was hardly ever used by Chinese Muslims, out of fear of persecution.

## Growth of Muslim Institutions

Before the establishment of the People's Republic of China there were 42,000 mosques coupled with Islamic schools. These mosques existed all across the country wherever Muslims were present. A city like Kashgar, the Muslim metropolis of Eastern Turkestan, had 400 mosques. The capital, Peking, then had forty-nine mosques. There were also twenty-seven mosques in Nankin, fourteen mosques in Shanghai, eleven in Tching-tou, eleven in Hankow, ten in Tien-Tsin, eight in Urumchi and four in the city of Canton.

There were also tens of thousands of *imams* active in educating the people. These are called *ahungs*, and there were many women-*imams* among them as well. The *imams* were trained in four great centers of Islamic learning at the level of the Azhar University of Cairo. The first was in Eastern Turkestan, in the city of Kashgar which acted as the center for spreading Islamic culture to the whole of China. The second was in Ho-Tcheou in the Khansu where students came from all across China to study Islamic sciences. The third, the High Studies Institute, was in Peking; and the fourth in the city of Houai-King in the Province of Honan which had the highest number of Muslims among the Chinese provinces.

Finally, since the nineteenth century a considerable amount of Islamic literature has been produced by the Muslims in the Chinese language. Among the early Muslim writers in Chinese, one should mention Liu Chih who in 1724 wrote a treatise about the life of the Prophet. Liu Chih called upon the Muslims to follow the Prophet's exemplary life if they wanted to be better Muslims. Other Muslim writers in Chinese such as Wang Tai-yu (died in 1660) and Yusuf Ma Chu (died in 1711) wrote dozens of books about the Islamic faith and philosophy. Interest in the Arabic language and its teaching to the children started in the nineteenth century. Ma Te-hsin (died in 1874) the great *imam* and Muslim leader of Yunnan who led its 1856–72 rebellion and independence movement wrote in Chinese about Muslim law, philosophy and history, as well as about Arabic grammar and rhetoric. He was also a prolific writer in the Arabic language which he had mastered. Imam Ma Te-hsin was also the first to attempt the translation of the meanings of the *Holy Quran* into Chinese, but he died before finishing the work. The latter was finished by the political leader of the Muslim rebellion of Yunnan, Tu Wen-hsiu, and was published before the turn of the century. During the beginning of this century primers were written for the education of Muslim children and teenagers in Chinese. Thus, by the mid-twentieth century, a Chinese Muslim could become a fully-fledged *alim* and *imam* within his own language.

All this changed during the People's Republic; especially during the Cultural Revolution. Practically all mosques have been closed, demolished, or turned into clubs, warehouses, cinemas, barracks, etc. The rare exceptions were a lone mosque in Kashgar and the famous Tungzu Mosque of Peking. These were mostly opened for foreign dignitaries. Religious instruction and all religious meetings and worship were greatly curtailed. Most Muslim schools have been closed down or their curricula changed to include Communist indoctrination. Muslim religious leaders were tortured and humiliated. Anti-Islamic posters were hung in most Muslim districts and cities, and religious books were confiscated and often burned in the public squares.

## The Case of Eastern Turkestan

Eastern Turkestan, or Sin-Kiang (i.e. New Dominion) as called by the Chinese, is an autonomous region within the Popular Republic of China. This territory has an area of 1,646,800 square kilometres and a population of 12,500,000 in 1982. Historically, Eastern Turkestan enclosed a much larger area. Actually, this territory is no more than a Muslim state converted into a Chinese colony. Its true inhabitants are mostly Turkish, who speak several Turkish dialects, especially Uighur written in Arabic script. They are all Muslims of the Hanafi school.

Muslim armies opened Kashgar for Islam in the year 96 A.H. (714 C.E.) under the leadership of Qutaybah Ibn Muslim as seen before. Since then Eastern Turkestan became a Muslim province with Kashgar as capital. The Arabic language and Islamic culture became widespread in the country which produced in the Abbasid times such distinguished scholars as Sadiduddin Kashgari and Mahmud Kashgari.

In the year 466 A.H. (1073 C.E.) Turkish tribes invaded Northern

Turkestan and were followed in the thirteenth century by the Mongol armies of Chingis Khan, whose capital was Karakorum (Black Sands) in Eastern Turkestan. Eastern Turkestan became an independent state under Islamized Mongols and Turks until the seventeenth century when it was invaded by China's Manchu rulers.

In 1289 A.H. (1872 C.E.) a revolution was successfully carried out against the Manchus, leading to the independence of the country under King Yaqub-Beg. This independence lasted only four years. The country was invaded again by China in 1293 A.H. (1876 C.E.) which converted it in 1301 A.H. (1884 C.E.) into a Chinese province.

This state of affairs did not change with the fall of the Manchu dynasty and the establishment of the nationalist state. In 1350 A.H. (1931 C.E.), a new revolution took place led by Khoja Niyaz Hajji which succeeded in liberating the country. The Russians, however, were not in favour of establishing a Muslim Turkish state to the east of their Muslim Turkish colonies. They helped the Chinese to destroy the new state. Eventually, the Muslims overcame the combined forces and declared the Islamic Republic of Eastern Turkestan on 12 November 1932. Mr Khoja Niyaz Hajji was elected first president and Mawlana Thabit prime minister. On 27 December 1933, a Russian army invaded the young Republic supported by the air-force and succeeded in defeating the forces of the Islamic Republic in July 1934. A campaign of massacres against the Muslim population followed which led to the death of hundreds of thousands of Muslims, including Hajji Khoja Niyaz, Mawlana Thabit and all the Muslim leaders.

Muslims revolted against this Russian colonization in 1933 and established a republic under the leadership of Ilyas Khan and Sultan Sharif Tayji; then in 1937, they revolted again under the leadership of Abdullah Al-Niyaz; and once again in 1940 under the leadership of Uthman Batur. The latter succeeded in defeating the Russians and establishing an independent Muslim state which lasted until 1943. In that year, the Nationalist Government of China took over the country. They were followed in 1949 by the People's Republic which continues to rule over the region to this day.

Persecution of Muslims by the People's Republic in Eastern Turkestan started in 1950. They carried out land reforms concurrently with mass execution of local noblemen and religious leaders. However, persecution was not carried out further after this event until 1958.

In 1958, the regime carried out total collectivization followed by mass detention of innocent people in labour camps. The aim was to obtain free labour for the 'Great Leap Forward' programme. This had a disastrous effect on the economy of the region, which was further aggravated by mismanagement. The result was a famine which took the lives of millions in Muslim areas, such as the southern part of Eastern Turkestan and the neighbouring provinces of Khansu and Szechwan.

During the 'Cultural Revolution', in 1966, the regime openly declared its intention to destroy Islam in China. In Eastern Turkestan—as elsewhere—Red Guards committed acts of unprecedented vandalism by burning the *Holy Quran* and other Islamic religous books, by damaging the mosques, and assaulting the *imams*. As an example, Imam Muhammad Amin of the village of Kypek in the Kuldja district, organized a mass prayer for rainfall (*istisqa*) in the arid year of 1968. Contrary to the official weather forecast, the rain fell. As a result, Imam Muhammad was executed in 1969 for 'counter-revolutionary activities'. Most of the mosques were closed in this period, and thousands of refugees fled the country.

In 1953, 90.7 per cent of the population were Muslims out of a total of 4,420,000 people. There were only 454,000 non-Muslims, mostly Chinese settled after 1949. Indeed, before 1949 the non-Muslim population was numerically negligible. After 1953, the regime started a programme of de-Islamization of Eastern Turkestan by bringing great numbers of Chinese settlers to the region. In 1968, the population was eight million, of whom 5,700,000 (71.2 per cent) were Muslims and the remaining 2,300,000 non-Muslim Chinese settlers. In 1982, the total population could be estimated at 12.5 million with only nine million Muslims; the Muslim percentage remained almost stabilized, mostly because of a high Muslim natural growth rate.

The events in Eastern Turkestan during the last half century led to an outflow of refugees. Indeed in 1949, 40,000 Muslim Kazakhs fled to the Indian sub-continent and most of them perished on the way. During the communization effort that created an artificial famine in 1959–62, another 200,000 Muslim Kazakhs and Uighurs fled to the Soviet Union. From 1976 some Tartar families were allowed to emigrate to Hong Kong and then to Australia, where they settled in a thriving Muslim community in Adelaide. In 1982, the Eastern Turkestan diaspora could be estimated at 250,000 people, of whom 220,000 are in the Soviet Union, 10,000 in Saudi

Arabia, 10,000 in Turkey, 2,000 in Pakistan, 1,000 in Afghanistan and the remaining are in India, Egypt and European countries. Most of these refugees took up the nationalities of their host countries. Prominent among them is Isa Yusuf Alp-Tekin who was the last Secretary General of the coalition government of Eastern Turkestan under the Chinese Nationalist Regime (1947–49). He lives in Istanbul and keeps the memory of Eastern Turkestan alive in the minds of the Muslims all over the world.

## The Situation of Muslims in the Post-Mao Period

The presence under a special category of sixteen religious leaders at the Fifth National Committee of the Chinese People's Political Consultative Conference marked an important departure from the anti-religious policy adopted since the Cultural Revolution. The meeting was opened on 26 February 1978 in Peking and grouped 2,800 deputies who arrived from all parts of China to approve a new constitution and new nominations for the high offices of the state. This meeting was held under the symbol of 'unity refound' and for the first time many religious leaders appeared in public since the excesses of the Cultural Revolution.

In fact since early 1977, the Chinese news media changed their tune towards religion especially among minority groups, most of them being Muslim. Since Muslims of non-Chinese nationality lived in strategically located areas along the borders with the USSR, Peking seemed determined to win their confidence by allowing the re-emergence of Muslim national associations. Indeed, a group of Hong Kong Muslims toured China in October 1977. They visited mosques in Hangchow, Shanghai and Peking where still the only open mosque seems to have been the Tungtzu Mosque. The Hong Kong Muslims met *imams* and were the guests of the resuscitated Chinese Muslim Association. They came back to Hong Kong to report a relatively satisfactory picture of the Muslim community in China. During the same year several mosques were reopened for service. For instance, in Kunming (Yunnan) four mosques were reopened in June 1977.

In fact, M. Hsu Teh-Cheng, the vice-president of the former National Committee of the Consultative Conference which was reconvened for a meeting on 24 and 25 February 1978, presented the key speech at the 24 February session. He accused the 'Gang of Four' of 'having fomented divisions among nationalities' and undermined the policy of the regime, especially in 'the matter of religion'. 'The consequences', he added, 'were serious'.

More recently, it was announced that postgraduate students are to be admitted to the newly established Chinese Academy of Social Sciences. There are to be ten institutes, including an Institute of World Religions where students will study Islam, Buddhism, Taoism and Christianity. In November 1978, Peking's Tungszu Mosque held the largest ever Id-ul-Adha prayers since the founding of the People's Republic. Besides foreign Muslims, a large number of the Chinese Muslims took part in the prayers. The Chinese congregation consisted of people of all ages including young teenagers. The prayer was led by the Imam of the Mosque, Imam Salih An Shih-Wei, member of the National Committee of the Chinese People's Political Consultative Conference. Also present at the prayer were Haji Muhammad Chang Chein and other leading members of the Chinese Muslim Association. The Chinese authorities said that 'as in previous years' they had done everything necessary to provide the Muslims with 'whole living and unblemished male sheep' for sacrifice. For the first time in the People's Republic, the prayers were filmed by the Chinese television.

In Eastern Turkestan (Sin-Kiang), the Provincial Revolutionary Committee held a gala party on 12 November 1978 to celebrate Id-ul-Adha. Representatives of all Muslim nationalities of the region (Uighur, Kazakh, Kirghiz, Uzbek, Tartar, Tajik, Huis, etc) were invited on the occasion to exchange greetings as Muslims.

Interviewed by the Agence France Presse in 1979, Imam Ma Congling of Kunming said that the Bureau of Religious Affairs in Yunnan Province had recently decided to allocate funds to publish copies of the *Holy Quran* in Arabic. He indicated that the work could begin as soon as the religious committee for Muslims in Kunming began operating again. The committee was disbanded in 1970 at the same time that the city's mosques were closed. The Imam said that a Quranic school would open 'at some time'. Such a school would be the first to reopen in the People's Republic of China.

## Conclusions

The Muslim community of China started almost with the very advent of Islam. The community passed through vicissitudes of fortune during the following centuries, from positions of great prestige and power in the entire country to periods of intense persecution and suppression. During the Cultural Revolution they passed through the worst period of their history. Today there are hopes of great improvement. But are these hopes well-founded?

If one looks at the Muslim community of China (excluding the case of Eastern Turkestan which is no more than a Muslim land conquered by a non-Muslim power) one notices the following unique characteristics of the Chinese Muslim minority. First of all this is a minority in the true sense of the term created by immigration and mass conversion of Chinese people to form a group of people sharing with others the Chinese culture but in the same time adapting it fully to the Islamic ideals. The existence of this Chinese Muslim minority was not the result of the conquest by China of a Muslim land whose population was reduced to the status of a minority within the empire. In this it differs completely from the Muslim community of the Soviet Union which is entirely the result of colonization of Muslim states after their conquest by a non-Muslim power. Second, the Chinese Muslim community is characterized by its continuity. Muslims were in China as an organized religious community continuously from the first century of Islam and without any break, and without ever establishing a Muslim state. Few other Muslim minorities could claim the same longevity. Third, the persistent identification of Muslim Chinese with China. The rare exception of wars of secession in the nineteenth century were only the results of extreme persecution of the Manchu dynasty which left the Muslims no other choice but to fight back for survival.

After a lapse of renaissance of thirty-eight years during the Nationalist establishment, Muslims passed by difficult situations during the People's Republic. It seems, however, that the community kept all the necessary conditions for survival: strong Islamic allegiance in the families; existence of Islamic tradition (if not literature due to its mass burning during the Cultural Revolution) in the Chinese language; survival (albeit weakened and reduced) of Islamic institutions, etc. The events after the death of Mao-Tse-Tung give good reasons for hope of great improvements.

One more situation which would certainly induce improvements for both the Muslims of the Soviet Union and those of China is the Sino-Chinese rivalry. The borders between both the countries pass through Muslim lands and, therefore, it becomes imperative for each one of these states to win the allegiance of Muslim populations by respecting their Islamic identity.

Finally, the Muslims of China would be happy within the People's Republic of China if they are given their religious freedom and if they are allowed to thrive as a Muslim community with its institutions and its cultural autonomy. They will certainly respond by more allegiance to their country China. Even Eastern Turkestan could be satisfied if its autonomy as a Muslim Turkic state is respected within the Chinese state. Once the Muslim community of China is satisfied, both China and the Muslim world would benefit from the friendship created by common bonds rather than suspicion created by persecution of members of the Muslim *ummah*.

## References

1. Marshall Broomhall, *Islam in China, a Neglected Problem* (London, 1910).
2. H. M. Delon, *Studies on Muslim Chinese* (Paris, 1911) (French).
3. A. Vissiere, *Chinese Muslim Studies* (Paris, 1911) (French).
4. G. Cordier, *The Muslims of Yunnan* (Hanoi, Vietnam, 1927) (French).
5. Pai Shou-i, *A Short History of Islam in China* (Chunking, China, 1944) (Chinese).
6. Claude L. Pekins, Jr. *References on Muslims in China* (Hankow Hopei Province, China, 1950).
7. Daud S. M. Ting, 'Islamic Civilization in China' Chapter 11 in *Islam, the Straight Path* edited by Kenneth W. Morgan (New York, 1958).
8. M. S. Ismail, *The Muslims of the Soviet Union and Popular China* (Cairo, Egypt, 1958) (Arabic).
9. J. P. Roux, 'Islam in New China' Chapter 4 in *Islam in Asia* (Paris, 1958) (French).
10. Imam Ibrahim Chiung, *What happened to Muslims in Communist China* (Beirut, 1962) (Arabic).
11. Chu Wen-Djang, *The Muslim Rebellions in North-West China 1862–1878* (The Hague, 1966).
12. F. Karam, *Islam and Muslims in Popular China* (Beirut, 1969) (Arabic).
13. M. A. Kettani, *Muslims in the Communist Camp* (Mecca, 1974) (Arabic).
14. R. Israeli, 'The Muslim Revival in 19th Century China' in *Studia Islamica* (Paris, 1976).
15. R. E. White, 'China' in *Religion & Freedom* (London, July 1978).

16. Anonymous, 'Peking Regime to Finance Reprinting of Holy Quran' *Hong Kong Muslim Herald*, II, No. 1 (April 1979).
17. S. E. Wimbush, *Nationality Research in the People's Republic of China: A Trip Report* A Rand Note (California, USA, August 1981).

# 5 Muslims in India

## Introduction

Islam was introduced to India for the first time when Muhammad Ibn Al-Qasim, the Arab general of the Umayyad period, opened up Sind with a Muslim army. Since then, and for more than one thousand years most of India was ruled by Muslims who were organized in Muslim states of various sizes and areas depending on the century considered. The last of these states was the Moghul Empire which at one stage established its control over almost the entire sub-continent.

When the British embarked upon their colonial enterprise, they were confronted with the Muslims as their opponents. Thus, from the beginning, British colonization of India has meant to Muslims the obliteration of Islamic political, economic, cultural and religious influence. This policy was pursued in a most systematic way after the failure of the 1857 Revolution which led to the fall of the Moghul Empire. Since then, the Muslims of India (including today's Pakistan and Bangladesh) have found themselves more and more pushed aside by the new British colonial establishment at the periphery of the social life of the sub-continent. The British preferred Hindus in their administration to such an extent that by the turn of the present century, Muslims had lost most of the influence they had wielded for more than one thousand years.

Nevertheless, a modern Muslim renaissance coincided with the British striving to destroy all Muslim influence. This attempt, however, could not receive enough guarantees from the Hindu majority to safeguard the identity, the culture and the religion of the Muslims. Many Muslims, therefore, opted for independence, for separation in the areas where Muslims were in majority. This led to the creation of Pakistan which eventually split into two states (Pakistan and Bangladesh). The Muslims found their lot greatly improved in the two independent states by gaining sovereignty and the freedom to live out their lives as Muslims. On the other hand, the Muslims of the areas under Hindu majority which constituted the Republic of India, witnessed a worsening of their situation since the achievement of independence.

The case of Kashmir is particularly appalling. Here, a state which had an overwhelming Muslim majority and would have normally joined Pakistan was illegally invaded by Indian armies. Two-thirds of the state is now under Indian domination. It has been included in this study since its Muslim population is de facto under non-Muslim rule and thus suffers from the same handicap that the Muslims of India suffer from. Their inclusion does not in any way represent a recognition of this unjust situation. The status of Kashmir will be finalized when the wishes of the people concerning their future is allowed to prevail as was resolved again and again by the United Nations, in the beginning even with the agreement of India.

At present, the Islamic culture of India, notwithstanding its overall homogeneity in comparison with the Hindu culture of the sub-continent, seems to have two somewhat distinct flavours in the northern and southern zones of India. In the north, the Muslims mostly follow the Hanafi school and their cultural languages are Urdu or Bengali. In the south, the Muslims follow the Shafii school and their language generally is Tamil. Indeed, the Muslims of the south grew out of the early Muslim immigration from South Arabia and their centre of influence is the Kerala State.

Despite their minor cultural differences – linguistic, cultural, etc. – Indian Muslims have a strong sense of common identity as Muslims. In addition to their strong attachment to Islam, they impress us with their large numbers and with the fact that despite heavy odds, their population percentage has been rising. In 1971, there were 61 million Muslims or 11.21 per cent of the total Indian population. This percentage was only 9.9 per cent in 1951. In 1981, there were about 82 million Muslims in a total Indian population of 685 million people, or a percentage of 12 per cent. Thus in 1982, the Muslims in India are estimated to be about 84 million. However, ever since independence, they have lived under persecution which, if it continues, will endanger the survival of the entire community. Indeed, Muslims are continuously eliminated from the administration where their percentage has dropped in

most ministries to a mere 1 per cent. Concerted efforts are made to
destroy their languages, to hinduize or secularize their schools,
and their lives and their properties are endangered by a continuous
string of violent riots by Hindu fanatics often encouraged by local
or even central government authorities. The persecution reached
its peak in the last years of the rule of the Congress Party (before it
came back again to power) when the Ulemas were imprisoned, a
major Islamic organization banned, many Muslims expelled from
their homes (e.g. in Delhi) and subjected in the northern states to
forced sterilization.

The percentage of Muslims in the different states of the Indian
Union varies greatly. In 1971, Muslims were in majority in two
territories: Lakshadwep Islands (94.4%) and Jammu-Kashmir
(65.9%). They formed more than 10 per cent of the population in
seven other territories: Assam (24.0%); West Bengal (20.5%);
Kerala (19.5%); Uttar Pradesh (15.5%); Bihar (13.5%); Karnataka
(10.6%); and Andoman-Nicobar (10.1%). Their numbers exceeded
the ten million point in Uttar Pradesh and the million point in
twelve other territories.

In 1971, only five cities in India with a population of more
than 100,000, had a Muslim majority. These are Srinagar (Jammu
& Kashmir), Malegeon (Maharashtra), Garden Reach (West
Bengal), Rampur (U.P.), and Moradabad (U.P.).

## Historical Background

The first part of the Indian sub-continent which was incorporated in the Muslim State was Sind (now in Pakistan) during the
Umayyad times by Muhammed Ibn Qasim in 711 C.E. (92 A.H.).
Muslim communities were also formed in these early centuries
around trading centres along the entire western shores of India
from Kerala in the south to Gujarat.

It was however, the Gahznavids, under Mahmoud of Ghazna
(999–1030 C.E., 388–421 A.H.) who brought parts of the present-
day India within the fold of the Ghaznavid Muslim State. During
his reign, this state came to include most of Gujarat, the Indus
Valley as well as the Valley of the Ganges, including Benares.
Eventually, Punjab became the core of the Ghaznavid State with
Lahore as the capital until the end of the dynasty in 1186 C.E. (582
A.H.).

The power of the Ghaznavids was inherited by the Muslim
Ghurids. Indeed Muizz-Din Muhammad took Ajmer and Delhi in

1192 C.E. (588 A.H.). He then put one of his Turkish commanders, Aybak, in charge of the Indian provinces of the Ghurid Empire. These included Punjab, Uttar Pradesh and later Bihar, Bengal and Assam. On the death of Muizz-Din in 1206 C.E. (602 A.H.), Aybak became independent. Thus Muslim India became an independent Muslim state with the capital at Lahore (now Pakistan). The capital of the state was moved to Delhi during the reign of Iletmish (1211–1236 C.E., 607–633 A.H.). Thus Delhi became the capital of a Muslim state known as the Delhi Sultanate, a state which lasted for about three centuries after which it was conquered by the Moghul Emperor Humayun in 1555 C.E. (962 A.H.). In course of time the Moghul Empire united most of northern India under the banner of Islam until it was conquered by the British in 1858 C.E. (1274 A.H.).

Other Muslim states were established elsewhere in the Indian sub-continent. Bengal, for instance, was part of the Delhi Sultanate. It became an independent Muslim state with a capital at Lakhnawati, in 1336 C.E. (737 A.H.). It was reunited to the Delhi State by the Moghuls in 1576 C.E. (984 A.H.). The throne of Kashmir was seized in 1335 C.E. (735 A.H.) by Shah Mirza Swati who established a Kashmiri Muslim State which lasted until 1589 C.E. (997 A.H.) when it was incorporated in the Moghul Empire. Gujarat was part of the Delhi Sultanate, but became independent in 1391 C.E. (793 A.H.) and remained so until 1583 C.E. (991 A.H.) when it was incorporated in the Moghul Empire. Other Muslim states were established in Jawnpur (1394–1479 C.E., 796–883 A.H.); Malwa (1401–1531 C.E., 804–937 A.H.); Deccan (1347–1948 C.E., 748–1367 A.H.); etc.

The British who came initially as traders, began to subjugate the sub-continent in the eighteenth century starting with the coastal regions. They subsequently extended their power through Bengal to Oudh, Central India, and Rajputana. The Moghul Emperor, Bahadur Shah (1837–1858 C.E., 1253–1274 A.H.) became a British pensioner. He was deposed by the British in 1858 after the Indian Army revolt, which completed the British occupation of India, and the country was formally declared a part of the British Crown.

To counter the British invasion, the Muslim masses took upon themselves the responsibility of defending their territories since their established states had failed. In the 1820s, the Mujahidin Movement was establishment by Syed Ahmad Shahid with the aim of ousting the British militarily. The years between 1858 (the year of the failure of the Muslim Revolt) and 1906 (when the Muslim League was established) were years of withdrawal for the Muslims of India, along with a thorough soul-searching effort.

In 1906, the Muslim League was formed to seek the political rights of the Muslims and to protect the Muslim community from Hindu domination and British persecution. The Muslim League co-operated with the Hindu-dominated Indian Congress to seek the independence of India. The idea of a separate Muslim state was put forth in 1930 by the great Muslim poet Muhammad Iqbal, but was resisted by the Muslims. However, in view of the fanaticism of the Indian Congress and its complete disregard of Muslim fears of subjugation, the League was forced in 1940 to adopt the achievement of a separate Muslim state in India as the major political objective of the Muslims of the sub-continent.

In 1946, the Hindu extremists started a chain of violence against Muslims, leading to huge losses of life and property and the mass movement of more than ten million people. On 14 August 1947, Louis Mountbatten, the last British Viceroy of India, transferred the power to the President of the Muslim League Muhammad Ali Jinnah, as the first President of the newly established Muslim State of Pakistan. At the time of concluding the agreement for the partition of India into a Muslim state and a non-Muslim state, the British Government declared that princely states could choose to join any of the two states, but they should take into account the religious composition of their states, their geographical situation, and the wish of the people. However, in the actual implementation of those conditions the Muslim state was reduced to the smallest possible dimension. The states of Punjab and Bengal were partitioned in spite of an overall Muslim majority in both. The State of Hyderabad in Deccan encompassed a large area where twenty million people choose to be independent as a Muslim State. It was invaded by India and incorporated forcibly in 1948. The State of Junagadh which is located in the Gujarat, opted for Pakistan in 1947. That state too was annexed by India by force of arms. Finally, Jammu and Kashmir, which had a preponderant Muslim majority and was contiguous to Pakistan, could not join Pakistan in spite of the wish of its populations because its Hindu prince wanted to join India. The population revolted against the Maharajah who massacred thousands of Muslims and forced emigration on hundreds of thousands of others. Pakistan then entered to free the territory but clashed with the Indian army. The war lasted until January 1949 when a ceasefire came to force, leaving about two-thirds of Kashmir (the most populated) in Indian hands, and one-third, Azad Kashmir which is administered by Pakistan. At the time of the conclusion of the ceasefire agreement under the aegis of the United Nations, it was agreed by all the parties concerned that the future of Kashmir would be decided by a plebiscite under the supervision of the UN. The UN has passed dozens of resolutions since then urging India to honour its commitment. All these resolutions have proved of no avail and the Indian occupation of Kashmir continues.

In 1911, the Muslims formed 21 per cent of the population of India. This percentage increased to 24 per cent in 1941. After partition, Muslim percentage in India fell to 9.9 per cent in 1951. Muslims in the newly established Muslim State of Pakistan found their lot greatly improved by winning the right to lead their Muslim lives without interference. Those of the Indian Union found that their lot had become more precarious, their leadership thinned out by emigration and their influence was greatly reduced. The effects were most harmful in northern India, whereas the south was not much affected by these events.

## Demographic Considerations

According to the 1981 census, there were 82 million Muslims in India (12 per cent of the total population). This percentage has been increasing steadily because of a higher rate of natural growth of the Muslim population. Indeed, in 1961, the Muslim percentage was 10.70 per cent whereas in 1951 it was only 9.9 per cent. Thus, Muslims increased from 1951 to 1971 by 64.3 per cent (there were in 1951 about 37,393,000 Muslims) while the Hindu population increased by 48.8 per cent in the same period. In 1951, Hindus formed 84.2 per cent of the population, whereas all other religious denominations besides Muslims and Hindus formed an overall 6.07 per cent. In 1971, these percentages became 82.72 per cent and 6.07 per cent (as in 1951) respectively. In 1982, the Muslim population can be estimated at about 84.7 million with a percentage of 12.0 per cent of the total population.

The Muslim population of India is more urban than the non-Muslim population, although it is by itself mostly rural. Indeed, the 1971 census reports that 19.87 per cent of Indians are urban, whereas the Muslim percentage rises to 28.8 per cent. Thus, although Muslims formed only 11.21 per cent of the total population of India in 1971, they formed 16.21 per cent of the total population of Indian cities. Actually, more Muslims live in rural areas in districts where they are in the majority or form an important minority and more of them live in cities in districts where their percentage is small. Indeed in such states as Tamil Nadu, Madhya Pradesh and Gujarat where Muslim percentages are below 10 per cent, more than 50 per cent of the Muslims are city dwellers. On the other hand, more Muslims live in rural areas in Jammu-Kashmir, West Bengal, Assam and Uttar Pradesh where their percentages are above 10 per cent. Also, Muslims are more urban in south India than in north India.

The effect of emigration on the Muslim population is negligible. Indeed, the flow of migration out of India to Pakistan which was significant in the late 1940s and the 1950s has practically stopped and Muslim emigration to America or to the Arab countries is extremely small compared to the total number of Muslims in India. On the other hand, cases of apostasy from Islam to Hinduism or other religions are extremely rare. The few marginal and isolated cases which occurred in Punjab, Haryana, Himalchal Pradesh and Uttar Pradesh after partition, returned to Islam when things settled down. Those areas illustrative of this phenomenon are Dinpuri and Mewat in the vicinity of Delhi. Anyway, the numbers involved are counted by the thousands only all over India. On the other hand, many Harijans in southern India are choosing Islam, but their numbers are still very small compared to the overall Muslim population.

The sex ratio in the Muslim population is 921 Muslim females for every 1000 Muslim males. This ratio is smaller than that of non-Muslims. There are indeed 935 non-Muslim Indian females for every 1000 non-Muslim Indian males. However, the female/male ratio of the Muslim population varies from one district to another. There are more Muslim females than males in thirty-three out of a total of 356 districts in India. In one district, there are 1356 females for each 1000 males in the Muslim population.

Since 71.2 per cent of the Muslims live in rural areas, farming constitutes the largest activity of the Muslim population. Next to farming comes handicrafts which occupy a good number of Muslims in the cities. Muslims are in this case artisans, craftsmen and menials. At a higher level come trade and commerce, but these are on a small or medium scale. There is an extremely small number, if any, of Muslim industrialists and businessmen with leading positions in any sector of the economy of the country.

Since the achievement of independence (and the partition of

the sub-continent) the Muslim community has been systematically pushed out of the public sector. They are woefully under-represented in all government departments, at all administrative levels: federal, state, and district. Muslims represent at best only 2 per cent of the middle and higher ranks of the country's administrative services. Often they are not represented at all. True, some Muslim individuals have reached the positions of the President of the Republic (mostly ceremonial), Chief Justices, or even Chief of the Air Staff, etc. But these seem to be isolated cases that cannot detract from the fact that the masses of Muslims are segregated in all walks of public life. There are also fewer Muslims in the professions. But it seems that Muslims have been able to keep their lead in sports and cultural activities.

There is obviously a great number of completely destitute Muslims. However, it is not possible to assess the percentage of such people in the Muslim population as compared with the percentage of destitutes in the other religious groups of India.

## Geographical Distribution

Muslims live in all the states and territories of India. However, their percentage in the total population varies widely from one entity to another. Table 5.1 gives the distribution of Muslims by state and territory, as well as their percentages for 1971. It also reports the number of Muslims grouped by districts where their percentages are above 50 per cent, between 25 and 50 per cent, between 10 and 25 per cent and below 10 per cent respectively. Muslims are in the majority in one state (Jammu and Kashmir) in the north and in one territory (Lakshadweep Islands) in the south. Outside these two areas, they are in majority only in two districts in the other states: the district of Murshidabad in West Bengal (area 5,341 square kilometres, total population 2,940,204 of whom 1,656,406 or 56.3 per cent are Muslims); and the district of Malappuram in Kerala (area 3,638 square kilometres, total population 1,856,362 of whom 1,186,675 or 63.9 per cent are Muslim).

Muslims form more than a tenth of the population in seven other states and territories: Assam (24.03%); West Bengal (20.46%); Kerala (19.50%); Uttar Pradesh (15.48%); Bihar (13.48%); Karnataka (10.63%); and Andoman-Nicobar Islands (10.12 per cent). Out of a total of 356 districts in India, Muslims form the majority in nine districts. They form more than the quarter of the population in nineteen other districts, and more than the tenth of the population but less than 25 per cent in ninety-four districts. In 102 districts, Muslims have percentages between 5 and 10 per cent; and in fifty-one districts between 2.5 and 5 per cent. Their percentages in the remaining eighty-one districts are small, being below 2.5 per cent of the total population of the district. The areas where Muslims form more than one-quarter of the population can be grouped into eight regions. 1. Kashmir, with the exclusion of the districts of Jammu and Kathua (2,952,135 Muslims, area 97,000 square kilometres, overall Muslim

*Table 5.1*    Muslims in India by state and district, 1971 census

| State or territory | Number of Muslims (thousands) in districts where they make up the following part of total populations: | | | | | |
|---|---|---|---|---|---|---|
| | More than 50% | 25–50% | 10–25% | Less than 10% | Total | (%age of total population) |
| Uttar Pradesh | | 4,030 | 8,225 | 1,420 | 13,675 | 15.48% |
| West Bengal | 1,656 | 1,881 | 4,747 | 782 | 9,066 | 20.46% |
| Bihar | | 1,562 | 4,838 | 1,197 | 7,596 | 13.48% |
| Maharashtra | | | 2,368 | 1,901 | 4,270 | 8.47% |
| Kerala | 1,187 | 645 | 2,093 | 238 | 4,163 | 19.50% |
| Andhra Pradesh | | 738 | 1,399 | 1,373 | 3,510 | 8.09% |
| Assam | | 3,111 | 281 | 115 | 3,508 | 24.03% |
| Karnataka | | | 2,184 | 927 | 3,111 | 10.63% |
| Jammu & Kashmir | 2,791 | 161 | 30 | 58 | 3,040 | 65.85% |
| Gujarat | | | 792 | 1,456 | 2,248 | 8.42% |
| Tamil Nadu | | | | 2,100 | 2,100 | 5.11% |
| Madhya Pradesh | | | 501 | 1,317 | 1,818 | 4.39% |
| Rajasthan | | | 194 | 1,581 | 1,775 | 6.90% |
| Lakshadweep | 30 | | | | 30 | 94.37% |
| Andoman & Nikobar | | | 12 | | 12 | 10.12% |
| Haryana | | | 298 | 104 | 402 | 4.00% |
| Pondicherry | | | 19 | 10 | 29 | 6.18% |
| Goa | | | 4 | 26 | 30 | 3.50% |
| Orissa | | | | 337 | 337 | 1.54% |
| Delhi | | | | 263 | 263 | 6.47% |
| Punjab | | | | 114 | 114 | 0.84% |
| Tripura | | | | 104 | 104 | 6.68% |
| Himalshal Pradesh | | | | 104 | 104 | 3.00% |
| Other | | | 119 | 119 | | |
| Total | 5,664 | 12,128 | 27,985 | 15,645 | 61,425 | (11.21%) |
| | 9.22% | 19.74% | 45.56% | 25.48% | 100.00% | |

percentage 81.2 per cent); 2. North-West Uttar Pradesh (3,563,903 Muslims, area 27,000 square kilometres, overall Muslim percentage 34.1 per cent); 3. North West Bengal and North East Bihar (5,099,635 Muslims, area 25,810 square kilometres, percentage 42.0 per cent); 4. Central Uttar Pradesh (466,022 Muslims, 6,900 square kilometres, percentage 27.0 per cent); 5. West Assam (2,427,928 Muslims, 25,779 square kilometres, percentage 35.9 per cent); 6. Central Assam (683,387 Muslims, 6,962 square kilometres, percentage 39.9 per cent); 7. Hyderabad (738,484 Muslims, 7,707 square kilometres, percentage 26.5); and 8. Central Kerala (1,861,735 Muslims, 7,399 square kilometres, percentage 46.6 per cent).

Thus, one can see that the Muslim population of India is fairly diluted in the mass of non-Muslims. Indeed, only 9.2 per cent of the Muslim population live in districts where they form the majority; 28.96 per cent live in districts where they form more than 25 per cent of the population; 45.56 per cent live in districts where they form more than 10 per cent but less than 25 per cent of the population; and the remaining 25.48 per cent live in districts where they form less than a tenth of the population. Thus, schematically one can say that one quarter of the Muslim population live in districts where it forms more than a quarter of the population; half of the Muslim population live in districts where it forms more than one-tenth but less than one-quarter of the population; and another quarter live in districts where it forms less than one-tenth of the population. Of these, 3,633,000 Muslims (5.92 per cent of all Muslims) are scattered in districts where their percentages are below 5 per cent. The few states and territories where Muslims form less than 5 per cent are: Punjab, Haryana and Himalshal Pradesh in the north-west, whose Muslim populations suffered greatly after partition and a great majority of whom had to emigrate to Pakistan; Orissa which came only briefly under Muslim rule; and Arauchal Pradesh and the neighbouring tribal states carved out of Assam.

Since 1951, the Muslim percentages have continued to increase in most states as they did increase all over India. If one compares only the censuses of 1961 and 1971, one finds that Muslim percentages increased from 14.7 to 15.5 per cent in Uttar Pradesh; from 10.3 to 13.5 per cent in Bihar; and from 7.7 to 8.5 per cent in Maharashtra.

Finally, about half (49.39%) of the Muslim population of India live in three states: Uttar Pradesh, West Bengal and Bihar; and

almost one-quarter (22.27%) of the Muslim population live in
Uttar Pradesh. Another quarter (25.25%) live in Maharashtra,
Kerala, Assam and Andhra Pradesh. The remaining quarter live
all over the rest of India.

## Religious Organization

About 90 per cent of the Muslims of India are Sunni and generally
follow the Hanafi school. Among the Sunnis, there are about four
million Muslims of the Shafii school, mostly in the southern states.
The remainder are mostly Shiah of the Jaafari school in the north-
western states, mostly in the Lucknow area of Uttar Pradesh, and
Ismailis of the Bohra branch (mostly in Bombay) or even Agha
Khanis. There is no friction whatsoever between the two existing
schools of Sunnism in India. As for the Shia-Sunni feud, it is now
by and large a story of the past. This mood of reconciliation is not
astonishing for there are no basic differences between the Jaafari
school and the schools of Sunnism. The feuds of the past generally
remained localized to the districts of Lucknow for more than a
century. Today, the Muslims form one single community and the
fact that they belong to one school or to another is no longer a
barrier to friendly relations and marriages. Even Ismailis are
coming closer to the main body of the Muslim community and
vice-versa, under the pressure of the non-Muslim community and
the non-Muslim establishment. A threat to any section of the
Muslim community is considered a threat to the entire community.

Religiously, the Sunni majority is divided into two schools: the
Deobandi and the Bareilvi. Deoband and Bareilly, located in the
area of Muslim concentration of north-west Uttar Pradesh, are the
seats of famous Islamic universities. The subjects of division are
of such a secondary nature today that they became a matter of
theological discussion rather than a concern of the community.

Two contemporary Muslim religious movements are affecting
the lives of Muslims in India: the Jamaat-e-Islami and the Tablighi
Jamaat. The Jamaat-e-Islami is centred in Delhi and its range of
interest extends to almost all the problems that face the Muslim
community. The Tablighi Jamaat, which is also centred in Delhi,
however, has more of an inward looking attitude to life, a tendency of withdrawal from all concerns except *ibadah* (worship), and
concentrates mainly on the spiritual welfare of Muslims.

The greatest concern of the Muslim community is to impart
Islamic education to the rising generations of Muslims. Efforts

were made in the eighteenth and the nineteenth centuries to build
up Urdu as the Muslim language of the sub-continent. Indeed
Urdu was closer to the spoken language of the masses, whereas
Persian, the then official language, was understood only by the
few. The family of Shah Waliullah of Delhi rendered the greatest
services in this regard and it is a member of this family who first
translated the meaning of the *Holy Quran* into Urdu for the first
time.

The famous Islamic University of Deoband, Dar-ul-Ulum, was
established by Maulana Qasim Nanavtvi after the fall of the
Moghuls. Other universities of the same calibre followed all over
India; the most known and effective being the Nadvatul-Ulema at
Lucknow (Uttar Pradesh); the Mazahirul Ulum of Saharanpur (in
the same district as Deoband in Uttar Pradesh); the Madrasat-ul-
Islah at Sarai Mir; and several others in other parts of India. These
universities kept Islamic knowledge alive in India. They are in full
contact with similar ones in the rest of the Muslim *ummah*, thus
ensuring that Islamic religious life in India remains in tune with
that in the rest of the World. They are also powerful seats of
propagation of the Arabic language among the educated members
of the Muslim community.

Basic religious education is imparted to Muslim children in
Islamic primary schools called *makatib* or *madaris* (Arabic for
schools). Jamaat-e-Islami has prepared about sixty textbooks in
various subjects for use in these schools. There are thousands
of such schools, but their number is still insufficient since they
seem to cover the needs of only about 25 per cent of the Muslim
children of India. The Jamiyat-ul-Ulama (seat Delhi), or Upper
Religious Council makes a great effort to remedy this situation for
all of India. At the state level, local Councils are carrying out the
burden, such as the Dini Talimi Council (Council of Religious
Education) in Uttar Pradesh, the Muslim Education Standing
Committee of Tamil Nadu, the All-India Muslim Educational
Society; etc.

There are tens of thousands of mosques in towns and villages all
across India. These include such outstanding pieces of Islamic
architecture as the Masjid Jami of Delhi built in the sixteenth
century and the Mecca Masjid of Hyderabad built in the seventeenth century as well as a multitude of more discreet buildings.
All the mosques are also seats of education imparting Islamic
knowledge to children as well as to adults.

The meaning of the *Holy Quran* has been translated not only in

Urdu, the Muslim language par excellence, but also into Hindi and the other national languages, namely: Marathi, Kashmiri, Bengali, Kanari, Tamil, Malayalam and Telugu. Religious books on Islam are available in many languages, but the greatest numbers are in Urdu and Hindi.

Indian Muslims are free to perform *hajj*. About 20,000 of them do perform it yearly. Furthermore, Muslim personal laws are in force. But, as will be seen later there is recurrent threat from the non-Muslim Government to tamper with such laws.

Finally, the effect of all-India Muslim organizations in bringing the Muslim community of India into one single united community should be mentioned. Besides those in Uttar Pradesh and Delhi mentioned above, one should add The All-India Muslim Council at Hyderabad (Andhra Pradesh), the Majlis Ittihad-ul-Muslimin, at Hyderabad also, and the All-India Muslim League of Madras (Tamil Nadu). The latter is the survivor of the pre-partition Muslim League, but its effect has remained important only in the southern states.

## Cultural Persecution

Since Muslims live in all the states of India, each one of the sixteen constitutionally recognized languages is spoken by one group of Muslims or another. In fact, each one of these languages has a Muslim variety which is more influenced by Arabic and Persian and is often written in the Arabic script. Urdu is the first Muslim tongue of India. It is the mother tongue of the Muslims of Uttar Pradesh, Bihar, Madhya Pradesh, Haryana, Punjab, Himalchal Pradesh, Rajasthan and some of the Muslims of West Bengal, Orissa, Andhra Pradesh, Maharashtra, Gujarat, Karnataka and Jammu and Kashmir; i.e. it is the mother tongue of about 38 million Muslims in India, or about 62 per cent of the total Muslim population. But it is spoken as a second language by almost as many other Muslims, making it understood by about 90 per cent of the Muslims of India. The other important Muslim languages arc Bengali, Gujarati, Kashmiri, Tamil, and Malayalam. Urdu has become an international Muslim language, being the official language of Pakistan as well as the language of the Muslim communities of Fiji, Mauritius, Trinidad, Guyana and South Africa. It has the richest Islamic literature among Indian languages in all fields of learning. The importance of this language in the survival of the Muslim community is the basis of the great concern among

Muslims in the World about the efforts of undermining it. Indeed, both the Indian federal government and the governments of the states seem to do all that is possible to strangle Urdu and to deny it all opportunities of existence and growth. This situation is considered by the Muslims of India as one of the greatest tragedies that has befallen them since 1947. The wisest among the Muslims, such as the Jamaat-e-Islami, while defending the rights of Urdu are already making available basic Islamic literature in all official languages, including Hindi.

Muslims have greatly contributed to all the civilized facets of Indian life: the music, the architecture, the cuisine, the dress fashions, in short, the cultural life of the country. Modern Indian nationalism, although declaring itself secular, has a tendency to rewrite the history of India by de-Islamizing and Hinduizing it instead. This chauvinist attitude can sometimes go to the ridiculous extreme of claiming that the prestigious Muslim architectural monuments including the Taj Mahal of Agra (Uttar Pradesh) were built by Hindu Kings and Hindu architects. This anti-Islamic attitude often reaches the textbooks in use in schools and colleges.

Ever since they were put under the colonizing degradations of the British Empire, the Muslims made a great effort in education. Muslims established hundreds of schools and many colleges. The leading university established by Muslims is the Muslim University of Aligarh (Uttar Pradesh), established in 1920. Another Muslim university in the North is the Jamia Millia in Delhi. In Tamil Nadu, the New College was established in 1951 at Madras and the Islamiah College in 1903 at Vaniyambadi. The State of Hyderabad established universities of the first quality, the most famous being the Osmania College (now University) established in 1916 at Hyderabad (now Andhra Pradesh).

Since the independence of India, the governments, both federal and state, have taken all actions possible to deny the Islamic character to the institutions established by Muslims. These eventually become like any other Indian universities with minority Muslim enrolment, minority Muslim faculty and no specifically Islamic oriented curriculum. The biggest victims of this policy are those most famous universities such as Aligarh University, Osmania University and Jamia Millia, among many others. The present government presented an amending bill on Aligarh Muslim University restoring some of the autonomy of the previous bill (under Gandhi's rule). But the bill fell short of accepting the Muslim demand to give the University a minority institution status within

Article 30 of the Indian Constitution. When the Minister of Education who presented the bill was asked why that was so, he answered that 'although Muslims had originated the concept of the University and the University came into being through their efforts, since it had been aided by the Government of India, it cannot be described as a minority institution in strictly legal terms'. This so-called government aid is always taken as an excuse to take over Muslim institutions.

Muslims are instead encouraged or forced to enroll in secular Indian institutions. These schools are actually Hinduized institutions where the religious beliefs and the mythology of the Hindus are freely introduced in textbooks with an aim to indoctrinate young Muslims into the religious beliefs of the majority. No wonder, then, that Muslims are making huge efforts to establish new schools and new colleges.

Nevertheless, the discriminating efforts of the Indian governments after Independence and of the British Colonial Establishment before Independence led to the present dismal situation of the Muslim Community. The literacy ratio of the Muslims is half the national average which is itself very low. Out of 2716 colleges in the country, only fifty-four are under Muslim control or slightly more than 2 per cent of the total, in spite of a percentage of the Muslim population of 12 per cent.

To give a clearer picture of this situation, consider the state of Tamil Nadu in Southern India where the formation of the Muslim Educational Association of Southern India at Madras in 1902 constitutes an important achievement of the Muslim community. In 1972–73, out of 172 colleges in the State, eleven colleges were founded and administered by Muslims. However, out of 30,000 students attending the Muslim colleges, only 6,500 students were actually Muslim (22 per cent of the total!). With about 2,000 Muslim students in non-Muslim colleges, the total figure for college education among Muslims compares well with their percentage in the population. Indeed, there were 193,779 students in colleges in Tamil Nadu in 1972-73. There were about thirty high schools under Muslim management with about 8,000 Muslim students out of a total enrolment of about 20,000 students. About 24,000 Muslims studied in non-Muslim high schools. Thus, the total number of Muslims in high schools in the State was 32,000 students, instead of about 80,000 if they were to equal the Muslim percentage in the state. In primary education, the situation was even worse. There were seventy-five recognized Muslim primary schools and 300 unrecognized religious schools. The total Muslim enrolment in these schools was about 25,000. Assuming 75,000 student enrolment of Muslims in non-Muslim schools, the total Muslim primary enrolment was 100,000, instead of about 300,000 if they were to equal the overall Muslim percentage in the population. About 20 per cent of all Muslim children of school age attend school whereas the average in the State was 40 per cent. This situation did not improve since 1972-73, and the same story could be told in the other states of the Union.

## Social Persecution

In a majority community based on the caste system, the egalitarianism of the Muslim community in all aspects of communal life or social intercourse marks them out clearly from the majority. Traditionally, the Muslim women had more rights than Hindu women, even in the context of Indian practice. Muslim girls are quite numerous in schools and colleges and often outnumber boys in higher education. Muslim personal law, with some changes, has been in force since the days of British rule and contributes to the strengthening of the homogeneity of the Muslim community.

There were intermittent attacks on all aspects of Muslim community characteristics by different sectors of the majority as well as by the mass of Hindus. Muslims are often considered as a caste worse than that of untouchables. There was even talk of a uniform law for all Indian citizens. It was a clumsy attempt to abolish Muslim personal law. A flow of propaganda is often produced claiming the lower status given to women by Islamic laws and thereby paving the way for destroying the legal aspect of the Muslim entity in India.

This assault had the effect of bringing the different sections of the Muslim community closer together. Indeed, the Bohra community (sub-sect of Ismaili Shia Muslims) would be considered by both the Shia and the Sunni as sectarian, almost on the fringe of the Muslim community (the Quadianis/Ahmadis are considered by all to be non-Muslims). This community has a small following of traders, mainly located in Bombay, Gujarat and other parts of Western and Central India. The community is headed by a *dai mutlaq* who enjoys absolute temporal and spiritual authority over the members (here lies one of the basic infringements on Muslim law as understood by most Muslims). But, when the community faced a crisis due to the rebellion of a section of its members against its un-Islamic practices, the entire Muslim *ummah* of India stood by the Bohra community against any interference from the non-Muslim State. The latter was just too eager to take advantage of the split, by nominating the Bombay-based 'Citizens for Democracy' to enquire into the state of the human rights in the Bohra community in 1978. The Muslims were wise enough to react as one body against this infringement by the secular state and their unwillingness to let it take advantage of its diversity. Indeed, the matter is a religious one and it is the business of the Muslim community alone to settle it. Any interference by the secular state of India is in contradiction with its supposed religious 'neutrality' which could dangerously extend to all the affairs of the Muslim community. After all, the Bohra Muslims who feel that the behaviour of their sect is against their genuine personal Islamic beliefs are free to join another school of Islam without any outside interference.

One of the greatest tragedies of the Muslim community after Indian Independence is in the economic field. In agriculture, Muslims are mostly medium and small peasants. Their concentration is important only in the rice growing areas. These areas have been bypassed by the green revolution which, in India, concerned only wheat, thus creating a continually widening gap between the situation of the Muslim community and that of the Hindus.

The second largest occupation of the Muslims is handicraft. They have been the best craftsmen and artisans of India and still are. However, with the industrialization of the country in the hands of the government, i.e. the Hindu establishment, the handicraft industry became relegated to the most exploited and lowest paid sections of the economy. These artisans have not yet responded by organizing trade unions of their own to defend their rights.

The third occupation is trade and commerce. However, there are no Muslim business houses catering for all India. Nevertheless, in spite of all the handicaps, Muslims seem to be holding their own in this area. Muslim merchants are prosperous in the field of mines in Tamil Nadu; in ship-building in Kerala, and in several other sectors of the economy in Maharashtra and Gujarat. This relative success occurs in spite of the fact that in general, Muslims are not proportionately benefiting from the credit facilities from the banks (all nationalized). This sector of the Muslim community was also particularly hit by the continuous flow of its talented elite emigrating to Pakistan from 1947 to 1965.

In summary, Kuldip Nayar (a Hindu), Editor of the *Statesman* reported on 14 November 1974: 'In jobs or vocations, Muslims believe that they are discriminated against and that the government has done little to ensure for them equality of opportunity. It is claimed that the private sector is in particular reluctant to employ them because of old prejudices'. C. A. Abdussalam wrote in February 1975 in *Problems of Indian Muslims and their Solutions* the following: 'A study based on 831 public limited companies having a paid-up capital of Rs. 1,427.59 crores reveals that out of 6,465 directors there are only 119 Muslim directors, the percentage of which works out to be 1.8 only. Of the companies we find Muslim Managing Directors only eight companies (i.e. 1 per cent of the total number of companies). The paid-up capital of these eight companies is only 6.41 crores, i.e. 0.4 per cent of the total paid-up capital of the companies. Only in four companies (i.e. 0.5 per cent) there is a majority of Muslims on the directors' board. The paid-up capital of these four companies is only Rs. 3.31 crores (i.e. 0.2 per cent)'. Another study by K. L. Gauba points out that the Hindus of Greater Bombay (2,870,000 people) had 66,000 telephone connections, the Parsees (82,000 people) had 4,200 telephones and the Muslims (540,000 people) had 2,500 telephones. Thus, the percentages of telephone subscribers are 2.3 per cent among Hindus, 5.5 per cent among Parsees and 0.5 per cent among Muslims. The same could presumably be said about other parts of India.

In 1979, out of a total of 405 licences approved, only five were given to Muslims, whereas in 1980, the proportion did not rise much since six licences were approved for Muslims out of a total of 386 licences. Examples of this type could be given ad infinitum.

## Political Persecution

Ever since partition, the Muslim ratio in the services has followed a continuous slide down, to the point that their representation in every government department is today much lower than their percentage in the population. At the middle and higher scales of the government hierarchy, their percentage is no more than 2 per cent. Bias in employment against Muslims started actually since partition. Since 1947, there were secret circulars, executive policy decisions and 'understandings' barring recruitment of Muslims from the ranks of ordinary peons to the position of chief secretaries in the ministries.

Inder Malhotra reported in a leading Indian weekly in April 1973 'When all is said and done, there can be no escape from the stark reality that the share of the Muslims in public employment is abysmally low. Incredible though it may seem, according to the latest available statistics (1965), there were only six Muslim officers in the top two grades of the civil service out of 681. In the next grade, there were only four Muslims out of 2,000. As if this is not shocking enough, there were only twenty-one Muslims out of 9,900 clerks'. He goes on summarizing as follows: 'Twenty-five years after Independence our sixty million Muslims still feel alienated from the nation mainstream. They feel discriminated against, neglected and spurned. They do not get jobs easily, either in government or in private firms. Their share of seats in Parliament and State Assemblies is less than half of what is warranted by their population. They complain that their language, Urdu, is being throttled. They live in fear of communal riots and the Police'. In 1982, the number of Muslim members of Parliament was seventy-three out of a total of 788 members.

In the *Illustrated Weekly of India*, Rasheeduddin Khan reported in an article of the 14 May 1978 issue, the following: 'In the States, there were twenty-eight Muslim ministers out of a total of 345. The percentage today is probably a little less. From available data the position of Muslims in the all-India services is as follows: in the Central Secretariat: one secretary, one additional secretary, three joint secretaries, two deputy secretaries and three under-secretaries. In 1974, Muslims of the rank of secretary in the Government of India were six, by 1976 there were two, and now to none. The statewide distribution of Muslims and Christians in the IAS and the IPS show that Muslims are 3.09 per cent and 3.19 per cent in the two services, while Christians account for 2.44 per cent and 2.04 per cent respectively. This is even less than what it was in 1965, when the percentages for the IAS and the IPS respectively were: Muslims 5.3 per cent and 3.6 per cent and Christians 3.5 per cent and 4.6 per cent. The picture that one gets is equally dismal in education. It is stated that out of a total of 3,604 degree colleges in the country, only fifty-four are managed by Muslims, and that there are just 3.5 per cent Muslims in all the technical institutions in the country.'

What is, then, the political participation of the Muslim community? One line of action of the Muslim response is turning inward and trying to build itself outside the Indian State. Such an attitude has been taken by the influential Jamaat-e-Islami which reaffirmed in its May 1978 meeting that is members should not exercise their vote because the 'Indian State is a *taghut*' (i.e. despotic, anti-Muslim). The Muslim League which became practically defunct in the north, survived almost unscathed in the south. It is still an important political force in Kerala, Tamil Nadu and Maharashtra. A Muslim *majlis* has however been established in Uttar Pradesh to further the political rights of the Muslim community.

## The Communal Riots

The most dramatic single phenomenon that endangers the very life and property of the Muslims of India is the widespread occurrence of communal riots. These anti-Muslim riots, peculiar to India, are the work of Hindu mobs encouraged and organized by Hindu extremist parties such as the RSS. The police and the army made up overwhelmingly of Hindu elements join the mobs in killing Muslims and destroying their properties instead of protecting them. These riots have been the reality with which the Muslims of India had to live to this day since Independence in 1947. They keep the Muslims in a continuous pogrom, in a terrible state of fear for their lives and their property. These communal riots can occur anywhere in India, but are more concentrated in the north.

The Indian Home Ministry reports frightening statistics on anti-Muslim riots in its annual reports. In the two decades from 1964 to 1983, there occurred 7,287 anti-Muslim riots in India, i.e. an average of one riot a day. In the decade from 1974 to 1983 alone, there occurred 2,822 riots during which 2,398 persons were killed and 19,713 persons were maimed and injured, the great majority being Muslim.

After the bloodbath of Partition in which a huge number of Muslims were killed and almost ten million were forced to emigrate, there was a brief interlude. This was followed by a string of communal riots that climaxed at Jabalpur in Madhya Pradesh in 1961, and then the holocaust of Ahmadabad in Gujarat in 1969. The large Qamar Hostel, built in the city with Muslim voluntary donations of Rs.700,000 housing 200 students of which forty-seven were Hindus, was reduced to shambles. On its desolate walls were written the words: 'For Hindus Only'. The riots spread to neighbouring Baroda which was plastered with wall posters requesting the Muslims to 'Quit India'.

During the years of emergency before the end of the long period of the rule of the Congress Party, communal riots were stopped temporarily. But they were replaced by the persecution of the family planning zealots who ran wild against the Muslims in Delhi (Turkman Gate) and in the District of Muzaffarnagar (Uttar Pradesh) as well as elsewhere.

As soon as the old regime fell with a great relief to the Muslims, the communal riots started their ugly presence during the Janata Party rule. Uttar Pradesh witnessed communal riots in Banares, Sambhal, and as late as October 1978 in Aligarh. Riots also broke out in Bihar Sharif, near Patna (in Bihar), as well as in such peaceful areas as Tamil Nadu in the south, and later in Hyderabad. While this book was being written, a holocaust fell upon the Muslims of Bombay and Bhivandi in May 1984. The onslaught of Assam, however, in 1983, with about ten thousand Muslims – children and women – butchered in cold blood has all the characteristics of a new trend in mass extermination reminiscent of Hitlerian method, under the watchful eyes of complacent authorities.

To give an idea of how these riots come about and how much misery they bring to the Muslim community, let us describe two of the latest ones. In the Patna District (Bihar) a Muslim religious endowment (*waqf*) property was usurped by Hindus to establish a Hindu temple. First, they placed an idol under a peepul tree within the *waqf*'s precincts, then they took over the entire property with official blessings. Thus, when of 28 January 1979, Hindus tried to place another idol adjacent to a mosque in Mohalla Moghal Kunwan in Bihar Sharif, Muslims obtained court orders against building a Hindu temple on Muslim property, and tried to prevent the placing of the idol. The police arrived and opened fire on the Muslims, killing one Muslim and injuring fifteen others. Later, the police broke into Muslim homes and shops, and went about burning and destroying before arresting sixty more Muslims.

At Aligarh, in a wrestling match, a Muslim wrestler happened to defeat his Hindu counterpart. Scuffles then broke out among the supporters of the two antagonists. Hindu extremists started to incite the Hindu population and a chain of stabbings followed between Hindus and Muslims. On 5 October, a Hindu died in the hospital of stab wounds. A group of RSS fanatics then snatched the body and organized a funeral procession. The processionists, escorted by the official police called Provincial Armed Constabulary (PAC), were allowed to proceed towards the Muslim quarters of Chawraha Abdul-Karim and Upper Court shouting for revenge.

They then began looting and burning shops, houses and mosques. When the Muslims tried to organize resistance in the nearby Muhammed Ali Road, they were cut down by a barrage of gunfire from the PAC. Then, the processionists marched over the Muslim quarters of Bani Israelian and Manek Chowk where for four hours they killed, burned and looted; with the result that four Muslims were killed in Bani Israelian and the whole of Manek Chowk was destroyed. Later a Muslim woman was stabbed, tied to a cot and then burnt to death. The same fate was meted out to a Muslim rickshaw puller, and a newly married young man. At the same time the PAC were firing at the courtyard of the Moti Mosque while the mob was setting fire to the Mosque's gate. Other Muslims were killed in Halwaian Mosque and Chatari Mosque. On 6 November, the PAC started gunning down peaceful Muslim shoppers killing more Muslims. On 7 November, the PAC started searching Muslim houses taking seventy-five young men into custody. In the evening Sultani Serai Muslim quarter was attacked. On 8 November, the PAC killed six more Muslims in Serai Mian and another near Turkman Gate. By the evening on 8 November, eleven Muslims were killed. On 10 November, Hindus attacked Serai Rahman, Serai Hakeem and Rasulganj. By then, the Muslims were organized enough to repulse the attackers without loss. But on 12 November, Muslims prayed in local mosques the *Id-Al-Adha* and there was no sacrifice or celebration.

## Conclusions

This report might have depicted a dismal picture of the situation of the Muslims in India. However, if one is to take a static picture, one sees that the situation of the Muslim community is certainly far better than that of their brethren in Popular China or even the Soviet Union. Nevertheless, the basic cause of concern is the continuously deteriorating situation of the community. This deterioration lies in the great hypocrisy of the modern democratic, secular system. A democracy that does not protect the right of the minorities is certainly of no advantage to such minority. And a secular system that is a cover for fusion of religious minorities within the standard point of view of the majority is certainly abhorrent to any justice-conscious mind. It would have been much better for India to have declared a state religion and then make sure to protect the religious minority, just as Islam always sought to do and just as the modern Muslim States are doing as well as some European countries such as Sweden and Belgium. The effects of such persecution are not all negative. They help give a challenge to the Muslim community which have gone a long way to increase its own cohesion, overcome its contradictions and seek the solution to its problems within a movement of self-help. One thing is certain, however, the Muslim community is in India to stay, not because of any weakness in its Islamic conviction, but on the contrary because of the strength of this conviction. Muslims of India are Muslims and they are Indians, and they will not bow to the persecutions and the riots and move out of a land that has seen Muslim presence for more than one thousand years.

One aspect of Muslim response is to try to unite all efforts of the community in all-India, all-parties Muslim Council, known as Majlis-e-Mushawarat (i.e. Consultative Council). The first all-India Muslim Convention was held in Aligarh in 1953. More efforts of cohesion and self-help were made after the Jabalpur riots in 1961. The Consultative Council came into existence with the efforts of the Islamic organizations, especially the Jamaat-e-Islami, with the understanding that it would be non-political. The Council was entrusted in the all-India meeting of 1974 with the task of social, economic and educational reconstruction of the Muslim community. Another and much wider meeting was held in Delhi in October 1977, the Delhi Milli Convention.

Finally, it must be said, that in spite of all the problems it is facing, the Muslim community of India did overcome the traumatizing effects related to the division of the sub-continent into a Muslim majority and a Muslim minority state. It has now all the elements necessary for the survival of the community. It is dynamic, and although its economic, political and to some extent cultural position *vis-a-vis* the majority has been worsening due to bias and outright persecution, the Muslim community strengthened itself on cohesiveness and organization. It also started to solve its own problems, especially in education and welfare. After this slide down, the future will certainly see a bigger role for the Muslim community in the affairs of India in one way or another.

## References

1. C. Smith *Modern Islam in India* (London, 1946).
2. *Proceedings of the Tamil Nadu Muslim Educational Conference*,

published by the Tamil Nadu Muslim Education Standing Committee (Madras, Tamil-Nadu, 1973).

3. K. Nayar, *Statesman* (India, 14 November 1974).
4. C. A. Abdussalam *Problems of Indian Muslims and their Solutions* (Delhi, February 1975).
5. *Proceedings of the 5th All India Muslim Educational Conference* (Delhi, 1975).
6. R. Zakaria, the *Illustrated Weekly of India* (7 May 1978).
7. R. Khan, the *Illustrated Weekly of India* (14 May 1978).
8. I. A. Ansari, *Condition of Muslims in India,* International Seminar on Muslim Communities in Non-Muslim States (London England, July 1978).
9. M. Anwar, 'The Muslim Minority in India', *Muslim World League Journal* (Mecca, October 1978).
10. Students Islamic Movement of India, 'What Happened in Aligarh', *Impact International* (London, 22 December 1978–11 January 1979).
11. A. Ahmad, *Muslim Community in India, A Social & Economic Profile* IRTI of IDB (Jeddah, Saudi Arabia, February 1984).

# 6 Muslim Minorities in the Rest of Asia

## Introduction

Asia could be divided into five large sections as far as Muslims are concerned: Muslim States; India; China; the Soviet Union; other Muslim minorities. India, China and the Soviet Union have been treated elsewhere in this volume; only the other Muslim minorities will be treated in this chapter.

The question now is what is a Muslim state as opposed to non-Muslim states where Muslims live as minorities? It is certainly not always easy to answer the question. The most accurate definition of a Muslim state would be the state whose entire philosophy of existence is based on the teachings of the *Quran* and the *Sunnah*. Such a state should have as its model the state established by the Prophet Muhammad in Medina. Such a state should be a sovereign entity and exercise authority over all lands where Muslims have populations that are large enough to invest them with the governmental power. It should be the protector and the refuge of Muslims all over the world, independent of race, colour, national identity or school of law (*madhhab*). A state that commits itself more towards such an ideal could also be considered a Muslim state. Thus, a corollary of this definition is that no Muslim can be a foreigner in the Muslim state; there could be either one single Muslim state or no Muslim state at all.

However, there are states which recognize themselves in one way or another as belonging to the Muslim *ummah*. The clearest indication of this is membership of the Conference of the Foreign Ministers of Muslim Countries. This organization was established as a kind of Islamic League by the Muslim heads of states at Rabat

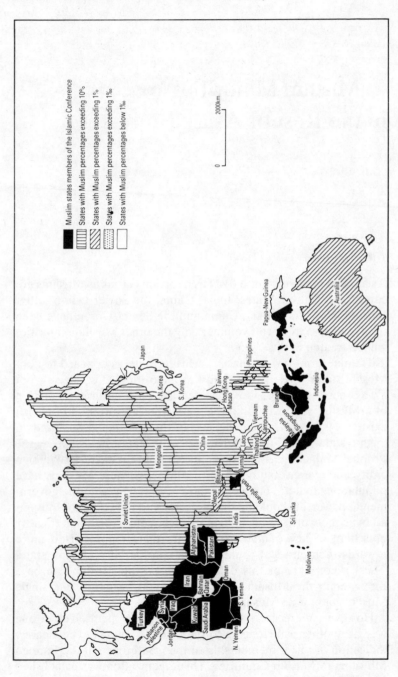

(Morocco) on 25 December 1969 in response to the burning of the Aqsa Mosque in Al-Quds (Palestine). The Conference has been growing ever since and has served as a forum for bringing the member states closer together and closer to Islam. The permanent secretariat of the conference is located in Jeddah (Saudi Arabia). It has forty–five member states of which twenty-two are Asian states and twenty-three are African. These states will be considered as the Muslim states; all other communities will be considered minorities independent of the Muslim percentages. The population of the Asian Muslim states totalled 522,720,000 people in 1982 of whom about 474,780,000 were Muslims. The list of these states and their Muslim populations are shown in Table 6.1. (See Figure 2.)

Islam entered most of the regions of Asia during the first century of the *Hijrah*. The first nuclei of Muslim communities were

*Table 6.1*   Muslim countries of Asia, 1982

| State | Population in thousands | | |
|-------|-------|-------|-----|
| | Total | Muslim | |
| Indonesia | 157,230 | 141,500 | 90% |
| Pakistan | 91,580 | 88,830 | 97% |
| Bangladesh | 95,710 | 81,350 | 85% |
| Turkey | 47,920 | 47,440 | 99% |
| Iran | 40,610 | 39,760 | 99% |
| Afghanistan | 15,740 | 15,740 | 100% |
| Iraq | 14,270 | 13,840 | 97% |
| Saudi Arabia | 10,980 | 10,430 | 95% |
| Syria | 10,700 | 9,100 | 85% |
| Malaysia | 14,760 | 7,970 | 54% |
| North Yemen | 5,420 | 5,420 | 100% |
| Jordan | 2,840 | 2,700 | 95% |
| Palestine | 5,300 | 2,330 | 44% |
| South Yemen | 2,040 | 2,040 | 100% |
| Lebanon | 3,080 | 2,000 | 65% |
| Kuwait | 1,590 | 1,430 | 90% |
| Oman | 940 | 930 | 99% |
| United Arab Emirates | 1,020 | 920 | 90% |
| Bahrain | 370 | 330 | 90% |
| Qatar | 230 | 220 | 95% |
| Maldives | 160 | 160 | 100% |
| Brunei Darussalam | 230 | 160 | 70% |
| Total | 522,720 | 474,780 | 91% |

established by Arab and Persian merchants, especially sea-farers from southern Arabia. In fact, the influence of southern Arabia is such that all Muslim communities of the Indian Ocean and further, from East Africa to Indochina are of the Shafii school which is predominant in southern Arabia.

Muslim immigration to South-East Asia and the Far East is at present negligible and does not contribute much to the growth of the Muslim communities. More important than immigration are growth by conversion (which remains important notwithstanding the difficulties) and natural growth which is usually higher than that of non-Muslims.

Many minority communities in Asian states were in fact independent Muslim states which were forcibly incorporated into bigger non-Muslim entities. Furthermore, Muslims are persecuted in many of the Asian states as will be seen in this chapter.

Table 6.2 shows that there were 18,782,000 Muslims in the Asian states outside the Muslim states, India, China and the Soviet Union, in 1982. In that year, the percentage of Muslims over the total population exceeded 10 per cent in five states: Singapore (17%), Mongolia (15%), Philippines (12.2%), Thailand (12%) and Burma (10.7%). It exceeds the million point in four states: Thailand, Philippines, Burma and Sri Lanka.

*Table 6.2*　Asian Muslim minorities, except India, China and the USSR, 1982

| Country | Population in thousands | | |
|---|---|---|---|
| | *Total* | *Muslim* | |
| Philippines | 51,200 | 6,250 | 12.2 % |
| Thailand | 50,020 | 6,000 | 12.0 % |
| Burma | 36,000 | 3,560 | 10.7 % |
| Sri Lanka | 15,360 | 1,168 | 7.6 % |
| Nepal | 15,680 | 500 | 3.2 % |
| Singapore | 2,440 | 420 | 17.0 % |
| Cambodia | 5,560 | 335 | 6.0 % |
| Mongolia | 1,740 | 260 | 15.0 % |
| Taiwan | 18,550 | 75 | 0.4 % |
| Bhutan | 1,430 | 75 | 5.2 % |
| Vietnam | 55,900 | 55 | 0.1 % |
| Hong Kong | 5,210 | 30 | 0.5 % |
| Japan | 119,200 | 30 | 0.03% |
| Other | 64,710 | 24 | 0.04% |
| Total | 443,000 | 18,782 | 4.2 % |

## The Philippines

In the sixteenth century, the islands which make up today the Philippines were in an advanced state of Islamization. Three Muslim states extended their influence on these islands: The Sulu Muslim State, including Sulu, Basilan, Palawan, Negros, Panay, Mindoro and Iloco in the north of Luzon Islands; The Maguindanao Muslim State, including the entire Island of Mindanao; and the Muslim state of Manilad (today's Manilla) including the Centre of Luzon. The Spanish were in the midst of their infamous Inquisition against the Muslims (Moriscos) in the Iberian Peninsula. They attacked the Muslim states of Sulu, Maguindanao and Manilad with the same fanaticism and ferocity with which they treated their own Muslim population in Spain. King Philip, after whom the islands were later to be named, gave the following order to his Admiral-in-Chief: 'Conquer the lands and convert the people (to Catholicism)'. It is against this background that the Muslims of the so-called Philippines (called Moros, the name given by the Spanish to the Muslims of Spain) had to struggle for survival to this day, for more than four centuries. The first victim of this colonial attack was the Muslim state of Manilad. But Muslim resistance organized itself in the south in the islands of Palawan, Sulu and Mindanao. These islands became part of a united independent Muslim state of the Sulus. Spain could never conquer this state in spite of continuous warfare, and had to recognize its independent existence.

In 1896, President McKinley of the US decided to occupy the Philippines to 'Christianize and civilize' the people as he put it. The Americans succeeded in conquering the Spanish Colony in 1899, but the Muslim state of Sulu resisted. It fell to the American arms in 1914 after a long and heroic struggle. For the first time in its history the Bangsa Moro (Muslim name for their homeland in the Philippines) fell to non-Muslim armies and lost its independence. On 11 March 1915, the Muslim King (Sultan) was forced to abdicate, but was recognized as head of the Muslim community. It was only in April 1940 that the Americans abolished the Sultanate of Sulu and incorporated Bangsa Moro in the Philippines.

Thus, Bangsa Moro is a Muslim land whose population follows the Shafii school. It was colonized by the Philippines in 1940 and has remained so ever since. After independence from the US, the indigenous populations of the northern islands which had been converted forcibly to Catholicism by Spain, followed up the same policy of genocide against the Muslims which they had inherited from the Spanish colonial establishment and which has been encouraged and supported by the US. Indeed, as soon as the US completed the occupation of Bangsa Moro in 1915, it opened it up for Christian immigration from the north. In fact, the Bangsa Moro formed half the area of the islands. Immigration was slow in the beginning, but after 1939 it grew to alarming proportions and was even more encouraged by the government of independent Philippines. Indeed, this government encouraged and tacitly supported hords of criminals which killed the Muslims and burned their villages, then took the emptied lands for Chiristian settlement. The Catholic Church remained the moving power behind the brutal de-Islamization and Christianization of the south in the same way as it had been the moving power behind the Spanish Inquisition.

This situation has forced the Muslims in recent years to take up arms once again to defend themselves. The struggle is led by the Moro National Liberation Front (Chairman: Professor Nur Miswari). The Muslim population has been suffering great hardships for the last ten years because of the fierceness with which the Philippino Army has been trying to crush the urge of the Muslims to survive and to live honourably as Muslims. A large number of Muslim villages have been destroyed. Many Muslim refugees fled to Sabah (Malaysia). The OIC and Libya played the roles of arbitrators between the Philippino Government and the Bangsa Moro National Liberation Front. There was an agreement for the autonomy of thirteen provinces in the south with large Muslim percentages. But, it seems that the Philippino Government never wanted to find a just solution. No wonder the negotiations soon broke down, and the Government resumed its genocidal war against the Muslims. From March 1968 to March 1982, more than a hundred thousand Muslim civilians were done to death by the Philippino Army, more than three hundred thousand Muslim houses were destroyed and more than fifty major villages, towns and cities have been razed by the Philippino Army, including the old Muslim capital of Jolo. This Army was swollen to about three hundred thousand soldiers from fifty thousand in the beginning of hostilities in 1972. About three million Muslims have been displaced (of whom a hundred thousand have found refuge in Sabah, Malaysia and hundreds of thousands live in misery around Manila) and a very large number of mosques, schools and plantations were destroyed. The entire Muslim population is in a state of disarray and shock. The struggle of the Muslims of Bangsa

Moro however goes on, in spite of all these atrocities and the weight of the entire Philippino Army.

In 1982, there were about 6,250,000 Muslims in the Philippines (12 per cent of the population). The government recognizes the existence of only 2,200,000 Muslims. Muslims are in majority in the thirteen provinces about which an agreement had been reached that they should constitute a Bangsa Moro Autonomous State. These are: Palawan, Tawi-Tawi, Sulu, Basilan, Zamboanga del Sur, Zamboanga del Norte, North Catabato, Maguindanao, Sultan Kudarat, South Cotabato, Lanao Sur, Lanao Norte and Davao Sur. The government accepts that Muslims are in the majority only in Tawi-Tawi, Sulu, Basilan, Maguindanao and Lanao Sur. It also claims that they form more than one-tenth of the population but less than 50 per cent in Zamboanga del Sur, North Catabato and Sultan Kudarat. Actually there are large Muslim communities in all the other provinces of Mindanao as well as in the region of Manila. Many Christian Philippinos convert to Islam in spite of the war. Muslim lands have a total area of 117,000 square kilometres (total Philippines 289,000 square kilometres) and the area of the thirteen provinces is approximately 60,000 square kilometres, comprising the Sulu Archipelago, the island of Palawan and the western part of Mindanao. Muslims belong to several ethnic groups: the most important being the Tausugs (Basilan, Sulu, Tawi-Tawi) and the Maguindanaos (Lanao-del-Sur).

There are about three thousand mosques in the country, especially in the south. Marawi City and Jolo could be considered the religious centres of the Muslim community. The meaning of the *Holy Quran* has been translated by Dr Ahmad Domocao Alonto into Maranao, the most common language among Muslims. The work was sponsored by the Institute of Islamic Studies of the Philippines Muslim University in Marawi City. There is no Muslim literature in local languages but Arabic is spread among the educated. About a thousand Muslims from the Philippines perform the *hajj* every year and the Shariah Courts are functioning in the south. There are about a thousand Muslim schools in the country in addition to special schools for training *imams* and *Quran* readers. The Philippines Muslim University at Marawi City imparts Islamic education at the University level and trains the *ulama*. It has five thousand students. In Jolo, the Philippines Muslim College played a similar role and had two thousand students. But the college has been closed because of the war.

Most Muslims are farmers and fishermen, among them the illiteracy rate is high, diseases and infant mortality are widespread and unemployment is much higher than the Philippino average. University graduates number about fifteen thousand people only. In the Philippines government's higher services, the number of Muslims is negligible. The most active Islamic Associations are the Muslim Association of the Philippines (Manila); Ansar Al-Islam (Marawi City), the Converts to Islam Society (Manila) and the Sulu Islamic Foundation (Jolo); etc. . . . In 1983, an Islamic Dawah Council of the Philippines has been formed to unify Muslim organizations in the north and the south.

## Thailand

There must have been about six million Muslims in Thailand in 1982. However, the official figures are much lower. These give an overall Muslim percentage of the population of about 4 per cent instead of a more probable figure of 12 per cent. Actually this is part of the Thai establishment's effort to reduce the importance of its Muslim population. Muslims live all over Thailand, but there are three areas of Muslim concentration: the south, from the Malaysian border to the Isthmus of Kra; the north, in the area of Chiang Rai; and the Capital region.

The south was not part of Thailand. In fact the Malay Peninsula was inhabited by Malays who were organized in small states. These Malays adopted Islam during the fifteenth century as did almost all other Malays. Since the fourteenth century, Thailand began a campaign of conquest of the Malay Peninsula which culminated in 1767 C.E. with the conquest of all Muslim states down to Ligor (Nakhom Sri Thammarat), thus incorporating the Muslim states of Jays (Chaiya), Grahi (Surat-Thani) and Ligor in the Thai Empire. From Ligor, the Thais extended their conquest to the south conquering more Muslim states, such as Bedelung (Pathalung), Senggora (Songkhla) and Setul (Satun). During the nineteenth century, competition for the conquest of the remaining of the Malay Peninsula started between Britain and Thailand. In 1832 C.E., the Thais conquered the Muslim state of Pattani, and this conquest was recognized by Britain in 1909. At first, the Muslim states conquered by Thailand were allowed to be administered by their own Sultans. However in 1902, Muslim administrators were deposed; the Muslim lands lost all autonomy and became administered directly by the Thais.

Out of a total of six million Muslims in Thailand in 1982 about four million are Malay Muslims who live in the provinces of the south. The Muslims of Bangkok, numbering about 800,000 people, are descendents of prisoners brought from the Malay states. For instance, in 1789, four thousand Pattani Muslims were arrested and taken to Bangkok. These forced immigrants mixed later with other Muslim immigrants. In this process, they lost their Malay language and became Thai-speakers. Other Muslims of central Thailand are also descendants of Muslim prisoners who mixed with local converts. They may total about one million Muslims. Muslims in the north-east and some of the north region are descendants of Chams who were brought from Cambodia when it was conquered by Thailand. Many Thai converts live in these two regions. Finally, in the north, there are many Muslim descendants of Muslim immigrants from Yunnan (China) who had to flee when the Muslim rebellion was crushed in 1875. If the census of 1976 is taken into account with the estimates given by the Muslims the results shown in Table 6.3 are obtained which gives also the number of registered mosques by Region. This Table shows that there were 5,250,000 Muslims in Thailand in 1976. Muslims constitute half the population of the south region, one of the four regions of the Kingdom. In this region (72,961 square kilometres in area), they are actually in the majority in the provinces of Narathiwat, Yala, Pattani, Satun, Songkhla, Trang, and Krabi.

*Table 6.3*   Muslims in Thailand, 1976

| Region | Population in thousands | | | Registered Mosques |
|---|---|---|---|---|
| | Total | Muslims | | |
| Southern Region | 5,534 | 2,820 | 51.0% | 1695 |
| Central Region | 13,459 | 1,210 | 9.0% | 364 |
| North-eastern Region | 15,584 | 930 | 6.0% | 18 |
| Northern Region | 9,696 | 290 | 3.0% | 1 |
| Total | 44,273 | 5,250 | 11.9% | 2078 |

There must be about 2,500 mosques in Thailand, but in 1976, only 2,078 mosques were registered under the Royal Act of 1947 relating to mosques. There are 414 of such mosques in Pattani Province, 339 in Narathiwat Province, 213 in Songkhla Province, 196 in Yala Province and 139 mosques in the Capital Bangkok. By Region, there are 1,695 mosques in the south, 364 mosques in the central province, eighteen mosques in the north east and only one registered mosque in the eastern province. But there are very few qualified *imams*. The meaning of the *Holy Quran* has been translated into Thai. One version by Haji Ibrahim Qureshi has been published. Another version is by Sheikh-ul-Islam Haji Ismail. Copies of Malay translations are also imported from neighbouring Malaysia. Learned Muslims know Arabic, and the *Holy Quran* has constantly been printed in the country (in Arabic). However, Islamic literature in the Thai language is meagre.

Several thousand Muslims of Thailand perform the *hajj* every year. Muslim personal laws are in force in four southern provinces only (Pattani, Narathiwat, Songkhla, and Yala with an area of 14,010 square kilometres). Two *Qadis* are appointed by the Government for each of these provinces as well as a State Committee for Islamic Affairs for all of Thailand headed by a Sheikh-ul-Islam. Thus, the highest Muslim authority is not chosen by the Muslims, but appointed by the state.

There are about four hundred Muslim schools (*pondoks*). Islam is not taught in state schools. The government established its own Islamic education institutions (*ponoh*), and an Islamic College, thus trying to control Islamic Education as well. Few Muslims reach the college level of education. There are only a few hundred college graduates among Muslims, among whom about forty are physicians and thirty are engineers. Muslims are mostly farmers, fishermen and traders; their representation in the government and the services is weak, and the majority community seems to have had a biased attitude towards them. In 1976, there were fourteen Muslim deputies in the parliament and two deputy ministers in the government.

There are many local Muslim organizations, but there is no national organization which might unite all Muslims. The most important of these associations are the Thai Welfare Association (Bangkok), the Yound Muslim Association of Thailand, and the Thai Muslim Student Association.

The Muslims of Thailand feel persecuted and under the pressure of assimilation by the majority (e.g., they are forced to take Thai names). There is great discontent in the south with the lack of consideration on the part of the government for the national (Malay) and religious feeling of the population. The government tries to destroy Muslim schools and replace them by Thai ones; it also tries to destroy the influence of the Malay language among Muslims, it disregards Islamic festivals; it persecutes, imprisons and sometimes even puts to death Muslim religious and political leaders (between 1973 and 1975, about five hundred Muslims were killed by the Government in the south); and last but not least, the Government forces Muslims to take non-Muslim Thai names; thus diluting their Islamic identity.

In the south, resistance against Thai colonization has been continuously going on for long, especially since the government accelerated its policy of Thaization which helped reduce the Muslim majority in the Muslim southern region. In 1960, the Pattani Liberation Front (PLF) was formed and in 1968, the Pattani United Liberation Organization (PULO) was established. Both of them seek independence for the four southernmost Muslim provinces by armed guerilla struggle.

## Burma

Islam reached Burma through many routes. First, there were Muslim Arab traders who settled on the shorelines during the first *Hijrah* century (7th C.E.) or later, first on the Arakan coast, and later more to the south. More recently, Indian and Malay traders have been effective in spreading Islam. Finally, refugees from Yunnan (China) in the nineteenth century settled in the northern parts of the country.

A Muslim state was established in Arakan when the Sultan of Muslim Bengal Naseer-ud-Deen Mahmud Shah (1442–59 C.E.) helped King Sulayman Naramithla establish a Muslim Mrauku state. Muslim rule lasted for several centuries in Arakan and extended as far south as Moulmein during the tenure of Sultan Salim Shah Razagri (1593–1612 C.E.). Persian was the state language of the Arakan Muslim state. The Capital was Myohaung. It was in 1784 that Buddhist Burma conquered the Muslim state, followed between the years 1824 and 1826 by the British. When Burma became independent in 1948, Arakan was incorporated within it.

The total area of Arakan is 36,762 square kilometres, with a total population in 1969 of 1,847,000 people. These are today divided into two religious communities: the Muslims (called *Rohingyas*) and the Buddhists (called *Moghs*). By 1982, there were about 2.6 million people living in Arakan of whom about 1,460,000 were Muslims (56 per cent of the population); another 2.1 million of the overall Muslims lived in other parts of Burma, bringing the total Muslim population estimate to 3,560,000 people, or 10.7 per cent of the overall Burmese population (Burmese Muslims estimate their numbers to be double the above figure). The population of Tenasserim Division (Capital; Moulmein) is about 20 per cent Muslim (600,000 Muslims in 1982). The remaining Muslims live mainly in the Rangoon Region and in the northeast. The cities where Muslims are in the majority outside the Arakan Region are numerous, the most important being Moulmein (Tanasserim Division); Moulmeingyun (Irrawaday Division); Pyinmana and Kyaukse (Mandalay Division); and Shwebo (Sagaing Division). However, there are no detailed statistics on Muslims in Burma.

The Muslims of Burma consist of two ethnic groups. Those who are of Indo-Pakistani origin, live mainly in the large cities, have strong links with the Indian sub-continent and speak Urdu and Tamil fluently. The others are of Burmese origin. There are more than five thousand mosques in Burma. In large cities, there are several mosques, many of which are several centuries old. The meaning of the *Holy Quran* has been translated into Burmese by a team of well-versed Muslim *ulama*. Some books on Islam have been translated into Burmese, but there is not enough Islamic literature in that language. About five hundred Muslims used to perform *hajj* yearly before 1962. Muslim personal laws are in force in the country. There is also a large number of Muslim schools covering about 60 per cent of Muslim children. There are six institutions for *Quran* teaching. Islam is not taught however in public schools.

Muslims were running three high schools which were nationalized in 1964. There are many Muslim university graduates, but their percentage in the community is about half that of the non-Muslims. There are Muslim lawyers, engineers, physicians and university professors; many of them, however, are reduced to emigration. The number of Muslims in the government and the armed forces is now negligible.

At present the Muslim community of Burma is highly persecuted. Their businesses have been nationalized, their lands seized, their schools de-Islamized. They are forbidden from performing *hajj* and their links with the Muslim world have been greatly curtailed. Even securing copies of the *Quran* is becoming a problem: publishing it needs the permission of the government and then paper is not available. Since 1973, Muslims have not been allowed to receive free copies from abroad. Since 1982, many of them were stripped of their Burmese nationality or officially reduced to second class citizens.

Before the Burmese armed forces took over the country in 1962 and established their brand of socialism, Muslims were well itegrated with the population. They were in top positions in the army and the government (e.g., Haji M. A. Raschid, once Burmese Central Minister). There were two Muslim judges in the High Court and four Muslims were ministers at one time or another. The mass of Muslims were farmers but many others were rich traders. Muslims established a free Muslim hospital (in the 1930s) and a Muslim Central Fund Trust. There were also many Muslim organizations. At present the leading ones are the Jamiat Ulema-e-Islam, the All-Burmese Muslim Organization and the Islamic Religious Affairs Council.

The brunt of the Burmese persecutions fell on the Arakanese Muslims. The efforts of the different governments of Burma were concentrated on reducing their majority. Four major expulsions were carried out against them since 1942. Indeed, after the departure of the British in 1942, a wave of hatred against the Muslims drenched the Arakan Region in blood. Muslims were massacred en masse and two hundred thousand of them had to flee to East Pakistan (now Bangladesh), West Pakistan and even Saudi Arabia, whereas about eight thousand Muslims lost their lives. Before the Japanese arrived, the Muslims tried to establish an Islamic Republic in Arakan but failed. New pogroms were led against the Arakanese Muslims in 1958, in 1962, and in 1974 with thousands of victims and tens of thousands of refugees. However, the most criminal activity led by the Burmese Government with the use of its army is what it called 'Operation Dragon King' which started out in February 1978. The Rangoon Government introduced national identity cards but refused to give them to the Rohingya Muslims. They were offered, instead, foreigners' registration cards in spite of the fact that the Rohingyas have been citizens of Arakan for more than a thousand years. Even those who accepted these cards subsequently saw them confiscated and destroyed. Burmese political commisars aided by armed forces launched upon an orgy of Muslim killings and Muslim village burning, especially in the two sub-divisions of Buthidaung and Maungdaw. Thousands of Muslims were thus killed and the remainder fled in terror across the border to Bangladesh. 71,000 Muslims were thus evicted by 1 May 1978, of whom 16,000 crossed the border on 30 April alone. There were 313,000 refugee Muslims by 1 August 1978. Of these 283,000 people were housed in make-shift camps and the others outside the camps. In August 1978, Bangladesh and Burma concluded an agreement for the repatriation of the refugees and 'Operation Hintha' started. Eventually, all Burmese Rohingyas were repatriated after more than ten thousand of them died of disease and malnutrition. However, once back home they faced again the most inhuman treatment as well as disease and misery. Many found their lands confiscated and their citizenship denied. And while some of their brightest sons think of armed struggle to recover the right to their homeland under the United Islamic Organisation, Burma (UIOB), another page of Muslim sufferings seems to have been turned.

Since 1980, Muslims of other areas were forced out of the country by persecution. Thousands found their way to Malaysia and Thailand.

## Sri Lanka

Islam entered Sri Lanka in the Seventh Century C.E. with Arab traders from south Arabia. From the beginning, Muslims were well received by the local kings and they soon became a trading community with necessary international links. With the fall of Baghdad in 1258 C.E., their links with the heartland of Islam became weak, and were replaced by stronger links with the Muslims of south India, many of whom emigrated to the island and fused with the earlier Muslim elements. Thus, the present Muslim population of Sri Lanka received from south Arabia its school (*Shafii*) and from south India, its language (Tamil) which is different from the language of the majority (Sinhalese). By the sixteenth century the Muslims were well concentrated in the south-west coast with main centres at Colombo, Beruwala, and Galle.

The Portuguese who landed in Colombo in 1502 hit the Muslim population very hard. They broke both their political power and economic prosperity, and then embarked on a systematic policy of terror and expulsion. Muslims were officially expelled in 1526 and some more remaining Muslims were expelled in 1626. They found refuge in territories on the island which were not under Portuguese rule such as Kandy, Sitawaka and all towns and villages of the interior, as well as on the northern (Purralam) and eastern coasts (Kalmunai). They eventually became agriculturists on the eastern coast where many of them became soldiers in the Sinhalese armies to fight the Portuguese.

The Dutch replaced the Portuguese in 1658 and followed the same policy of persecution and suppression against the Muslims. Muslims were expelled again from Galle and Matara (in 1659) and from Colombo (in 1670). They were not allowed to buy land and were forced to labour without due compensation. However, these discriminatory rules were rescinded in 1832 by the British. With the Dutch came also a new element in the Muslim population: Javanese refugees, prisoners, soldiers, exiles, etc. These Malays have kept their language to this day.

Meanwhile the Sinhalese Kandyan Kingdom became a refuge for Muslims. They were well treated in it and they became influential in their area of excellence: commerce.

In the late eighteenth century the Dutch introduced a bill promulgating 'Islamic personal laws' for the Muslims. These were retained when the British replaced the Dutch in 1796. The British treated the Muslims reasonably well during their colonial tenure. By 1937, a system of 'domestic relations' courts presided over by *qadis* (Muslim judges) were established and *waqfs* were organized under the aegis of Muslims.

In 1901, the number of Muslims was 248,000 people and they formed 6.9 per cent of Sri Lanka's population. In 1963, they kept the same percentage as their number grew to 731,000. By 1971, they became 910,000 Muslims (7.2% of total population) and by 1981, there were 1,134,000 Muslims (or 7.6% of the total population). The total population was 14,850,000 in 1981, when the Muslim population comprised 1,057,000 Ceylon 'Moors' (Tamil-speaking); 43,000 Malays (Malay-speaking); 29,000 Indian 'Moors' (Gujrati-speaking); and 5,000 Muslims Bohrahs and Memons. By 1982, the Muslim population could be estimated at 1,168,000. Table 6.4 shows their distribution by province in 1971 and 1981 censuses. Muslims form more than 10 per cent of the population in seven districts out of twenty-four districts. They are more than 20 per cent of the population only in four districts. Muslims are concentrated in four areas where they form more than 10 per cent of the total population; the east coast (Trincomalee, Bathicaloa, Amparai); the north-west coast (Mannar and Puttalam); Colombo; and Kandy; with the highest concentration in the agricultural east coast. No district has a Muslim absolute majority. Almost all Malays are concentrated in Colombo (western). From Table 6.4 it is clearly seen that Muslim percentages are decreasing in the two districts of highest Muslim concentration: Amparai and Trincomalee. This means that the Muslim

*Table 6.4*    Muslims in Sri Lanka by province

| District | Muslim population | | | |
|---|---|---|---|---|
| | 1971 | | 1981 | |
| Amparai | 126,033 | 46.2% | 161,754 | 41.6% |
| Trincomalee | 62,613 | 32.4% | 75,761 | 29.5% |
| Bathicaloa | 62,519 | 24.2% | 80,000 | 24.1% |
| Colombo | 187,987 | 7.0% | 168,956 | 10.0% |
| Gampaha | | | 47,850 | 3.4% |
| Kalutara | 49,600 | 6.8% | 62,781 | 7.6% |
| Kandy | 104,469 | 8.8% | 125,646 | 11.2% |
| Matale | 21,825 | 6.9% | 26,603 | 7.4% |
| Nuara Eliya | 9,609 | 2.1% | 15,791 | 3.0% |
| Kurunegala | 48,881 | 4.8% | 64,213 | 5.3% |
| Puttalam | 39,548 | 10.4% | 50,246 | 10.2% |
| Jaffna | 15,520 | 2.2% | 14,169 | 1.7% |
| Mannar | | | 30,079 | 28.1% |
| Vavuniya | 28,009 | 16.2% | 6,764 | 7.1% |
| Mullaitivu | | | 3,816 | 4.9% |
| Galle | 22,555 | 3.1% | 26,000 | 3.2% |
| Matara | 14,960 | 2.5% | 16,853 | 2.6% |
| Hambantota | 7,634 | 2.2% | 9,333 | 2.2% |
| Annuradhapura | 27,274 | 7.0% | 43,801 | 7.5% |
| Polonnaruwa | 11,603 | 7.1% | 17,621 | 6.7% |
| Ratnapura | 10,218 | 1.5% | 15,441 | 1.9% |
| Kegalle | 30,151 | 4.6% | 36,548 | 5.4% |
| Badulla | 24,888 | 3.9% | 28,759 | 4.5% |
| Moneragala | 4,195 | 2.2% | 5,750 | 2.1% |
| Total | 910,091 | 7.2% | 1,134,556 | 7.6% |

*Table 6.5*    Muslims in Sri Lanka by region

1, percentage of Muslims in region; 2, percentage of total number of Muslims in Sri Lanka

| Region | Muslim population 1971 | | Muslim population 1982 | |
|---|---|---|---|---|
| | 1 | 2 | 1 | 2 |
| Eastern Region | 254,936  35.3% | 28.0% | 317,177  32.5% | 28.0% |
| Mannar/Puttalam | 60,444  13.5% | 6.6% | 80,325  13.4% | 7.1% |
| Colombo | | | 168,956  10.0% | 14.9% |
| Kandy | | | 125,646  11.1% | 11.1% |
| Other | 594,561  5.2% | 65.4% | 442,452  4.2% | 38.9% |
| Total | 909,941  7.2% | 100.0% | 1,134,556  7.6% | 100.0% |

population, dispersed as it is, tends towards more dispersion, either through government policy of colonization of Muslim lands as some claim, or by natural forces on population movements, or both. Table 6.5 shows Muslim percentages by region.

There are about two thousand mosques in Sri Lanka, with sixty-three mosques in Colombo alone. Large mosques are governed by boards of trustees and most mosques are administered by the Waqf Board (around fifteen hundred mosques). The Waqf Board is a government department and the Waqf Commissioner is appointed by the government. *Quran* is taught in all mosques. Its meaning has been translated into Tamil and more recently into Sinhalese. There is a shortage of Islamic books and restrictions have been imposed on the import of books. There are also restrictions on *hajj* because of foreign exchange shortage. Still several hundred Sri Lanka Muslims manage to reach Mecca every year. Muslim personal laws are in force.

All schools, including Muslims schools, have been nationalized. But in the Ministry of Education there exists a Muslim School section which controls two hundred primary and high schools. In these schools the same official curriculum is taught along with Arabic and Islamic education. There is only one single private Muslim School left, the Zahira College, which was established in Colombo in 1892. It is constituted of a primary and a high school and has an all-male student body of two thousand. There is a Muslim Ladies' College (Government-run) and one Muslim Training College for teachers in the Eastern Province. Muslim percentage in the University barely reaches 4, thus lower than their national percentage.

There are six *imam* schools, five for boys and one for girls. These are in Amparai District (Addlaichani); in Galle (Galle and Weligama); in Colombo (Maharagama); in Puttalam and in Kandy (Galeliya for girls). These schools have a total enrolment of five hundred and dozens of students are enrolled in Islamic universities abroad.

Muslims have the lowest percentage of education in Sri Lanka and are at present poorer than the rest of the population. About 90 per cent are farmers and labourers, 9 per cent traders and 1 per cent government employees.

Muslims are reasonably well treated, but from time to time communal problems arise due to political polarization (e.g., the anti-Muslim riots of Puttalam in 1976 and Galle in 1982). Relations between the Muslims and the Sinhalese Buddhist majority are much better than with the Hindu (Tamil) minority with which they share the same language. There is always one Muslim minister in the government, sometimes two. The Mayor of Colombo is traditionally a Muslim and Muslims had twenty-one representatives out of the 151 constituencies in the country (double their national percentage). Muslims are completely integrated in the country and serve it most sincerely as they did for one thousand years. However, the new Constitution of 1978 implies proportional representation only when a community forms a high percentage of the electoral district. The dispersion of the Muslim community works against them under the new constitution. Thus, their representatives end up being chosen for them by other communities. Many Muslims resent this situation.

The most important Muslim organizations are the Muslim League, the Ceylon Moors League, the Islamic Socialist Front, the Jamaat-e-Islami, the All-Ceylon Council of *ulama*, the Muslim Youth League; the All-Ceylon Muslim Educational Conference, the University Muslim Majlis, etc. However, there is no overall Muslim organization representing all the Muslims of Sri Lanka.

## Cambodia

In the Middle Ages, Indochina was divided into three kingdoms: Annam (the Vietnam of today); Cambodia; and Champa. Annam consisted only of the northern plains of Tonkin, i.e., the delta of the Red River. It was a Buddhist state. Cambodia was of Hindu tradition and occupied a much larger area than today's Cambodia. It enclosed also Cochinchina, i.e., the delta of the Mekong River. The central part of today's Vietnam was the domain of the Kingdom of Champa. This Kingdom which existed for more than fifteen centuries had Hindu culture.

There was continuous warfare between the three kingdoms, with Annam as the invading and agressive power. In 1471, the new capital of Champa was destroyed; by the turn of the sixteenth century Annam conquered the area of Hue; and by the end of the same century, it absorbed all of the Champa Kingdom. Annam then proceeded to absorb Cambodia as well by conquering the entire Mekong delta during the eighteenth and nineteenth centuries. Total absorption of Cambodia was halted by the French.

The Kingdom of Champa had affinities with the Hindu states of Java and Malacca. When these regions adopted Islam, the Chams, persecuted and subjugated by the invading Vietnamese, embraced

Islam en masse. They also emigrated in large numbers to the kingdom of Cambodia where they found protection and refuge. Thus, the greatest majority of the Muslims of Cambodia today are Chams; i.e., the real indigenous population of Indochina before the Vietnamese invasion from the north.

In 1971, the number of Muslims in Cambodia would have been about 500,000 people, of whom 480,000 were Chams and 20,000 were of Javanese origin whose ancestors emigrated to Cambodia in the thirteenth century. All these Muslims follow the Shafii school. By 1974, just before the onslaught of the Khmer Rouge on the country, there must have been about 550,000 Muslims in Cambodia. Muslims lived in fourteen of the seventeen provinces of the country, with the highest concentration in Kampong Cham where they formed about 36 per cent of the total population (about 300,000 Muslims). There were also high percentages of Muslims in the following provinces: Kampot, Kandal, Phnom-Penh, Kampong Chhang, Kampong Thum, Kracheh and Batdambang. The Chams speak their own language and the Javanese speak the Cambodian language. There were, in 1974, about 185 mosques in the country of which fifty-nine were in Kampong Cham Province and nine in the city of Phnom Penh. About half the Muslim population must have been slaughtered by the Khmer Rouge. In 1982, the number of Muslims is estimated to be no more than 335,000.

A majority of the Muslims lived in compact villages. Some live in the cities and engage in trade and industry. The spiritual centre of the Muslims is Chruoy Changvar, near Phnom Penh, where most of the high Muslim officials live including their supreme chief. Most Muslims are farmers; others are butchers, fishermen and boat-builders. Most of the Muslims of Javanese origin live in Chruoy Changvar. All Muslims were members of the Islamic Association whose headquarters were in Phnom Penh and whose sections enclosed all Muslim villages. Historically, the Cambodian King bestowed his favours on the Muslims, and the Supreme Chief of the Muslim community was appointed by the King and was considered a member of the royal court.

The Muslim community of Cambodia was well organized. Each Muslim village was headed by a *hakam*, helped by a *kalik* (*qadi*). The *imam* led the prayers, the *ketip* (*katib*) taught *Quran*, the *bilal* calls the people for prayer. The *hakam* is elected by the community. Each village had an Islamic school. The most advanced students were sent to Malaysia, Saudi Arabia and Egypt for higher

Islamic education. Several hundred Muslims from Cambodia went yearly to Mecca for pilgrimage.

This situation changed dramatically when Khmer Rouge took over in 1974. Since the take-over of power by these modern-day brutes, hundreds of thousands of citizens have been killed, millions displaced and all forms of religion banned. Many citizens have fled the country and narrated horrifying stories of the brutal treatment that has been meted out to them. Among them there were about 25,000 Muslims who were received by Malaysia and settled mostly in Kelantan. Some emigrated to Thailand, and scores went to Saudi Arabia, France and the USA.

These Muslim refugees narrated horrifying tales of killing, forced labour and the breaking of the family units. Murders hit more specifically the leaders of the community such as Colonel Hamzah; Colonel Sit Met; Second Lt Lee Seman; Nong Mat Cit; Captain Yok Rani and the representative for Serirod constituency in Phnom Penh, Oh Sulaiman. Mosques have been closed and Muslim religious leaders who resisted this step were shot dead. Thus were killed Imam Tabib Ahmad and Tuan Syahed Ali of Tebor among many others. Muslim girls were defiled by the savage Khmer Rouge and when they resisted in such places as Kompong Deras, the whole community was massacred. The Chief Qadi of the Muslim community Serong Yusof was killed along with other leading Imams such as Ustaz Yaakub; Ustaz Sulaiman (who had studied in Cairo); Ustaz Ahmad (who had studied in India); etc.

The fall of the Khmer Rouge in January 1979 was certainly good news for the Muslims; but it is not clear whether the damage done in four years of brutal persecution would be lasting or if the new regime would restore the religious freedom which they had enjoyed up until a few years ago. The trend is however good, since the Islamic Development Bank was able to contact the surviving Muslims and bring them some humble relief, with no objection from the government.

## Nepal

The first Muslim presence in Nepal occurred at the end of the fourteenth century when Sultan Shamsuddin of Bengal launched an attack on the Kathmandu Valley. Under the Moghul Emperor Akbar, however, Muslim influence increased. The first Muslim settlers came to Nepal in the fifteenth century, especially as traders, teachers of Islam, and were allowed to stay in the country by the Nepali Kings. Some of these Muslims rose to prominence in government circles in the eighteenth century.

Today, the Muslims of Nepal have very strong links with those of India, one evident manifestation of which is the use of the Urdu language as the main language of culture. Muslims of Nepal are also of the Hanafi school which is predominant in Northern India. In the 1971 census, they numbered 351,156 people, or 3.04 per cent of the total population of Nepal. They could be estimated in 1982 at 500,000 Muslims, or 3.2 per cent of the total population.

Muslims are mostly concentrated in the Tarai region along the eastern border with India. They formed in 1971 more than 10 per cent of the population in six of the seventy-five districts of Nepal. These are Banke (19.3%), Kapilbastu (16.9%), Parsa (13.3%), Bara (11.6%), Rantahat (14.2%), and Mohotari (11.0%).

It should be noted that the Muslim population of Nepal increases at a slightly faster rate than the rest of the population. Indeed. in 1953, Muslims numbered 208,900 or 2.53 per cent of the total population.

The majority of the Muslims of Nepal are agriculturists. Some Muslims are artisans in the public sectors and others work with government agencies. In Kathmandu, most Muslims are traders.

A small group of Muslims are Shia, especially concentrated in the Sunsari district of Eastern Nepal. Ethnically, some Nepali Muslims claim Arab, Afghan and Turkish origin, but the majority are Nepali descendants of converts. The Muslims of Kathmandu are known as Kashmiri Muslims, most probably because of their Kashmiri origin. Muslims in Nepal speak many languages. In Kathmandu, Urdu is the mother tongue of Muslims, although most of them speak Nepali and Newari. In Western Nepal, Muslims speak also Urdu. However, in the districts of Bara and Parsa, Muslims speak Bhojpuri, whereas those of Eastern Nepal speak Maithali.

The state religion of Nepal is Hinduism. In this system the state promulgated in 1852 the Muluki Ain code distinguishing between foreign Muslims (highest among the empire castes) and native Muslims (lowest). This caste system has been abolished in 1963, but it is still prevalent socially, giving the Muslim community a great handicap. The law prohibits Hindus to convert. Nepal does not accord any official recognition to Islam, but Muslims are free to exercise their customs and have been treated as an integral part of Nepalese society. Muslims are in general free to build mosques and perform their religious duties, but Muslim personal law is not in force.

Until a generation ago, Muslim children were not allowed in school, being considered impure, nor were they allowed to build their own schools. However, this situation has now changed. Muslim children are in increasing numbers in public schools and they have now about twenty Islamic schools. Islamic education for children is imparted in these schools as well as in mosques, covering only 40% of the Muslim children. There are no *imam* schools, and most *imams* are trained in India. Thus, Muslims are being assimilated in remote areas and their illiteracy rate is higher than the average in the country. There are several hundred Muslim students at the University and about 200 university graduates. There is a Muslim Deputy Minister and two Muslim university lecturers.

There are scores of mosques in the country, including two major ones in the capital Kathmandu: the Nepali Jama Masjid and the Kashmiri Mosque. There are mosques in most villages having a Muslim community. Muslims are free to perform *hajj*; under the aegis of the Home Ministry about sixty Nepalese Muslims become *hajji* yearly.

The most active Islamic organizations are the All Nepal Anjuman Islah Samity, the Muslim Seva Samity, the Bajme Adab and the All-Nepal Muslim Sudhar Samity.

## Singapore

Singapore, which is an island Republic of 544 square kilometres, was part of the Muslim State of Johore when the British made a bid for its conquest. Pressures on the Sultan of Johore in 1819 forced an agreement on ceding the island to the British. The latter took over effectively in 1824. By then the island had a small population, but was totally Malay Muslim. The British opened the door wide open to Chinese immigration which resulted in the dwarfing of the original population. Most of the Chinese immigrants were non-Muslim. In 1963, the State of Singapore joined Malaysia as one of its fourteen states. However, this union did not last long. Thus, agreement was signed for Singapore to secede as an independent Republic. This became effective on 9 August 1965, thus creating a new Muslim minority.

The census of 1980 showed a total population of Singapore of 2,414,000 persons of whom 400,000 were Muslims. In 1982, the number of Muslims can be estimated to be around 420,000 or 17 per cent of the population. In the 1980 census, of the 400,000

Muslims, about 360,000 were Malays, 34,000 were Indians, 6,000 were Chinese and of different origins.

There are about 155 mosques in Singapore, the oldest being Masjid Molaka erected in 1820. The biggest mosques, which are real national monuments in Singapore, are the Sultan Mosque and Chulia Mosque. The Majlis-Ul-Ulama is building a series of modern new Islamic centres around the island. Of these, four are already completed. There is complete free movement of Islamic literature in English, Malay and Tamil (language of Indian Muslims) and freedom to go to *hajj* (1,000 pilgrims yearly).

Muslim personal laws are in force and Shariah Courts have been established since 1958. In 1968, a Majlis-ul-Ulama (Ulama Council) was established. It supervises mosques, *awqaf*, Islamic schools as well as Muslim cemeteries. The Council supervises the Shariah Courts as well as collecting the *zakat*. Islamic education is imparted in some mosques as well as in the Government Malay schools as an optional subject. There are ninety schools for Islamic education but they cover only 15 per cent of Muslim children. There is no *imam* school. Most *imams* are trained abroad. Arabic is taught by some Islamic organizations.

Muslims are less advanced than the rest of the population in all fields. The number of Muslim graduates of universities formed only 2.7 per cent of the total number of graduates. The percentage of Muslims in the professions and higher services is also much below their national average. However, the government has usually at least one Muslim minister in the Cabinet, such as the Acting Minister of Social Affairs (Dr Mattar) at present. Some Muslims occupy high positions in the legal sphere and in the university.

Economically, Muslims are among the poorest. Muslim youths face difficulties in seeking employment. Only a small percentage among them is called up for national service. There is neither open persecution of Muslims nor much effort to help them as a minority and to protect them until they reach the level of the rest of the population. It is clear that the present level at which they found themselves is a result of a century and half of colonization and unrestricted immigration of non-Muslims. There are ten Muslims in the parliament out of a total of sixty-nine members (14.5 per cent Muslims).

The leading Islamic organization is the Muslim Missionary Society, established in 1932. It has erected a large Islamic Centre: King Faisal Memorial Hall. It also runs a medical clinic and a legal centre. They had imparted Islamic education (including the Arabic language) to more than 6,000 students by 1982. They also have a welfare department, a ladies' department and a youth section. Other important Muslim societies are the Muslim Convert Society (Dar-ul-Arqam) which is the main *dawah* organization in the country and which managed to bring to Islam more than 8,000 people since 1982. Others are Yayasan Mendaki, the Scholarship Fund Board, and the Tamil Muslim Jamaat which erected an Islamic Hall: the Shahul-Hameed Muslim Lecture Hall, among many others.

## Other Countries

There are Muslims in all other countries of Asia and they are organized in most of these countries. In the following pages we will consider specifically the situation of Muslims in each one of the remaining countries.

When the Mongol armies conquered a good part of the Muslim world, the Muslim element became very important even in the heartland of the new empire. Almost all Turkish peoples adopted Islam and many Mongols did the same. The present-day Mongolian People's Republic has been carved out from regions which were for long under Islamic influence. Muslims were always present in these areas. In 1982, they amounted to approximately 260,000 people, or 15 per cent of the population of the Republic. These Muslims are all traditionally of the Hanafi school. Ethnically, they comprise three main groups: Kazakhs (80,000); Ghor (60,000); and Mongols (120,000). Mongolia became a People's Republic in 1921 and abolished all forms of religion in the 1930s. Therefore, it is not quite clear what happened to the Muslims. The fact is that they are at present completely cut off from the rest of the Muslim *ummah*, and none of them had come to *hajj* for a good number of years. High Muslim officials who visited Outer Mongolia mentioned meeting ministers in the government who were said to be Muslim.

Islam entered Taiwan in a first wave in 1661 C.E. in the era of the Ming Dynasty, when a Chinese army landed in the island and freed it from Dutch colonialism. There were among the Chinese soldiers many Muslims from the Fukien Province. These Muslims grew in numbers with time and when the Japanese took the island in 1895 they followed a policy of persecution against the Muslims which continued until they left in 1945. With the defeat of the

Nationalist Chinese and their emigration to Taiwan a new wave of Chinese Muslims arrived with them, numbering about 20,000 people. These Muslims came from all parts of China (Khansu, Yunnan, Ninghsia) and even from Eastern Turkestan. Many of these were high officials of the Nationalist Chinese Army and Government including General Ma Ching-Chiang. There was, in 1982, in Taiwan a total of no more than 75,000 Muslims, including the descendants of the first immigration. They are all of the Hanafi school. Muslims are united in a Chinese Muslim Organization, headed by Mr Abu Bakr Chao Ming-Yuan. They have five mosques, two in Taipei and one in each of Chungli, Taitung and Kaohsiung. There is no Islamic teaching in public schools. However, Muslims are treated equally with all others and there are Muslims in the legislative body (Yuan) and in the National Assembly of Taiwan. Most of the Muslims are in the independent professions. Some are in the government and the armed forces.

Bhutan had a total population of 1,430,000 in 1982 of whom 75,000 were Muslims. These Muslims are in contact with the Muslims of West Bengal and Assam in India. There seems no evidence of their being persecuted.

Muslims in Vietnam are in the majority from the same ethnic origin as those of Cambodia, i.e. Cham. They are the original inhabitants of what is called Vietnam today. There were about 55,000 Muslims in 1982. Two-thirds of the Muslims are Chams, the others are from different origins including Vietnamese converts or Vietnamized Muslims, especially in the city of Saigon (Hoshiminville). The Muslims in Vietnam lived in 1982 in three little groups: about 20,000 Chams in the provinces of Ninh-Thuan and Binh-Tuan living in a multitude of small villages with Chams who are still Hindus (50,000 in Vietnam); about 25,000 Chams of Cochinchina in the Mekong Delta; and about 9,000 Muslims of Saigon of different origins. There is also a small Muslim community and a mosque in Hanoi. Before the communist take-over in 1975, the Muslims of Vietnam had lived peacefully in the country in spite of continuous warfare. Since then, many Hoshiminville Muslims have left the country. They were indeed of diverse origins and they did not feel welcome in the new state (1750 Muslims came to Yemen in 1976 and settled in Taiz). Many Chams are requesting to emigrate to Malaysia. The Cham Muslims were not subjected to physical extermination but the fact that their mosques were closed, Islamic schools were prevented from functioning, made the Muslims fear that their culture might be destroyed.

There were 30,000 Muslims in Hong Kong in 1982. The first wave of Muslims came from the Kwantung Province of China. They were followed by a new wave in 1949, and a trickle of Muslims from India and Indonesia. The Muslims of Hong Kong are mostly tradesmen, most of their children go to non-Muslim schools and they are worried about their future. There are several Muslim organizations, all united into one national body. The most important organizations are the Islamic Union, the Pakistan Association of Hong Kong, the Dawoodi Bohra Association, the Chinese Cultural and Fraternal Association, the Hong Kong Islamic Youth Association, the Hong Kong Muslim Women Association, the International Islamic Society, and the Islamic Social Service Association. The Muslim community has a Muslim secondary school, the Islamic college, four mosques, of which the Kowloon Mosque is the largest, and several newsletters and magazines (*Muslim News, Strive, Muslim Herald*, etc.).

Islam was introduced in Japan around the turn of the present century by Muslim Tartars from the Russian Empire. One of the first such preachers, Abdul-Rashid Ibrahim arrived in Japan in 1909. More Tartar Muslims arrived and more Japanese converted to Islam. In 1935, the Muslims established the first mosque in Japan in Kobe, and in 1938 they built the Tokyo Mosque. There are at present about ten Muslim associations gathering the community in the following cities: Tokyo, Kyoto, Kobe, Naruta, Tokoshima, Sendai, Nagoya and Kamizawa. The number of Muslims in 1982 was about thirty thousand, of whom fifteen thousand were Japanese, and the rest were from a wide variety of origins. Many Japanese are presently embracing Islam, and the number of Muslims is expected to rise. There is complete freedom of religion in Japan.

The case of South Korea has been treated in detail in Chapter 1. The first Muslims of South Korea embraced Islam during the Korean War via the Turkish army. Their number increased to 3,000 in 1971 and there were about 22,000 Muslims in 1982, all Korean converts. These are organized under the Korea Muslim Federation. They built three mosques, one in Seoul, another in Pusan and a third in Kwanju. Their number is expected to increase greatly.

In Laos, there were about one thousand Muslims, Chams and Chinese in 1978. Many of the Chams requested to emigrate to Malaysia.

Macao has a Muslim population which is in close contact

with that of Hong Kong. Their number decreased to less than a hundred in 1982. They are organized and have a mosque. In North Korea, there are several hundred Muslims, but they do not seem to be organized.

## Conclusions

If we consider the large Muslim communities in the rest of Asia, i.e. Philippines, Thailand, Burma and Sri Lanka, we see that they all share one single characteristic: their Muslim population is indigenous to the country. In all these states, there are regions where Muslims are in majority, or near majority. In the Philippines, Thailand and Burma, these regions have been parts of fully-fledged Muslim states that have been absorbed by neighbouring non-Muslim powers. The situation of Muslims is tragic in the three above-mentioned states. In two of them (Philippines and Thailand) wars of liberation are waged by the Muslims to free their lands from foreign domination. Those Muslims would have been happy if only they could receive some autonomy and safequard of their Islamic identity. In Burma the Muslims are being eliminated by the terrorism of the state and mass expulsions. It is only in Sri Lanka where Muslims never established any state and where their situation remains satisfactory. In all these states the Muslim communities are very old, and can be traced almost thirteen centuries back for Burma and Sri Lanka and six centuries in Thailand and the Philippines, i.e. since the beginning of the Islamization of the Malay people.

The Islamic institutions of all these states are well established and their link with the Muslim world is solid. Only Burma's Muslims have been cut off for more than one decade from the rest of the Muslims of the world. The Muslim cultural language is Malay in Thailand and the Philippines, it is Urdu in Burma and Tamil in Sri Lanka. Islamic literature is available in all these languages. Arabic is also known among the educated. Muslim personal law is applied in all the above-mentioned countries.

The Muslims of Cambodia and Vietnam are mostly Chams; i.e. the original people of the area. Their Islamization took place after the fall of their empire. Their situation at the present is most tragic so much that their very survival is in question. In Mongolia, again a Communist state, Muslims are suppressed and cut-off completely from the rest of the *ummah*. Muslims in Nepal live peacefully, but are not recognized as a national religious community; the

same could be said about Bhutan. Muslims in Singapore became
a minority in their own country because of mass Chinese immigration. They are however treated relatively well. In Taiwan,
Hong Kong, and Macao, the Muslims are part of the Chinese
world and their numbers are small. They suffer no persecution.
The greatest hopes for the future of Islam are indeed on Japan
and Korea. Both the Muslim communities are characterized by a
fast expanding convert population. The Japanese Islamic dream
is more than eithty years old, the Korean one is less than ten
years old. Both dreams are still far from being fulfilled. There
is also complete freedom of religion in both Japan and South
Korea.

## References

PHILIPPINES

1. C. A. Majul, *Muslims in the Philippines* The University of the
   Philippines Press (Quezon City, 1973).
2. J. T. Poland, 'La Guerre Ignoree des Philippines' *Le Monde*
   (France, 16, 17, 18 December 1976)
3. M. A. Kettani, *Muslims in the Philippines* Problems Confronting Da'wah Activities in Muslim Societies and Strategy for the
   Future (Kuala Lumpur, Malaysia, 23 November–3 December
   1981).

THAILAND

1. PULO, 'Pattani' Brochure, 1976 (Arabic).
2. Liberation National Front of Pattani 'Muslims in South
   Thailand' Brochure, 1977 (English).
3. Hamzah Ibn Abdel-Mutalib, *Understand our Case Oh
   Muslims!* (Al-Balagh, Kuwait, 3 April 1977) (Arabic).
4. Muslims in Thailand, Publication of the Thai Ministry of
   Foreign Affairs (Bangkok, April 1978) (Arabic).

BURMA

1. R. P. Paringaux, 'Les Nouveaux Refugies du Bangladesh' *Le
   Monde* (9 July and 11 July 1978).
2. K. Ikramullah Khan, *Plight of Muslims of Burma* International
   Seminar on Muslim Communities in Non-Muslim States
   (London, July 1978) (English).

3. Anonymous, 'Operation Dragon King' *Impact International* (London, 26 May–8 June 1978).
4. Anonymous, 'The Hintha Dragon' *Impact International* (London, 26 January–8 February 1979).

SRI LANKA

1. H. M. Z. Farouque, 'The Ceylon Muslim Community' *Times of Ceylon* (Sri Lanka, 12, 13 December 1972).
2. M. A. M. Hussain, 'Muslim in Sri Lanka Polity' *MWL Journal* (September, October, November, December, 1982).

CAMBODIA

1. G. Maspero, *The Champa Kingdom* (Paris, 1930s) (French).
2. J. P. Roux, 'Muslim Life in Indochina' Chapters in *Islam in Asia* (Paris 1958) (French).
3. Anonymous, 'Muslims in Cambodia: The Taste of Horror' *Impact International* (London, 23 June, 13 July 1978).

NEPAL

1. H. Ansari, 'Muslims in Nepal' *Journal of the Institute of Muslim Minority Affairs*, Summer 1981, Vol. III, No. 1.

OTHER COUNTRIES

1. P. G. Going, 'Islam in Taiwan' *Aramco World* (Saudi Arabia, July/ August 1970).
2. Y. K. Sun, *Islam in Korea* Ph.D. thesis, The Hartford Seminary Foundation (Hartford, Con., USA, June 1971).
3. A. B. Morimoto, 'The Tokyo Mosque' *Islamic Forum* (Japan, February 1976).
4. S. M. Samarrai, *Islam in Japan* (Al-Balagh, Kuwait, 2 May 1976) (Arabic).
5. 'Supplement on Islam In Korea' in the *Korea Herald* (Seoul, 21 May 1976).
6. A. B. Morimoto, 'Islam in Korea' *Islamic Forum* (Japan, December 1976).
7. A. A. Al-Shareef, *The Story of a Yemenite who lived in South Vietnam for 32 years* (Ukaz, Saudi Arabia, Muharram 13, 1397 A.H.) (Arabic).
8. A. K. Saito, 'The Coming of Islam to Japan and the Muslim Community Today' International Seminar on Muslim Communities in Non-Muslim States (London, July 1978).
9. Muti-Rahman, 'Muslims in South Asia' International

Seminar on Muslim Communities in Non-Muslim States (London, July 1978).
10. Tan Sri Abdul-Aziz bin Zain, 'Muslims in Viet-Nam, Laos, Kampuchea and Thailand' International Seminar on Muslim Communities in Non-Muslim States (London, July 1978).

# 7 Muslim Minorities in Africa

## Introduction

Like Asia, Africa is the home of the heartland of the Muslim world. We defined a Muslim country in Chapter 6 as a state which identifies itself to be Islamic and the minimum factor for such an identification is its full membership in the Organization of the Islamic Conference (OIC). Forty-five countries are members of OIC, of which twenty-two countries are in Asia and twenty-three others are in Africa. The twenty-three African Muslim countries are reported in Table 7.1. They had, in 1982, a total population of 192,400,000 of whom 161,940,000 were Muslims. It is to be noted that among these African Muslim countries, Muslims are numerically in minority in three of them (Uganda, Benin and Gabon), but their percentage is increasing dramatically. In the rest of Africa, Muslims are *de facto* in the minority regardless of their numerical percentage. (See Figure 3.)

The Muslim minorities of Africa came into being by three different ways: Muslim lands which have been conquered by colonial powers and enclosed into larger units where they found themselves in minority; movement of conversion of non-Muslim populations to Islam; and Muslim emigration to low Muslim-density areas.

The Muslims in Africa follow two main schools of Islamic law: the Maliki school in West, North and Equatorial Africa, and the Shafii school in the greatest part of East and South Africa. There are important pockets which follow the Hanafi school in Algeria, Tunisia, Libya and Egypt (since the establishment of Ottoman rule over these states) as well as in South Africa (for those Muslims who are of Indian origin).

Muslims have suffered greatly under the colonial regimes in

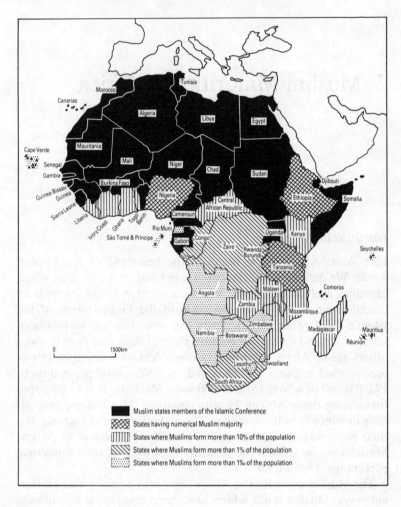

Muslim states members of the Islamic Conference
States having numerical Muslim majority
States where Muslims form more than 10% of the population
States where Muslims form more than 1% of the population
States where Muslims form more than 1‰ of the population

0        1500km

Africa. In fact, almost all wars of resistance to colonial encroachment in Africa were inspired by Islam and led by Muslims. As
soon as the colonial powers were able to overcome such resistance,
they embarked on an effort of 'pacification' by the army and the
church. Indeed, most schools in Africa have remained under the
control of the Christian missions. Thus, for fear of losing their
children to Christian evangelism, Muslims were forced to keep out
of these schools. After the independence of African countries,
Muslims often found themselves in such a backward state that they
could not compete with the graduates of the mission schools.
Thus, the influence of Muslims as well as other non-Christians as
compared with the Christians became marginal in most of the
countries where they were not in overwhelming majority. In such
countries, Muslims are often among the poorest classes of the
society and the least schooled. The situation is more serious in

Table 7.1    Muslim countries in Africa, 1982

| Country | Population in thousands | | |
|---------|-------|--------|------|
|         | Total | Muslim |      |
| Egypt | 44,370 | 40,820 | 92% |
| Morocco | 22,230 | 22,000 | 99% |
| Algeria | 19,920 | 19,720 | 99% |
| Sudan | 20,320 | 17,280 | 85% |
| Tunisia | 6,760 | 6,690 | 99% |
| Mali | 7,100 | 6,390 | 90% |
| Uganda | 14,550 | 5,820 | 40% |
| Senegal | 5,960 | 5,360 | 90% |
| Cameroon | 8,930 | 5,350 | 60% |
| Niger | 5,760 | 5,190 | 90% |
| Guinea | 5,750 | 4,880 | 85% |
| Burkina Faso | 7,160 | 4,300 | 60% |
| Chad | 4,810 | 3,850 | 80% |
| Somalia | 3,800 | 3,800 | 100% |
| Libya | 3,210 | 3,180 | 99% |
| Sierra Leone | 3,540 | 2,120 | 60% |
| Mauritania | 1,660 | 1,660 | 100% |
| Benin | 3,700 | 1,480 | 40% |
| Gambia | 640 | 625 | 98% |
| Djibouti | 500 | 500 | 100% |
| Guinea-Bissau | 670 | 470 | 70% |
| Comoros | 390 | 388 | 99% |
| Gabon | 670 | 67 | 10% |
| Total | 192,400 | 161,940 | 84% |

East Africa, where Muslims were subjected to Christian missionary proselytization, and both the colonial powers and the Christian
missions let loose a flood of propaganda aimed at distorting and
defaming their beliefs and their past.

In spite of all handicaps, Islam has continued to spread in
Africa. The strength of the truth in it, its logic, its insistence on
equality of all men, the coherence of its doctrines make it a
formidable competitor to the Christian foreign missions.

The Muslim minorities of Africa are reported in Table 7.2 for
1982. They totalled 114,200,000 Muslims. About 48 per cent of
them were Nigerians, and 93 per cent lived in eight countries:
Nigeria, Ethiopia, Tanzania, Kenya, Mozambique, Ghana, Ivory
Coast and Zaire. Actually, Muslims were in numerical majority in
three of these countries: Nigeria, Ethiopia and Tanzania. But

Table 7.2   Muslim minorities in Africa, 1982

| Country | Population in thousands | | |
|---|---|---|---|
| | Total | Muslim | |
| Nigeria | 91,440 | 54,860 | 60  % |
| Ethiopia | 34,100 | 20,460 | 60  % |
| Tanzania | 18,930 | 10,410 | 55  % |
| Kenya | 17,780 | 5,330 | 30  % |
| Mozambique | 10,930 | 4,920 | 45  % |
| Ghana | 12,910 | 4,240 | 33  % |
| Ivory Coast | 8,580 | 3,000 | 35  % |
| Zaire | 31,150 | 2,800 | 9  % |
| Malawi | 6,370 | 2,550 | 40  % |
| Centre-African Rep. | 2,460 | 980 | 40  % |
| Madagascar | 8,930 | 890 | 10  % |
| Liberia | 1,960 | 880 | 45  % |
| Zambia | 6,190 | 740 | 12  % |
| Togo | 2,680 | 670 | 25  % |
| South Africa | 29,610 | 510 | 1.7% |
| Rwanda | 5,460 | 380 | 7  % |
| Burundi | 4,510 | 230 | 5  % |
| Mauritius | 810 | 162 | 20  % |
| Zimbabwe | 7,770 | 62 | 0.8% |
| Ceuta & Melilla | 130 | 47 | 36  % |
| Mayotte | 53 | 37 | 70  % |
| Congo | 1,640 | 33 | 2  % |
| Reunion | 546 | 14 | 2.5% |
| Others | 11,411 | 15 | 0.1% |
| Total | 316,350 | 114,200 | 36.1% |

while Muslims are partners in the Nigerian establishment, albeit well below what their percentage in the population entitles them to, their situation is different in Tanzania and worst in Ethiopia where they are completely at the margin of public life. Muslims in these countries will still be considered the minority, because they are as such in all domains except in numbers. Muslims form more than a quarter of the population in nine other African states, where they are also more numerous than the Christian populations which control these countries. The number of Muslims exceeds ten million people in three states: Nigeria, Ethiopia, and Tanzania.

In 1971, the total number of Muslims in minority in Africa was about 86 million people, while the total Muslim population of Africa amounted to about 202 millions. In 1982, there were about 276,190,000 Muslims in Africa of a total African population of 508,700,000. Thus, with a Muslim percentage of 54 per cent, Africa is the Muslim continent of the world. About 41 per cent of all African Muslims live with minority status.

It should be stressed that the figures mentioned above are the best estimates. Exact figures are difficult to come by, and official censuses often give unacceptably lower figures.

## Nigeria

The heartland of Islam in Nigeria is in the north. Indeed, this region saw the development of the Empire of Kanem in the eleventh century. This Empire extended both to the east and the west of Lake Chad. Islamization of the Empire started by that time and by the fourteenth century it was almost complete. By then the Empire became reduced to Bornu which was one of its provinces. Meanwhile, Muslim states were established at Kano, Zaria, Daura, Gobir and Katsina, which all became centres of learning and civilization of no less importance than the Muslim cities of the Mediterranean and the East.

In the sixteenth century, these small Muslim states were all united by the Muslim state of Kanem and then by the Songhai Empire whose capital was Gao (on Niger River, in Mali today). The architect of this great unitary effort was Mohammed Askia the Great, one of the greatest Muslim leaders of all times. The unity, however, did not last long, and the state broke up into small units which were reunited again by the Muslim states of Bornu and Kebbi.

By the end of the eighteenth century a great Islamic revival took place under the leadership of Imam Othman Dan Fodio. Imam Othman was a learned and a pious Muslim. He performed the pilgrimage to Mecca and travelled widely in Muslim lands. He united most Muslim states into a large unit, promulgated Islamic law and defeated the enemy of the Muslims, the King of Gobar in 1802. He was declared 'Sarkin Musulmi' (Amir Al-Muminin) and built up a Muslim state, extending from Gandu to Adama and including temporarily the Bornu State. Othman was succeeded by his son Bello (Sultan of Sokoto) who became the suzerain of all the Fulani Muslim states. Bornu gained independence under Mohammed Al-Ameen Al-Kanemi who was succeeded by his son Omar. In 1893, Rabah Zubayr took over to lead a war of resistance against European penetration, but was killed by the French.

By 1850, a stream of European Christian missionaries preceded the European armies to what is now Nigeria. The first British colony was established in Lagos in 1861. In 1884, the Royal Niger Company was established. The British then proceeded to conquer the southern non-Muslim kingdoms and in 1900 established the Protectorate of Southern Nigeria. The Muslim north became a zone of British influence by agreement with the French. The British then set about conquering the Muslim north between 1902 and 1906 and consolidated the Protectorate of Northern Nigeria. In 1912, Northern and Southern Nigeria were united to form the present-day Nigeria, thus bringing large non-Muslim and Muslim populations together under one state. This unity helped the spread of Islam toward the southern regions, especially in the south-west among the Yoruba.

Nigeria became an independent Federation in 1960, made of three states: North, West and East. In 1963, a Mid-West State was carved out of the Western State. The Federation is a member of the Commonwealth and a Republic since 1963. The first Prime Minister was a highly respected Muslim Abu-Bakr Tafawa Balewa. He was assassinated in a military coup in 1966 along with the Premier of Northern Nigeria, another Muslim leader of international repute, Ahmadu Bello. In 1975, another Muslim, General Murtala Ramat Mohammed became head of state but was assassinated in an attempted coup in 1976. In the early 1970s the country was divided into nineteen states instead of the original four states.

The census of 1963 gave the total population of Nigeria as 55,670,000 people of whom about 48 per cent were Muslim and 34 per cent were Christian. By 1982, the total population was

about 91,440,000 of whom 60 per cent were Muslims, or about
54,860,000 Muslims. However, there is considerable uncertainty
about the total population and the values of the percentages are
also highly doubtful. The 60 per cent figure is the most probable
estimate.

There are about 250 linguistic groups in Nigeria. However, sixty
per cent of the population speak one of the following four languages: Hausa, Fulani, Yoruba (south-west) and Ibo (south-east).

The Muslim groups are the Hausa, the Fulani, the Kanemis, the
Kanuris, the Bagirmis, the Wadayans, etc. The most numerous are
the Hausa, whose Islamization started in the fourteenth century
but became complete only in the twentieth century. They numbered in 1982 about seventeen million people and are concentrated in the northern states. Their language has a deep Islamic
tradition. It was written in the Arabic script and was used by many
Muslim states. It is also spoken in the neighbouring Niger. The
Fulani (Peuhl) are spread all over West Africa; they are one of the
most ardent agents of Islamization and they were great empire
builders in the past. Their Islamization was completed by the
seventeenth century. In Nigeria, they numbered about nine
million people in 1982 mostly in the northern states. The Kanuris,
numbering about four million in Nigeria live mostly in the Bornu
State. About 40 per cent of the Yoruba, or nine million people, in
the south-west have adopted Islam. The remaining sixteen million
Muslims of Nigeria are made up of such groups as the Kanemis,
the Bagirmis, the Wadayans, the Nupe, the Mandara, the Kotoko
and parts of all other groups of Nigeria, including the Ibos of the
south-eastern states. There are also about 400,000 Arab speakers.
Islam is still in a state of dynamic growth due to large scale
conversion; the growth rate of Muslims could be estimated at
about double the national average.

The Muslims of Nigeria are of the Maliki school. Muslim Courts
exist in the northern states and also a Council of Nigerian Ulama.
The Muslims inherited their organization from the pre-colonial
Muslim states. Mosques are found all over the country in tens of
thousands. Nigerian Muslims maintain good contact with the rest
of the Muslim world. Thousands of pilgrims go to Mecca every
year.

During colonial days, all modern education was in the hands of
the Christian missionaries. Thus, most non-Muslim Nigerian
leaders were educated by Christian missionaries. These schools
received government grants-in-aid. This situation did not change

much after independence, but Muslims made great efforts to catch up with others by developing Islamic education. Quranic schools were and are widespread in areas of Muslim concentration. There are also advanced Arabic training centres in Ibadan, Ilorin, Agege, Owo, Kuta, Iwo, Ikirun and Abeokuta. Higher Islamic education on the modern style was pioneered by Al-Hajj Abdullahi Bayero, the late Emir of Kano who initiated a school of Qadis in 1934 which was named the Northern Provinces Law School. In 1947, it became the School of Arabic Studies. Later it became Abdullahi Bayero College and eventually Ahmadu Bello University (at Zaria). In the south, university level Islamic studies were developed at the University of Nigeria (Nsukka), the Ife University and the Ibadan University. Many Muslim organizations were established with the purpose of spreading Islamic education, among which are the Ansar-ud-Deen Society, established in 1923, and the Zumrat-Al-Islamiyah. Islamic education is at present imparted in all schools in the north and most secondary schools in the south.

Muslims are important partners in the Government of Nigeria. The President is usually Muslim, as well as many of the ministers. However, Nigeria has only an observer status in the Organisation of the Islamic Conference. Indeed, Muslims are represented at a lesser level than their percentage in the population warrants, but Islam is growing in the country. It is ony a matter of time before Nigeria becomes a fully-fledged member of the family of Muslim states. For a country where about 20 per cent of all Muslims of Africa live, this time could never be too early.

## Ethiopia

During the first years of Islam, Axum, now in the Province of Tigre, was the capital of a Christian state. It became the first refuge of Muslims from pagan persecution in the fifth year of the Bithah (the beginning of the Prophet's mission in 615 A.C.). The refugees were led by the cousin of the Prophet, Jafar Ibn Abi Talib. The King treated the Muslims well, protected them and eventually himself embraced Islam. During the Umayyad times the islands of Dahlak were occupied by the Muslims as well as the port of Musawwa. From this first bridgehead, Islam spread inside the continent. By the twelfth century the entire coast of Eritrea had been Islamized. In 283 A.H., a Muslim state was established in eastern Shoa (region of Addis-Ababa) under the Makhzumi

Dynasty. Other smaller Muslim states followed suit in the same region. By the late thirteenth century all these states were united by Ali ibn Wali Asma (Walashma) under the name of Awfat State. In the fourteenth century more Muslim states were established in the southern fringe of today's Ethiopia, namely in Harar and Arusi regions. One of the most important of these states was the State of Adal.

In the fifteenth century, Muslims witnessed a great renaissance under the leadership of Imam Ahmad ibn Ibrahim Al-Ghazi (1506–43) who united all the Muslim states of Ethiopia and then proceeded to unite all the country under Islam. In 1531, Muslims occupied Dawaro and Shoa and in 1533, Amhara and Lasta, and the Christian state of Abyssinia was abolished. However, this Muslim Ethiopia did not last long under the attacks of the Portuguese and the invasions of the Pagan Gallas.

Since then Ethiopia was stabilized as two states, a Muslim state in the south with capital at Harar (since 1520) and a smaller Christian state in the north. On the Red Sea coast, the struggle went on between Christians (Portuguese) and Muslims (Ottomans). But since 1557, the Portuguese threat was repulsed and Musawwa became the centre of an Ottoman Province, to become Eritrea later.

In the nineteenth century, the growth of colonial ambitions in Africa encouraged the Christian state of Ethiopia to share in the spoils and embark on an expansionist policy against the Muslim state of Harar in a crusading spirit. Muslims were massacred in Wollo in 1855, and the Egyptians (representing the Ottomans) defeated in Eritrea. The latter became the prey of Italian colonial ambition. The Italians took Asab in 1869, Musawwa in 1885 and Asmara in 1889. The last catastrophe to the Ethiopian Muslim state occurred when its capital Harar was occupied in 1887 by the Christian Ethiopians. The Muslim state was abolished; the main mosque of the capital was converted into a church and it remains so to this day, and the Muslim population was practically enslaved. In 1916, the Christian Emperor, Lij Yasu, converted to Islam and lost his throne. In 1930, Haile Selassie (the Force of the Trinity) took over, and, except for the 1935–47 Italian occupation, remained until he was deposed by a military coup in 1974.

Eritrea remained an Italian colony until 1941 when it came under British administration. It was federated to Ethiopia in 1952 by a UN resolution that did not take into account the wishes of its population. In 1962, the Emperor destroyed all semblance of

Eritrean autonomy and integrated it as a province of Ethiopia. In 1965, the Haud area of Ogaden, part of Somaliland under British occupation, was also handed over by the British to Ethiopia against the wishes of its people.

The population of Ethiopia (and Eritrea) amounted to 34.1 million in 1982. Of these about 20.5 million, or 60 per cent of the population, were Muslims. Out of the fourteen provinces of Ethiopia, Muslims are in the majority in Eritrea, Wollo, Harrage, Bale, Arussi and Sidamo. They contribute more than 25 per cent of the population in Gamu-Gofa, Shoa and Tigre and form substantial minorities in the remaining six provinces. The most important Muslim linguistic groups are the Somalis in Harrage and Bale, and the Galla Muslims in Sidamo and Arussi. Harar itself speaks a Semitic language close to Arabic. Afar (Danakil) is spoken in Eastern Wallo and Southern Eritrea, whereas Saho (Kushitic) Beja (Kushitic) and Tigre (Semitic) languages are spoken in the north. All Muslims follow the Shaffi school.

Muslims in Ethiopia are a persecuted majority. They lived under conditions reminiscent of the medieval fanaticism during the rule of Haile Selassie and they are faring no better under the present leftist military rule. Their presence in the government and the armed forces is practically non-existent and they are subjected to continuous suppression and discrimination. Suppression of Islamic schools is widespread; the use of Arabic is discouraged; Muslim leaders are persecuted and harrassed, Christian missionaries are given a free hand to take advantage of Muslim poverty and helplessness; alcohol and prostitution are encouraged in Muslim areas; Muslims are discouraged from pursuing their studies at university level whether within the country or abroad; etc.

Most Muslims are agriculturists or pastoralists; some are small businessmen. In spite of their poverty and persecution, they were able to establish Islamic institutions which they are supporting despite their miserable situation. Most important of these are the Islamic Centre in Asmara, the Al-Khulafa Mosque in Asmara which includes an Islamic library and an Islamic religious school; the Islamic institutes of Keren Agordat at Musawwa, the Al-Fath Islamic School in Addis Ababa; and the Muslim schools of Harar. Mosques and Islamic schools exist in all areas where Muslims are present.

Muslims could not work within the system to better their lot. Many of them turned to armed struggle to free themselves from oppression, colonization and suppression. However, their efforts remained divided into national secession movements instead of being a struggle for the rule of the Muslim majority in the entire Ethiopian State.

The most striking example of the division of the Muslims can be seen in the Eritrean liberation movement. The Eritrean Liberation Front (ELF) was established in 1961 with the aim of liberating Eritreans from Ethiopian colonial domination. It split in 1970, and the breakaway group called itself the Popular Front for the Liberation of Eritrea (PFLE) which produced another split group in 1976 called the 'Eritrean Liberation Front called Popular Forces for the Liberation of Eritrea' (ELP–PFLE). These organizations (especially the first two) succeeded in temporarily liberating most of Eritrea, but they could not attain final victory due to their divisions. They are still trying to unite their ranks but the efforts seem of little avail. The Eritrean people (including a minority of Christians) braved great sufferings in this war of liberation: out of a population of 1,600,000 people in 1982 (area 117,600 square kilometres) about 50,000 civilians died, more than one million people were displaced and almost 300,000 people found refuge in the Sudan. Thus the entire population has been decimated with the active support of the world powers.

Similarly, the Somali populations (Muslim) of Sidamo, Harrage and Bale led a war of liberation under the Liberation Front of Western Somalia (LFWS). This Front freed the entire region in 1977, but was eventually defeated by Ethiopian forces with the help of Cuban and Russian soldiers. The Front is still active with the aim of liberating the Somali-speaking areas and uniting them to Somalia. There is also an Afar Liberation Front which is much less active than the others as well as a Tigre Liberation Front.

## Tanzania

Since the tenth century C.E. the coast of what is known today as Tanzania became the domain of a string of Muslim city states whose population depended largely on trade. In the fifteenth century, the Muslim position was undermined by the Portuguese who took the island of Zanzibar in 1498 C.E. but had to relinquish it after about twenty-five years. By the end of the seventeenth century the Portuguese threat was completely eliminated with the help of Oman (in Arabia). In the eighteenth century, the area eventually united with Oman as a province with capital at Kilwa.

The King of Oman Sayyid Said moved his capital in 1832 from Muscat (in Arabia) to Zanzibar. In 1861, five years after the death of Sayyid Said, the African part of the Kingdom of Oman seceded due to British intrigues. By then, Muslims had reached Lake Tanganyika (in the 1840s) bringing all of modern Tanzania within the Muslim state of Zanzibar.

In 1886, an Anglo-German agreement forced the Sultan of Zanzibar to a ten mile strip on the African coast. They also made him renounce in favour of Portugal all claims to the coast to the south of Cape Delgado. In 1887, the Sultan was forced to hand over the administration of the coast north of River Umba to the British (which became part of Kenya). In 1888, a similar concession was granted to the German East Africa Association for the southern territories (to become part of Tanganyika). In 1890, the German Government bought these territories outright for 4,000,000 Marks. The same year, Zanzibar (and Pemba) became a British Protectorate, thus putting an end to the East African Muslim state.

Germany declared a protectorate on the territory it took and named it Tanganyika. After World War I and the defeat of Germany, the territory became a British mandate. However, the Kionga triangle was handed over to Portugal (part of Mozambique) and Ruanda and Urundi (Burundi) to Belgium. Tanganyika became fully independent in 1961. Zanzibar became independent on 10 December 1963. However, the Government was overthrown in January 1964 by six hundred mercenaries led by a foreign Christian Communist, John Okello who had been trained in Tanganyika. The Arab and Asian populations of the islands were subjected to massacres and humiliation. They had to flee the islands in large numbers. Eventually the islands united with Tanganyika on 27 April 1964 under the name of the United Republic of Tanzania.

In 1982, the population of Tanzania amounted to 18,930,000, of whom 535,000 lived in Zanzibar and Pemba and 18,395,000 in Tanganyika. Of this total about 10,410,000 people (55 per cent of the population) are Muslims. Muslims are in overwhelming majority in all the coastal provinces and in Zanzibar. Their language, Swahili, a heavily Arabized Bantu language, is the official language of the country as well as of Kenya and Uganda. Their main city Dar-es-Salaam (an Arabic compound word meaning City of Peace) is the capital of the land. Muslims are present in all the 120 tribes of the country. All Tanzanian Muslims of African origin are of the Shafii school; some Indian Muslims are of the Hanafi and Omanis of the Abbadi schools.

There are about two million Christians in the country, mainly a product of the Christian missionary schools. The real power is in their hands. The head of the state, although a devout Christian, professes a leftist doctrine. Islamic activity is discouraged and Muslims find themselves as second-class citizens in spite of being in the majority. One of the two vice-presidents is a Muslim. In 1982, about a quarter of Cabinet Ministers were Muslims. All others were Christians.

All Islamic associations in Tanzania have been abolished by the government except the Muslim Welfare Society. The government has put all the Islamic schools under the care of this association. In fact this association was put under full government control and Islamic and Arabic education was reduced to only a few hours per week. This Society is the only one allowed to send people to pilgrimage to Mecca. It sends delegations to Muslim countries from time to time.

There are mosques all over the country and many Muslim ulama are very learned and extremely respected by the population. Most noted among them is Shaykh Hasan Bin Umayr Al-Shirazi. There are, however, few contacts left between the Muslims of Tanzania and the rest of the Muslim world.

In Zanzibar, the coup led by the mercenaries in 1964 had anti-Islamic overtones. It led to the closing down of the famous Zanzibar Islamic Institute and its transformation into an ordinary secondary school, its Islamic characteristics having been destroyed. However, Islamic education is imparted in all the mosques of the island just as on the mainland. Nevertheless, Islam is still making headway in spite of official discouragement, even suppression.

## Mozambique

The history of Islam in Mozambique is more than one thousand years old. As seen in the sections on Tanzania and Kenya, the coast of Mozambique was part of the Muslim world. It was made of a string of Muslim city-states living on trade, the most important of which were Sofala (near present-day Beira) and Al-Sambiq (Mozambique, named after Sultan Musa Al-Sambiq). These Muslim states eventually expanded up to the Zambezi River.

By the end of the fifteenth century, the Muslim states of

Mozambique began to suffer the onslaught of the Portuguese. First Sofala was conquered, then Mozambique in 1508. Muslims resisted the Portuguese conquest up to 1629. In 1752, Portugal organized its conquest into a colony but was able to conquer the interior only in the twentieth century.

From the start, the Portuguese were only interested in destroying the Muslim community. Muslims were excluded from schools except those established by missionaries and the few Quranic schools which managed to survive. Those Muslim parents who were simple-minded enough to send their children to attend the Christian missionary schools found that often the children were induced to become Christians and were lost to the Muslim community.

Muslim resistance to Portuguese rule never stopped, and it was always put down with military atrocity. During the first two decades of this century tens of thousands of Muslims were forced to escape to neighbouring countries, especially to Malawi and Tanzania. When in 1960, the Portuguese murdered hundreds of people in Mueda in the Makonde country, Muslims joined hands with the Makondes and other Mozambicans to renew their struggle against colonialism. This eventually led in June 1962 to the formation of 'The Liberation Front of Mozambique (FRELIMO).

However, although FRELIMO was mainly composed of Muslim northerners, most of its leaders were southerners who have been educated in Christian missionary schools. These leaders were not able to free themselves from the anti-Islamic poison which had entered their minds during the period of their studentship in these schools. In spite of the overwhelming presence of Muslims in FRELIMO only two Muslims were admitted into the organization's Central Committee. Muslims of Mozambique believe that the anti-Islamic attitude of the Tanzanian leadership encouraged the leadership of FRELIMO to discriminate against Muslims. Muslims were squeezed out both from leadership positions and from the rank and file, many were murdered, and the movement became more Christian-Marxist and more anti-Muslim.

Mozambique gained its independence in June 1975 under the leadership of FRELIMO. The FRELIMO Government ruling the country now declares itself Marxist and atheistic. But its hatred is directed especially against the Muslims. All the members of the government are Christians, and there is not a single Muslim among them. The President himself takes every opportunity to insult

Islam and Muslims. He once entered a mosque in Nampula and refused to remove his shoes, and he insulted the Muslim who reminded him to do so. In the same city, he advised the Muslim Makuas to breed pigs. The government confined thousands of Muslims to 're-education camps' where many lost their lives. All this led to the complete alienation of the Muslim population.

The population of Mozambique amounted in 1982 to about 10,930,000 people, of whom about 4,920,000 (about 45 per cent of the population) were Muslims. The majority of the Muslims live in the four northern provinces: Mozambique (Nampula); Zambezia, Cabo Delgado, and Niassa. The Makua, Mozambique's largest tribe, which comprises about four million people is predominantly Muslim, and so are the Yao, the Angoni and other smaller tribes. Most of the Muslims are of the Shafii school.

The social condition of the Muslims is poor. Their areas were exploited more fully but were kept less developed by the Portuguese. Their level of education is low in comparison with the rest of the population. The Muslim child has to surmount unbelievable obstacles to obtain education. Some have been to the Quranic schools, but these are very few in number. The government schools are designed to lead Muslims away from Islam and the government is putting pressure against the Quranic schools.

The few Islamic organizations that exist are weak and their resources are meagre. There are practically no social, welfare and political organizations. The mosques are always doubled by the Quranic schools but basic religious education is imparted by poorly paid teachers. The most important organization is Anwar-ul-Islamo. Their contact with the rest of the Muslim world is poor and few Mozambicans perform *hajj*.

## Kenya

Like Tanzania, the Arab immigration toward what forms the coastal area of the present-day Kenya started from the earlier years of Islam. The Arab population mixed with the local Africans to form a distinct Muslim civilization of Swahili language and maritime vocation. One of the most important Muslim cities was Mombasa, the present port of Kenya, which was visited by Ibn Battutah, the well-known Moroccan traveller of the fourteenth century. The entire population of the coast was Islamized during the early period of Muslim history.

By 1806, the entire east African coast from Lindi (in Mozambique today) in the south to Warshih (in Somalia today) in the north became a part of the Muslim state of Oman. As mentioned above, the coast of today's Kenya was ceded in 1887 to Britain by the Kingdom of Zanzibar after it separated from Oman. The interior constituting today's Kenya was under the rule of pagan Masai tribes. Muslim tribesmen from the coast established, however, good relations with these tribes and reached Lake Rudolf by 1880 C.E. But Britain cut short any possibility of uniting the interior with the coast and annexed the territories which were under Zanzibari influence except for a ten-mile strip. The territories taken by Britain were then divided into Uganda and Kenya. The name Kenya was officially used for the first time on 23 July 1920. The interior became a colony and the coast a protectorate of Britain, nominally part of the Sultanate of Zanzibar. By a treaty with Italy in 1924, Britain ceded to Italy the Juba River and a strip from fifty to a hundred miles wide on the British side of the river. It is now part of Somalia. When Kenya gained independence in 1963, it forced Zanzibar to cede the coastal strip (Protectorate) to Kenya.

Kenya had a population of 17,780,000 people in 1982. Of these about 5,330,000 or 30 per cent of the population, were Muslims. Out of the eight provinces of Kenya, Muslims are in the majority in the coastal, the north-east and eastern provinces. The total area of these three provinces makes up two-thirds of the total area of Kenya. Muslims are also present in large numbers in all other provinces. The Muslims of Kenya comprise Arabs (50,000), the Swahilis (800,000), and Somalis (500,000). There is a large number of Muslims of Asian origin and most of the Boranas are also now Muslims. Muslims are present in all other tribes of Kenya including the Kikuyu, the Meru, the Makemba, the Bulahya, and the Massai. In Nairobi, there is a large Muslim population of Sudanese origin. Most Muslims of Kenya are of the Shafii school. The Muslims of Sudanese origin, however, are of the Maliki school and those of Asian origin are generally of the Hanafi school.

Christians are almost as numerous as Muslims but they virtually control the entire country. This is due to the fact that all schools were in the hands of Christian missions. Education is still mostly under the influence of the missions. Thus, Muslims end up being among the less schooled and the poorest in the country.

In the early 1960s, the Somali population of the north-east province staged a rebellion requesting union with Somalia. They were harshly dealt with. This war (of the Shifta) brought great misery to the Muslim population of the region since their herds were killed and many Muslims massacred. The Christian mission took advantage by establishing themselves among the Muslims and trying to raise the orphans in a different religion than their parents. There is now (in 1982) for the first time one Muslim minister in the government of Kenya. There are only about two deputy ministers and twenty-three Muslim deputies in the Parliament (i.e. only 14 per cent of the total number of deputies). There are some other Muslims in high positions, but they are few in number.

Government schools are neutral in terms of religion. But religious study can be sponsored in the school by the interested denomination if they have a qualified teacher and they are able to pay his salary. The government would pay the salary of the religious teacher if he is capable of teaching other subjects as well. Thus, the Christian missions were able to flood the government schools with their teachers, to the great disadvantage of the Muslims. Indeed, many of them had to take courses in Christianity since no courses in Islam were available and a grade in religion (any religion) was compulsory. Furthermore, education in Kenya is not free. Thus, the poorest sections of the population, including the Muslims, find themselves discriminated against because of poverty.

There are, however, Islamic schools all over the country. These are no more than makeshift schools, built by the Muslims near their mosques. The Kenya Welfare Society has launched since 1974 upon an ambitious programme of supporting these schools that would enable them to progress and modernize their Islamic curricula with the help of the population. These schools were also used as a means of improving the health conditions of the children. Few Muslim professors are in the university and only about 10 per cent of the students are Muslims.

There are more than 120 Islamic associations in Kenya. Some of these societies are *waqfs* of mosques, such as the society taking care of the main mosque in Nairobi. The Islamic Foundation, to mention another significant Islamic body, publishes Islamic books in the local languages, the most important being the Swahili interpretation of the *Holy Quran* by Sheykh Salih Al-Farsi. The Foundation also supports outstanding Islamic schools in Isiolo and Machakos. In 1976, the Supreme Council of Kenyan Muslims was established.

Islamic personal law is in force and *qadi* courts exist in areas where Muslims are in the majority. The most important *qadi* court is the one in Mombasa, but since 1978 there is one in Nairobi as well. About 500 Kenyans perform *hajj* every year and the relationship between the Muslims of Kenya and the Muslim *ummah* is good.

## Ghana

Britain started its infiltration into Ghana in the nineteenth century. The state of Ghana came into existence on 6 March 1957 as the union of four territories: the north which was a British protectorate; the Ashanti State also under British protection; the colony of Gold Coast; and the part of Togoland which was under British trusteeship. The entire area amounted to 238,305 square kilometres and the population amounted to 12,910,000 in 1982. In 1960, the country was declared a Republic within the Commonwealth of Nations.

Since the fourteenth century, Muslim Dyula traders played a major role in disseminating Islam in the lands which later became Ghana. These Dyula traders known in Ghana as Wangara created the nuclei of Islamization in most of the northern parts of the country. Muslim influence led eventually to the formation of states such as Dagomba, Mamprusi, Gonja and Wala. Islam gained a hold over the Dagomba and Gonja ruling classes; it has also penetrated some Mamprusi groups; it won over all the Wala and influenced Dagati and Lobe states. By 1750, Muslims had started to have a great influence in Ashanti where members of the Royal Court were converted. In 1780, King Osei Kwame of Ashanti himself became a Muslim.

The Islamization process continued under the British. In the north, the towns became the chief Islamic centres: Bawki (Mamprusi), Yemdi, Tamale (Dagomba), Saluga (Gonja), Wa (Wala), and Kete Krachi. On the coast Muslim nuclei were formed by Muslim immigration from the north and by conversion. By 1982, the total Muslim population of Ghana reached 4,260,000 and thus formed 33 per cent of the total population. By 1982, Muslims became a majority in the northern provinces.

In 1932, the Muslim Association of Ghana was formed. Its aim was to foster Muslim unity, spread Islamic education, and seek reforms giving greater recognition to Islam in the legal and educational systems. In 1939, it made its first entry into politics by sponsoring Muslim candidates for the Accra municipal elections.

In 1954, the Muslim Association claimed the support of the Muslims of the Gold Coast Colony and the Ashanti Protectorate. It also helped establish a Muslim Council which set up Muslim schools and sponsored Islamic education in government schools. Muslims are free to perform *hajj*, and about 2,500 do perform it yearly. The Muslim personal laws are in force in the country. There is a large number of mosques as well as Islamic schools. In 1956, there were seventy-one mosques, of which thirty-four mosques were Hausa-speaking, fourteen mosques Djerma-speaking, and the rest established by other linguistic groups. The number of mosques exceeded 250 in 1982.

Muslims are agriculturists, pastoralists and traders. They belong, economically speaking, to the middle class of the Ghanean society. However, there are some wealthy Muslims even in the capital Accra which has a beautiful central mosque. There are few Muslims in the professions. This is due to the fact that under the colonial rule, all modern schools were in the hands of Christian missions. Even after independence, about one third of the schools of Ghana remained in the nands of Christian missions.

This situation explains the overwhelming influence that the small Christian minority has in the country. While Christians, with all their denominations, do not make up the tenth of the population, they hold most of the ministerial posts in the government, and their presence is overwhelming in the administration and the army. In 1954, out of a total of 104 members in the parliament, only fifteen were Muslims (14.5%). This percentage did not increase much since then. Some Muslims reached the position of cabinet ministers from time to time, once a head of state was Muslim; but in general, the Muslim presence in the higher services is minimal.

A great majority of the Muslims of Ghana belongs to the Maliki school. The Qadiri Sufi brotherhood is very influential in the country. Islam is spreading in spite of all the handicaps. The principal Muslim organization at the present is the Ghana Muslim Representative Council with its branches, especially the *dawah* branch, the youth branch, and the ladies' branch.

## Ivory Coast

France infiltrated that part of the African coast that was to become the Ivory Coast in 1842. In 1882, the territory was conquered, and it was formally declared a colony in 1893 within Occidental French

Africa. In January 1933, a portion of Upper Volta was added to the Ivory Coast, but in 1948, the districts of Bobo-Dioulasso, Gaoua, Kondougou, Ouagadougou, Kaya, Tenkodogo and Dedougou were transferred back to the reconstituted Upper Volta. The territory became independent in August 1960 as the Republic of the Ivory Coast. The most important ethnic groups are the Agnis-Ashantis, the Kroumen, the Mande, the Baoule, the Dan-Gouro and the Koua, and seventy-two different languages are spoken in the country.

It was the great Muslim leader Samory Toure who first tried to establish a Muslim state in the north of the present-day Ivory Coast. But his efforts failed because of colonial pressure. He was eventually defeated by the French and imprisoned in September 1898 C.E.. However, since the eighteenth century traders established Muslim communities in the northern districts which became centres of Islamization for the entire region. The most active of these traders were the Dyula Muslims.

In 1982, the total population of the Ivory Coast reached about 8,580,000 of whom about three million were Muslim (35 per cent of the total population). All Muslims of the Ivory Coast are of the Maliki school. Ethnically, all the Dyula are Muslims; Muslims are among the Kulango, the Mande and the Fulbe; Mossi immigration brings with it Islamization, since most Mossi people leave their pagan beliefs and become Muslims when they emigrate.

Muslims constitute a majority in the northern districts of the country (departments). Indeed, the city of Bouake (200,000 inhabitants), the second in the country, is a Muslim city. Immigration from the north to the coast has created new Muslim nuclei. Indeed, most of the shepherds in such places as Port-Bouet and Marcory on the coast are Muslim Peuhls (Fulani) and Mauritanians. In Abidjan, the capital of the country, Treichville is a Muslim quarter.

Muslims in the Ivory Coast made a very serious effort to Islamize the pagans. For instance, in 1948, Sekou (Sheikh) Sangare made a systematic effort in the regon of Seguda to educate the pagans in Islamic beliefs. In the 1930s, Yacouba Silla created a sufi agricultural community at Cagura which became a centre of Islamic learning and training. The first efforts at overall organization started in 1957 with the establishment of the Muslim Cultural Union with branches at Bouake and Abidjan. There is a multitude of mosques in the country which are all combined with Quranic schools. The Muslim district of Treichville in the capital Abidjan has three such mosque/school facilities. Efforts at building modern schools imparting Islamic education in the primary and secondary levels have however been made. Most important among these are the efforts of El-Hadj Mori Kamara with his schools at Dalon and Bouake and the efforts of Mr Kabine Diane. Muslims are also free to perform *hajj* and there is no specific discrimination against them.

However, just as in other African countries, but at a level less than in the former British colonies, Muslims have been handicapped in the educational field during colonial days. The Christians who barely constitute one tenth of the population are the most educated, being the product of the well financed missionary schools. They control the entire country. The president of Ivory Coast is a Christian and out of thirty ministers in the government in 1977, seven were Muslims (23%) and twenty-three were Christians (77%). Similar percentages are to be found in the administration and the army.

## Other Countries

Zaire, one of the largest countries of Africa, became independent in 1960. In 1982, it had a population of 31,150,000, with 9 per cent being Muslim. Islam first entered Zaire from the east through Kivu and Oriental-Kasai provinces. More recently, Islam has been spreading in Shaba in the south and in the Equator Province in the north. The centres of Islamization are at present Kasongo (Kivu); Kisamgaru and Bunia (High Zaire); Kinda (Occidental Kasai) and Kalemi (Shaba) where a large mosque has been built recently. New communities have been organized in Bombo-Kosangi near Kananga, the capital of Occidental Kasai as well as in Kananga. Kasongo is however the Muslim centre of the entire country. In Kinshasa, the capital of Zaire, the Muslim community, started with Senegalese and Nigerians, is spreading to the local citizens. They are all organized in a Muslim community. There are several mosques in the city and a Muslim school. Islam is now spreading fast in Zaire.

Malawi, which won its independence in 1964, had a population of 6,370,000 people in 1982, of whom about 40 per cent or 2,550,000 were Muslims. Half of the population is Christian and the remainder are animists. Most Muslims are concentrated in the Lake district in Central and in Southern Malawi. Cities such as Mulanji, Dedza, Chiradzulu, Lilongwe (the capital), Zomba,

Salima and Nkhota-Kota are centres of Muslim concentration. Muslims are economically poor, being mainly farmers and labourers. Some Muslims are professionals who were trained in Christian missionary schools, and some are in trade and commerce. The principal Muslim organizations are the Limbe Muslim Association, the Zomba Muslim Association; the Blantyre Muslim Association; the Lilongwe Muslim Association; the Kanyenda Mohamedan Schools Association; and the Nuru Muslim Association. They are all under the Muslim Association in Malawi which has also a youth branch. Every Muslim district has a small mosque/ Quranic school complex, but teachers are poorly trained and receive very low support for their work by the poor community. However, two new religious training centres have been established to train teachers. Education has been and still is in the hands of Christian missions who are extremely biased against Islam. The Christian graduates of these schools run the country and are highly prejudiced against Muslims. The result is that there is only a small Muslim participation in the government.

The Central African Republic became independent in 1960. Its population amounted in 1982 to about 2,460,000 people. Of these about 980,000 were Muslims (about 40 per cent of the population). Muslims are not present in the government, and the leadership of the country is in the hands of the Christian minority.

Madagascar became independent in 1958. In 1982, its population amounted to 8,930,000. About 10 per cent of this population were Muslims, or about 890,000. Islam entered the island in the thirteenth century from the Persian Gulf and South Arabia, as well as from East Africa. These eventually settled in the south-east of the island forming the present-day Antaimoro tribe. Other Muslims live on the west coast. New Muslim arrivals are Indians and Comorans. There are about a hundred mosques in the country along with Quranic schools. But Muslims are segregated against by the Christian leftist leadership of the country. The most dramatic occurrence was the riot against the Muslims of Majunga (a city which has had a Muslim majority) which led to the massacre of more than six hundred Muslims, and injury to thousands of them, as well as to an exodus of tens of thousands of refugees outside the island and untold loss of Muslim property and incalculable human misery and suffering. During these events the Muslims received no protection from the government.

Liberia was established by the US in 1847 as a state to accommodate the liberated American slaves. To this day it is ruled by a small minority who are descendants of these Christianized and Americanized freed slaves. There is not a single Muslim in the government or in any important position in the country. In 1982, the population amounted to 1,960,000, Muslims forming about 45 per cent of the population, their number being about 880,000. Islam spread in the country since the eighteenth century. There are three mosques in the capital, Monrovia, and hundreds all over the country. Most of the time these are makeshift structures. Islamic law is in force among Muslims who are free to perform *hajj* (about 150 people every year). There are five Quranic schools in the capital and a few elsewhere. Islamic education is in the mosques but not in the government schools. The principal Muslim organization is the National Muslim Council of Liberia which is in good contact with the rest of the Muslim *ummah*, especially with the Muslims of Sierra Leone.

Zambia became independent in 1964. Its population amounted to 6,190,000 people in 1982. Of these about 740,000 were Muslims (12 per cent of populaton). Muslims are concentrated mostly in the Copperbelt Province, especially around its capital Ndola. There is also a Muslim community and a mosque in Luanshya. Most of the Muslims are Africans, but there are also Muslims of Indian origin. These have their own Islamic Indian Associations in Ndola and Lusaka. There is also a large Muslim community in the Eastern Province, especially in its capital city Chipata. The Indian Muslims are mostly traders whereas the African Muslims are mainly labourers in copper mines. There is a Muslim school in Lusaka and another one in Ndola. There are Quranic schools and mosques in other parts of the country but they are few in number. Muslim participation in the running of the country is practically nil.

Togo became independent in 1960. In 1982, its population amounted to 2,680,000. Of these some 25 per cent or about 670,000 people were Muslims. Northern Togo came under the same Islamic influence as northern Ghana. The Muslims are the Hausa, Djerma, Kotokoli, and Tchokossi people in the north and 'Brazilian' Muslims in the south. Quranic schools are present all across the country, but Muslims have practically no share in the government.

The Union of South Africa was established in 1909 as a land of Christian white European supremacy. It became a republic in 1961. In 1982, its population was about 29,160,000. The Muslims numbered in the same year about 510,000 people, or 1.7 per cent of the total population. About 85 per cent of Muslims are descendants of settlers from: Indonesia, India, Malawi, Zanzibar and Mozambique. The first batch of Muslims were political prisoners brought by the Dutch in 1667 from Java (at present a part of Indonesia). They were integrated with the first elements of Swahili Muslims who preceded the European colonization. Muslims are largely concentrated in the Provinces of the Cape, Natal and Transvaal. Muslims are to be found in most towns and villages of these provinces but with higher concentration in Durban, Cape Town, Johannesburg and Pretoria. About one-third of Muslims are traders, others are workers, some are professionals. There are more than 150 Islamic organizations which have joined together to form an Islamic Council of South Africa. There are about 200 mosques/Islamic schools and four orphanages. There is an Institute of Islamic Law Studies in Cape Town. The racial policy of the government forced division on the community into Indian, black, coloured and white components. Muslims are however free to observe their religious observances within each group and their contacts with the Muslim world are good.

Rwanda became independent in 1962. It had a population of 5,460,000 in 1982, including about 380,000 Muslims or 7 per cent of the total population. 30 per cent of Muslims live in the capital, Kigali, where they form half the population. There are about fifty mosques in the country, of which five are in the capital. All Muslims are organized under the 'Association of Rwanda Muslims' established in 1964 and recognized by the government as representing the Muslims.

Burundi became independent in 1962 and had a population of 4,510,000 in 1982. The Muslim portion amounted to about 230,000, or 5 per cent of the total. The most important centre of Muslim concentration is the capital Bujumbura where they are concentrated in the Muyanzi quarter. Islam is spreading in Burundi from Tanzania. There are Arab and Indian traders, but most Muslims are African traders and agriculturists. The Muslim community has complete respect of the authorities and is free to perform its religious duties. There are three important Muslim associations: The Sunni Muslim Association (mostly Indian); the African Muslim Association which is the most active; and the African Muslim Students Association. There are many Quranic schools in the country along with the mosques.

Mauritius is an island in the Indian Ocean which became independent in 1968. In 1982, its population amounted to about

810,000 people, of whom 162,000 were Muslims (20 per cent of the total population). Most Muslims are of Indian origin with Urdu and Gujrati as their languages, but they also speak French and English. There are ninety-one mosques on the island and some 200 perform *hajj* yearly. Islamic law, however, is not enforced on Muslims. Quranic schools are attached to the mosques, and there is an Islamic Institute, but Islam is not taught in government schools. Most Muslims are agriculturists. There are some who are in business and the professions, but their percentage among others is less than the percentage of Muslims on the island. There are usually two or three Muslim ministers in the government. The most important Muslim organizations are the Board of Waqf Commissioners, controlling the management of mosques and *awqafs*; the Islamic Welfare Foundation; the Islamic Circle; etc.

Zimbabwe, which became independent in 1980, had a population of 7,770,000 in 1982. The Muslim population is estimated at 62,000 of 0.8 per cent of the total population, 90 per cent of them are descendants of immigrants from Malawi, India, Somalia and Mozambique. Most Muslims are farmers in the midlands and south-eastern districts or traders in such towns as Salisbury, Bulawayo and Que Que. There are about fifty mosques and prayer halls in the country, to which the Quranic schools are attached. Muslims have no share in the administration of the country. The most important associations are the Bulawayo Muslim Youth Movement, the Muslim Students Association (Que Que), the Zimbabwe Islamic Youth Council, and the Zimbabwe Islamic Mission.

Many locations in northern Morocco are still under Spanish colonial rule. These include the towns of Sabtah and Maliliyah and the minor territories of Nakkur, Badis and Al-Jaafariyah Islands. They total 130,000 people of whom 47,000 are Muslims (36 per cent of the population). Muslims are Moroccan, although many of them received Spanish citizenship. They have their mosques and strong ties with Morocco. But they constitute the poorest elements in the society.

Mayotte is part of the Comoro Islands. It was illegally separated from the rest of the islands when they received their independence in 1976. In 1977, it became an overseas department of France. Its total population amounted to about 53,000 in 1982, of whom about 37,000 were Muslims (70 per cent of the population). The language of the people is Swahili; a small Christian minority of immigrants agitated for separation from the rest of the islands. The

United Nations recognize the State of Comoros as representing Mayotte as well.

The Congo had a population of 1,640,000 in 1982. Of these about 37,000 were Muslims, 2 per cent of the total population. Islam is being introduced by Nigerian and Senegalese immigrants. Muslims have mosques and Quranic schools in the main cities, especially in Brazzaville, the capital of the country.

The Reunion is an overseas *department* of France. It is an island neighbouring Mauritius. It had a population of 546,000 in 1982. Of these about 2.5 per cent or about 14,000 people were Muslims. Islam was introduced to the island by Indian immigration since 1885. There are at present twelve Islamic schools and thirteen mosques in the island, including two mosques in the capital Saint Denis. Muslims are united under the Cultural Association of Reunion Muslims, and they have a magazine in French 'L'Echo de I'Islam'.

There are about 8,000 Muslims in Angola and at least one minister in the government is Muslim. Each of Cape Verde, Equatorial Guinea and Sao Tome and Principe has about 1,000 Muslims. There are 500 Muslims in Botswana who have two mosques, one at Lobatse and another at Gaborone. There are also two Islamic schools. Muslims are organized under the Botswana Muslim Association. Seychelles have about 200 Muslims of various origins. They are organized under the Seychelles Muslim Organization and have plans for a mosque in the capital Victoria. Finally there are about 2,000 Muslims in Namibia, Swaziland and Lesotho as a whole.

## Conclusions

As far as minority Islam in Africa is concerned, the continent could be divided into two areas: West Africa, and East Africa. In West Africa, Muslims have indeed been pushed aside by small Christian minorities trained during colonial days to the point where in all of the states treated in this chapter Muslim influence is considerably less than Muslim numerical strength. However, it seems that this position is only temporary and as time passes more people convert to Islam and more influence Muslims have in their country. The improvement of the stuation of Muslims in this area seems to proceed peacefully. One state in this area has Muslim numerical majority: Nigeria.

In East Africa, the situation is altogether different. The area has been constituted in Muslim states for more than one thousand years. It witnessed Christian onslaughts since the fifteenth century. In a greater part of this region a policy of active segregation is being followed by the Marxist establishments which have inherited their hatred for Islam from the Christian missions or clergy, or have derived it from the inherent hostility of Marxism towards all religions. The most preoccupying situations are those existing in the states where Muslims are either in the majority or are close to being a majority: Ethiopia, Tanzania, Mozambique and Malawi.

In Ethiopia, many Muslims looked at war of liberation as the only way of avoiding the status of second-class citizens to which they were reduced in spite of their numerical majority. However, unfortunately for the Muslims of Ethiopia, they were unable to wage a united struggle to obtain their civil rights and the rule of the majority. Most wars of liberation in the country are of the secessionist type and are motivated as much by local national feelings as by the Islamic urge to revolt against oppression.

It is highly disturbing for Muslims to notice that some of the states of south-east Africa such as Tanzania and Mozambique which are most hostile to Muslims have been and are the same which had received support from Muslims in their fight against colonialism. However, it is hoped that the present situation is only a temporary one, since the mass of the population of the area, whether Muslim or not, does not share with this tiny minority that has been reared in the missionary schools their disdain for Islam. Indeed, even in East Africa, Islam is gaining new adepts every year.

In fact the real problem of the Muslim minorities in Africa is an educational one. During the colonial era, Muslims had been prevented from receiving modern education since they had been pushed to the position where they had to choose between their Islamic faith and modern education. They chose their faith. However, after the attainment of independence, the situation remained unchanged. Muslims have found themselves the least equipped to compete with the rest of the population, being the least educated and consequently the poorest. In order to tackle the problem at the roots it is necessary to help the African Muslims educate themselves. They are already making a gigantic effort which should be supported. Once Muslims in Africa are able to overcome their lag in education, without failing to emphasize Islamic education and developing deep understanding of Islamic principles, most of their problems are bound to be solved.

Muslims all over the world are coming to take notice of this problem. They have united their efforts to establish two Islamic universities, one in Uganda for East Africa and the other in Niger (in the town of Say) in West Africa. However, the problem has to be tackled from the earliest stages of education; the kindergarten; then the primary Islamic schools; then the secondary schools.

The problems of hunger, malnutrition and vitamin deficiency in children have hit Muslims more than anybody else in Africa; from the Sahel to the Horn. Muslims of the world should show their solidarity with their African brethren in this respect. The help given to Muslims in Africa should be direct and not through welfare groups related to European Churches which use such help to reinforce their own efforts designed to undermine the cultural roots of the Muslims.

Finally, one of the greatest tragedies of Africa is its decultarization by the European colonial powers. Why should foreign languages such as English or French, or Portuguese remain the languages of Africa? The Africans should develop their own languages as the bearers of their Islamic culture; Swahili, Hausa, Fulani, Wolof and many other languages have been written for centuries in the Arabic script and have been the carriers of great civilizations. For Muslims, attachment to the Arabic and at least the Arabic script is an integral part of their permanent cultural policy and is deemed a powerful guarantee for strengthening Islamic cultural unity at the global level.

## References

GENERAL

1. J. C. Froelich, *Muslims of Black Africa* (France, 1962) (French).
2. M. N. Al Ubudi, *In Green Africa* (Beirut, 1968) (Arabic).
3. R. Oliver and A. Atmore, *Africa Since 1800* (London, 1969).
4. V. Monteil, *Black Islam* (France, 1971) (French).

NIGERIA

1. J. Schacht, 'Report on the Position of Muhammedan Law in Northern Nigeria' Doc CHEAM, No. 1708 (France, 1950).
2. J. S. Trimingham, *Islam in West Africa* (London, 1962).

ETHIOPIA

1. S. H. Longrigg, *A Short History of Eritrea* (England, 1945).

2. J. S. Trimingham, *Islam in Ethiopia* (London, 1952).
3. A. de Borchgrave, 'Trouble on the Horn' *Newsweek* (27 June, 1977).
4. J. Darnton, 'Eritrean Rebel Army Set for Decisive Test' *New York Times* (11 July 1977).
5. G. Chaliand, 'Ethiopia, Key to the New Equilibrium in the Red Sea' *Le Monde Diplomatique* (July 1977) (French).

TANZANIA

1. J. S. Trimingham, *Islam in East Africa* (London, 1964).
2. P. J. A. Rigby, 'Sociological Factors in the Contact of the Gogo of Central Tanzania with Islam' in *Islam in Tropical Africa* edited by I. W. Lewis (London, 1966).
3. P. Lienhard, 'A Controversy over Islamic Custom in Kilwa Kivinje' in *Islam in Tropical Africa*, edited by I. W. Lewis (London, 1966).

MOZAMBIQUE

1. Anonymous, *Islam in Mozambique* King Abdul-Aziz University Seminar on Muslim Minorities (April 1977).

KENYA

1. P. T. W. Baxter, 'Acceptance and Rejection of Islam among the Boran of the Northern Frontier District of Kenya' in *Islam in Tropical Africa*, edited by I. W. Lewis (London, 1966).
2. M. A. Kettani, *Islam in Kenya* Report submitted to the Muslim World League (Mecca, 1973) (Arabic).
3. M. A. Eraj, *Basic Education in the Semi-Arid Areas of Kenya*, Workshop, Kenyatta University College (Nairobi, Kenya, 18–27 December 1977).

GHANA

1. I. Wilks, 'The Position of Muslims in Metropolitan Ashanti in the Early Nineteenth Century' in *Islam in Tropical Africa*, edited by I. W. Lewis (London, 1966).
2. T. Hodgkin, 'The Islamic Literary Tradition in Ghana' in *Islam in Tropical Africa*, edited by I. W. Lewis (London, 1966).

IVORY COAST

1. P. Marty, *Etudes Sur L'Islam en Côte d'Ivoire* (France, 1977).

OTHER COUNTRIES

1. P. Azam, *Dans le Togo, L'Islam Face a la Foret* Doc-CHEAM No. 888 (France, 1944).
2. J. Comhaire *Note sur les Musulmans de Leopoldville* II, No. 3 (Zaire, March 1948).
3. A. Y. Cava, *Muslims in the Republic of Zaire* WAMY Report, 1982.
4. P. Ceulemans, 'Introduction of Islam in the Congo' in *Islam in Tropical Africa*, edited by I. W. Lewis (London, 1966) (French).
5. G. Shepperson, 'The Jumbe of Kota Kota and Some Aspects of the History of Islam in British Central Africa' in *Islam in Tropical Africa*, edited by I. W. Lewis (London, 1966).
6. R. Rezette, *Les Enclaves Espagnoles au Maroc* (France, 1976).
7. J. M. Dewillard, 'An Eye-Witness Report on the Massacre of Comorians at Majunga' *Le Monde* (France, 16–17 January 1977).
8. F. Oozeerally & A. Bookuly, *Muslims in Madagascar* WAMY Report (1981).
9. I. Jadwat, *Muslims in Southern Africa*, International Seminar on Muslim Communities in non-Muslim States (London, July 1978).
10. O. H. Kasule, *The Situation of Islam and Muslims in the Republic of Rwanda*, WAMY Report (1981).

# 8 Muslims in America

## Introduction

The story of Islam in America started certainly before the conquest of the continent by European Christian powers which followed its discovery for them by Christopher Columbus. There is strong evidence that Andalusian Muslims visited the American continent long before Columbus as reported by Al-Sharif Al-Idrisi in the twelfth century C.E. Furthermore, there is certain evidence in the Caribbean of visits from the Muslim kingdoms of West Africa. Finally, it is a known fact that the Portuguese and Spanish discoverers were led by Andalusian Muslim mariners who knew better about the high seas. Some of the discoverers themselves were Moriscos, i.e., secret Muslims from Spain. It is also a known fact that the Andalusian Muslim immigrants of Al-Ribat and Sala (in Morocco) led the fight against the Spanish and Portuguese ships in the Atlantic down to the Caribbean coast.

However, the present formation of the Muslim communities of America can be traced to three main waves of immigration: the European wave; followed by the African wave; and then the Asiatic wave.

The Muslim European immigration to America started with the discovery by Columbus. Indeed, this discovery coincided in 1492 with the fall of Gharnatah (Granada) to Christian forces. Several years later, Cardinal Cisneros, head of the Spanish Catholic Church, imposed the Catholic religion on the millions of Muslims of Spain by force. Those among them who did not leave their homeland kept their Islamic religion secret. Thousands of these so-called Moriscos emigrated to America in the sixteenth century with the Spanish and Portuguese colonial armies, where in the new continent they declared their Islam openly. They even tried to convert the West Indians. The Catholic Inquisition (both Spanish and Portuguese) followed them and thousands of Muslims were burned on the stake for 'apostasy'. Among these Moriscos were Rodrigo de Lope, the colleague of Columbus and Estevanico de Azemor, the Spanish General who conquered Arizona. Only traces remained of this immigration. However, some new Muslim converts in Mexico, Argentina and Brazil declare themselves to be descendants of these first Muslims.

As soon as the first wave of Muslim immigration died out in blood and tears, a new wave started. This time it was from Africa and in no less dramatic circumstances. The Europeans, after destroying the local populations of the new continent started en-slaving the free Africans to make up for the shortage of manpower in the colonies of the New World. This movement of population started in the seventeenth century and lasted until the nineteenth century. A great number of these Africans were Muslim. They tried to keep their faith by all means, including sometimes armed struggle. Among these known Muslim revolts is the revolt of Makendal in 1758 in Haiti. This Muslim leader was burnt alive by the French colonial forces after his defeat. In 1830, the African Muslims of Brazil even succeeded in establishing a Muslim state which was destroyed after four years in a sea of blood. Due to this ferocious persecution against the Muslims which included the destruction of the family unit, Islam was on the verge of disappear-ing among the Blacks of America. However, things have taken an altogether unexpected turn, and the Africans have begun an en masse return to Islam.

The third wave started from Asia in 1830 C.E. Indeed the British and the Dutch replaced slavery by forced emigration from India and Java for 'indentured labour'. This was a barely disguised form of slavery. Islam remained firmly entrenched among the descen-dants of these immigrants. By the end of the nineteenth century a wave of emigration started from Greater Syria. It continues to this day. By the twentieth century Muslim immigrants arrived in America from all corners of the world, but more specifically from Asia, and Eastern Europe.

Table 8.1 shows that there were about 4 million Muslims in the American continent in 1982 or 0.74 per cent of the total popula-tion. They were only two million in 1971 (0.4%). Moreover, Muslim percentages exceed 10 per cent of the total population in three countries: Surinam (35%); Guyana (15%) and Trinidad and

Tobago (13%). The number of Muslims exceeds 100,000 in four other countries: the US, Canada, Argentina and Brazil. Muslims of the American continent are organized in twenty-five countries. The Muslim population is growing at a fast pace due to natural increase, immigration and conversion. Surinam, for instance, might soon become the first Muslim majority state of America. The distribution of Muslims in America is shown in Figure 4.

*Table 8.1*    Muslims in America, 1982

| Country | Population in thousands | | |
|---------|------|--------|------|
|         | *Total* | *Muslim* | |
| United States | 229,700 | 3,000 | 1.3 % |
| Argentina | 28,800 | 400 | 1.4 % |
| Brazil | 127,770 | 380 | 0.3 % |
| Trinidad and Tobago | 1,220 | 160 | 13.0 % |
| Surinam | 430 | 150 | 35.0 % |
| Guyana | 870 | 130 | 15.0 % |
| Canada | 24,300 | 120 | 0.5 % |
| Venezuela | 16,000 | 50 | 0.3 % |
| Colombia | 27,600 | 20 | 0.07% |
| Mexico | 71,690 | 15 | 0.02% |
| Jamaica | 2,330 | 14 | 0.6 % |
| Others | 91,100 | 26 | 0.03% |
| Total | 621,810 | 4,600 | 0.74% |

## The United States

It is almost certain that Muslims crossed the Atlantic as well as the Pacific long before Columbus reached the New World. But these visits did not have any lasting effects. Moriscos of Spain arrived in the sixteenth century with the Spanish armies to the region of New Mexico and Arizona. The most known of these is the Spanish General Estevanico de Azemor, whose Muslim name remains unknown. These first Muslims could not retain Islam among their descendants. During the same period an Egyptian prince by the name of Nasir-al-Din joined the Mohawk tribe in the territories which form today the state of New York. He reached a position of pre-eminence within this tribe.

Slavery was introduced into the lands which were to form later the United States in 1619 C.E. Hundreds of thousands of people were shipped from Africa across the Atlantic under the most

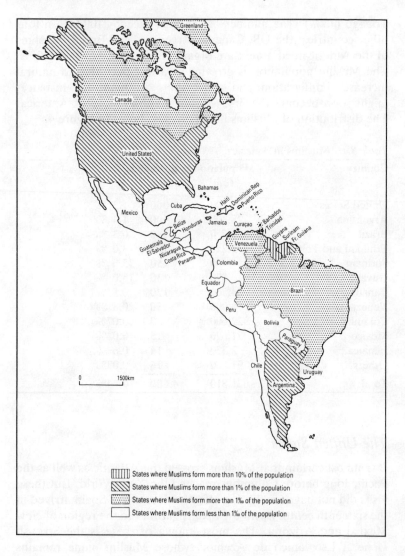

States where Muslims form more than 10% of the population

States where Muslims form more than 1% of the population

States where Muslims form more than 1‰ of the population

States where Muslims form less than 1‰ of the population

horrifying circumstances. Many of these were Muslims and their story can be followed along the entire history of the United States. For instance, in 1790, the state of South Carolina allowed the trial 'of some Moors subject to the Emperor of Morocco' in the tribunals using the current laws. There was during the same period a debate in the south on the right of worship of 'Catholics, Jews and Mohamedans'. Muslim names such as 'Ben Ali' are to be noted among those who fought with the Confederates in the Civil War in the nineteenth century. The conditions under which African Muslims were brought to America and how they were robbed of their dignity and religion, has been vividly described by Alex Haley in his book *Roots* which traces his own origin among the Muslims of Gambia. Islam never died completely in the hearts of the Americans of African origin and at present it is vigorously coming back.

Asian Muslim emigration to the US started in 1855 C.E. when a certain Hajd Ali was brought from Syria to oversee the introduction of camel breeding in Arizona. He has been followed by a continuous flow of immigrants from Greater Syria which goes on to this day. Many descendants of the first immigrants have been lost to Islam completely and have been assimilated in the majority.

European Muslim emigration started after World War I. It included Muslim Tartars from Kazan; Polish Muslims; but especially Yugoslavs and Albanians. After World War II, Muslim immigration to the US came from all over the world, but especially from India, Pakistan, Iran, Turkey and Egypt.

Conversion to Islam in the US has taken place throughout. Although most of the converts are those of African origin who are, in most cases, actually returning to their original religion, in addition to them, there are also converts of European, Mexican, Puerto Rican and even Jewish origins. Among the first converts of European origin one must note Mr Alexander Russel Webb, the US Consul in the Philippines who accepted Islam in 1888 C.E.

The organizational efforts of the Muslims started only in the twentieth century. The Afro-American returnees to Islam established their first Islamic association in 1913. As for the Syrian immigrants, they formed in Detroit their first Islamic association in 1912 and built the first mosque in 1919.

Efforts at establishing organizations on the national level started in 1952 when the 'Federation of Islamic Associations' was formed. However, this effort is far from satisfactory. Since 1976 a reorganization on two levels, one at the level of each state of the US and the second at national level, is in progress.

In 1971, there were in the United States about one million Muslims (or 0.5 per cent of the total population). They have been increasing at a yearly rate of about 10 per cent due to natural increase, immigration, and conversion. Their number reached about three million in 1982 making up about 1.3 per cent of the US population. Of these, about 1 million were of African origin; 900,000 were of Arab origin; 450,000 were of Indo-Pakistani origin; and the remaining 450,000 were of diverse, especially Yugoslav, Albanian, Turkish, and Iranian, backgrounds. There are at least 90,000 Muslim students in American universities.

About 90 per cent of the Muslims in the US are Sunni and 10 per cent are Shia. There is no area where Muslims are highly concentrated, but it seems that their numbers are larger in the bigger cities such as New York, Boston, Washington D.C., Detroit, Chicago, Los Angeles, Houston, etc. Many Muslims are professionals such as physicians and engineers, some of whom are highly outstanding. Others are workers or even farmers in the south-west.

Muslims of the United States are not yet organized on a national scale, and thus have only a negligible influence in the country. They are not represented in the Senate nor in the House of Representatives in spite of the fact that they are, in a good majority of cases, US citizens. However, Muslims are completely free to practice their religion, and their associations are treated in the same manner as Christian and Jewish religious organizations.

The Muslim organizations with nation-wide influence and activity are increasing in importance and influence. The main activity of the Federation of Islamic Organizations is its annual convention. The Muslim Students Association' was established in 1963 as a student organization and makes a laudable effort to spread Islamic literature. It established later many affiliated organizations dealing with the needs of the Muslim community. The World Community of Islam in the West concerns itself mainly with the Afro-American population which is coming increasingly closer to the Muslim mainstream. Since 1976, regional councils came into being gathering Muslim community organizations in several regions. Among these two councils especially deserve to be mentioned: The Islamic Council of Northern California and The Islamic Council of New England.

In the US, there are at least four hundred Muslim organizations and as many mosques, coupled with Quranic schools. Among these mosques some are fully-fledged community Islamic centres in the Islamic style such as the ones in Quincy (Mass.); Waterbury (Conn.); Detroit (Mich.); Dearborn (Mich.); Toledo (Ohio); Cedar Rapids (Iowa); Sacramento (California); Gary (Indiana); Phoenix (Arizona), etc. The Islamic Center of Washington D.C., with its beautiful mosque, is not a community mosque. It is rather a mosque established by the Muslim embassies of the capital and is run by them.

There are few fully-fledged Islamic schools in the US. Almost all Muslim children go to non-Muslim schools, either public or private, and tend to be assimilated. Two Muslim universities are, however, being established in Chicago. Islam is bound to grow in the US as more efforts are being devoted to establishing Islamic institutions which will cater to the needs of the rising generations and stop the nibbling effect of religious assimilation on the Muslim community.

## Argentina

The first Muslim immigrants to the areas which came to form Argentina are the Moriscos of Spain who arrived in the sixteenth century. Although Islam could not endure among these first Muslims they certainly left a lasting impact on the country such as the Gaucho tradition. Domingo Sarmiento, the Argentinian writer of the nineteenth century, exposed himself to the wrath of his fanatic compatriots when he claimed descent from the Muslim Bani Al-Razin in eastern Spain. Andalusian Islamic tradition has had great influence on the Argentinian writers.

Immigration from Greater Syria lasted from about 1880 to around 1955. In these seventy-five years, Syrian Arabs immigrated in such numbers that they became an important element in the constitution of the Argentinian population. In fact, they are the third element after the Spanish and the Italians. However, most of the immigrants were Christian; the Muslims being a mere minority among them. The Syrians constitute, nevertheless, the largest Muslim ethnic element of the Muslim community of Argentina.

In 1982 there were about 400,000 Muslims in Argentina who formed about 1.4 per cent of the total population. They were about 300,000 in 1971, and their increase is limited to natural growth. There is no Muslim immigration to Argentina at present and the number of Muslims who leave the country is very small.

Among the Muslims, about 200,000 live in Buenos Aires which has districts with high Muslim concentration. The remaining 200,000 Muslims live scattered throughout the country, most of them in the northern provinces.

About 65 per cent of the Muslims are of Syrian origin, 25 per cent of Lebanese and about 10 per cent of diverse ethnic origins including local converts. Religiously, they represent all the religious schools of Greater Syria: about 90 per cent are Sunnis and 10 per cent are Shias. Most of the Muslims are Argentinian citizens, with the exception of the old representatives of the first wave of immigration who cling tenaciously to their Syrian citizenship.

Most of the Muslims of Argentina are active in commerce. There are many professionals in the younger generations. These Muslims suffer from poor contact with the rest of the Muslim world. Outside Buenos Aires, they do not receive much help and Arabic language is dead among the younger people. Argentinian law forces them to carry Argentinian (i.e. Christian) names and it is impossible to recognize a Muslim by name, accent or physical appearance. Besides this nagging official policy aimed at the effacement of their Islamic identity, Muslims are free to organize as Muslims and have all their rights as Argentinian citizens. There are even among them governors of provinces and generals in the armed forces. However, as a religion with its institutions, Islam is practically ignored by Arentinian laws.

Earlier in the century, Muslims suffered from a status of double minority. In the first place, within the Arab population the Christian Arabs tended to infiltrate all their social activities, de-Islamize them, and steal from them all the attention of the Arab world. Secondly, they also suffered obscurity within the Argentinian population which forced them in the beginning to conceal their Islamic identity. This double persecution has now been greatly reduced, but if left the Muslim community weakened, its Islamic identity mixed up and its organization loose.

Organizationally, the Muslims are divided into a multitude of clubs hailing from different Syrian villages. These clubs are social gatherings which bring together both Muslims and Christians. They do hot help the Muslims retain their identity. Religiously, the first Muslim organization, the Islamic Centre was established in Buenos Aires in 1918. It used to meet in rented places and in 1968 it bought a building which is used as the spiritual centre of the entire Muslim community of Argentina. The centre has a qualified *imam* from Al-Azhar, and it is planning to build a large mosque/ Islamic centre in the capital. Other Muslim associations were established in the capital such as the 'Arab Argentinian Islamic Association' which was established in 1960. This association opened the first Muslim school in the country, which provides regular instruction along with instruction in Arabic and Islam. The Muslims of the capital have also a cemetery. Muslim organizations and Islamic centres were later established in other cities such as Mendoza (in 1926); Cordoba (in 1929); Rosario and Tucuman. However, these Islamic centres are closer to social clubs; they have no *imams,* no qualified teachers, and no regular prayers.

Thus, Muslims in Argentina are in real danger of disappearing by assimilation. Many have even been baptized in the Catholic religion. Most of the others have lost their Arabic language; yet others have been forced by circumstances to marry in the Catholic Church. All are forced to carry Christian names. Unless this trend is reversed soon, there is little hope of the survival of the Muslim community in Argentina.

## *Brazil*

When the Portuguese conquered Brazil in 1500 C.E., they specifically forbade their citizens of Muslim origin to emigrate to it. In spite of this ban, many Moriscos managed to reach Brazil. Their numbers became so large that by the end of the sixteenth century they openly declared their profession to Islam. This led the Court of Bahia to declare the Brazilian Catholic Inquisition against the Muslims in 1594 C.E. Thus, thousands of Muslims were burnt at the stake; others were enslaved; and the entire community eliminated with the most atrocious brutality.

In the seventeenth century, the Portuguese started capturing Africans and transporting them as slaves to Brazil. Many of these were Muslims of West Africa such as the Mandinguas, the Fulani, the Yoruba, the Hausa who had been caught by the animist King of Dahomey in his raids against the territories of the Muslim states and sold as slaves to the Europeans, including the Portuguese. Many of these Muslims were learned *alims* who were capable of keeping the knowledge of Arabic and the Islamic culture alive among the victims and their descendants. They even succeeded in converting to Islam other enslaved or oppressed people such as the American Indians. These Muslims were able to keep Islam alive in Brazil for more than two centuries. They were well established in the States of Bahia, Rio de Janeiro and San Luis do Marinon. Their mosques and Quranic schools were counted by the hundreds. In 1835, they felt strong enough to free themselves from the subservient status to which they had been consigned by the Christians. They led a war of liberation which lasted four years during which they established a Muslim state. They were finally defeated and persecuted mercilessly. The Christian authorities of Brazil then expressedly forbade any profession of Islam and declared the death sentence for any one who had allegiance to it. Hundreds of thousands crossed the Atlantic back to Africa where they form thriving Muslim communities in such ports as Porto-Norvo, Lagos and Freetown. Others have kept their religion in secret to this day. The area where their presence is conspicuously felt is in the state of Bahia.

Immigration from Greater Syria started in 1860. Most of the immigrants were Christians, but there were a number of Muslims among them as well. This immigration originated first from Syria, then Lebanon and more recently from Palestine. Immigration from Lebanon and especially from Palestine still goes on. These Arab Muslims have organized themselves since 1929.

There were in Brazil about 380,000 Muslims in 1982, among whom about 40 per cent were of Syrian origin, 20 per cent Lebanese, 20 per cent Palestinian and about 20 per cent of diverse backgrounds, including African. About 90 per cent of these Muslims are Sunnis, and 10 per cent Shias, and a great majority of them are Brazilian citizens.

Most of the Muslims of Brazil are in business, ranging from the roaming peddlers to the rich businessmen of Sao Paulo and Rio de Janeiro. Those who are of African origin are concentrated in the state of Bahia and not much information about their present situation is available. Those who are of Arab origin are concentrated mostly in the southern states, and more specifically in the two states of Sao Paulo and Parana. Most Syrians are in Sao Paulo and most Lebanese are in Prana whereas Palestinians can be found in Brazilia, Santa Caterina, and Rio Grande do Sul.

There is at present more freedom of religion for Muslims in Brazil than in Argentina, and Muslims in Brazil are better organized and have greater ties with the rest of the Muslim *ummah*. There are Muslim associations in seven Brazilian states and in ten different cities. Most associations have their mosques which often include a community centre as well as an Islamic school. There are seven mosques and others are under construction at present.

The associations owning mosques are in Curitiba, Londrina and Paranagua in the state of Parana, in Sao Paulo and Barretos in the state of Sao Paulo as well as in Rio de Janeiro (Gunabara), Cuiaba (Matto Grosso) and Brazilia. Muslim communities are organized at Manaus (Amazonas), at Campo Mourao (Parana) where the city donated a piece of land for the construction of the city's mosque; at Tubarao and at Criciuma in the state of Santa Catarina and at Porto Alegre in Rio Grande do Sul. There are also Muslim schools in Sao Paulo, Londrina, Curitiba and Paranagua.

Brazilian Muslims received some support from the Muslim world in the form of financial help for the construction of the mosques and the services of qualified *imams* were made available to them. Indeed the cities of Paranagua, Curitiba, Londrina, Sao Paulo, Cuiaba, Brazilia and Barretos, all have qualified *imams*.

The Muslims of Brazil are not yet organized on the national level. However, there are strong informal links between the different organizations, and there are periodic meetings between the leaders of the different communities. At this pace of development the future of Islam in Brazil, when the dark oppressive period of the nineteenth century has receded to the past, seems once more encouraging.

## Trinidad and Tobago

Trinidad and Tobago is about eleven kilometres from the Venezuelan coast in South America. Its overall area is 5,130 square kilometres of which 4,828 square kilometres make up Trinidad Island and 302 square kilometres cover Tobago and five smaller islands. In 1982, the total population was 1,220,000 people.

The islands were invaded by Britain in 1797 C.E. and received their independence on 31 August 1962. The official language is English. Racially, 43 per cent of the population is of African origin, 40 per cent of Indian origin, 14 per cent of mixed origin, and 3 per cent of Chinese and European origins.

As for most of the American continent, the first wave of Muslim immigration came from Africa in the form of slaves. These first Muslims lost their religion, but their descendants are today returning to Islam in large numbers. After the abolition of slavery, Britain introduced the institution of indentured labour by bringing workers from its Indian colony from 1844 C.E. until 1912 C.E. Many of these indentured labourers were Muslims who were able to keep their religion alive by forming secret Islamic societies since their arrival. But they have lost their mother tongue to the point that most of them speak English as their first language.

The different local Islamic societies started to organize on a national level in 1920. At this stage the *qadianis* were able to infiltrate the Islamic societies. It was only in 1935 that the Muslim community was able to free itself from this infiltration by forming the 'Anjuman Sunnatul Jamaat Association' (popularly called ASJA). This represents today almost the total number of Muslims of Trinidad and Tobago. The total number of Muslims amounted to 160,000 in 1982, or about 13 per cent of the total population. Of these about 10,000 are of African origin and the remaining are of Indian origin. They are all English speakers. There were 115,000 Muslims in 1971, or 11.5 per cent of the population. In 1951, the number of Muslims had amounted to 52,000 and made up only about 9 per cent of the total population. In 1978, the population of Trinidad and Tobago was 52 per cent Christian and 35 per cent Hindu.

At present, the Muslim community of Trinidad and Tobago is one of the best organized in America. The ASJA represents almost the total number of Muslims and manages all mosques and Muslim schools in the country. It is divided into seventy branches and is grouped into four regions. Its executive committee is elected by representatives from the seventy branches.

In Trinidad, the Muslims are better educated and are less poor than their brethren in neighbouring countries. The Muslims of Indian origin are of the Hanafi school. They are concentrated mostly in the southern part of the island. They are basically farmers but many have become professionals and businessmen. The influence of the Muslims in the country is proportionate to their numbers: the president of the Senate is Muslim as well as three government ministers and five deputies in the House of Representatives out of a total of thirty-six.

Muslims have eighty mosques in Trinidad and one in Tobago. They have fifteen full-time primary schools and three full-time secondary schools. To each mosque is attached a Quranic school to teach Islam. There is, however, a shortage of qualified *imams* and teachers which creates a basic problem for the growth of the Muslim community.

Many people of African origin return to Islam every year. This phenomenon does not occur as a result of any effort on the part of the Muslims of Indian origin to convert them. It is rather due to events in the United States which has a great cultural impact on Trinidad and Tobago. This creates friction between the two components of the Muslim community, which the leaders are trying their best to heal. Indeed, the Muslims of African origin find the way Islam is practiced by Indians too static and not necessarily in the spirit of the orignal Message of the Prophet. They complain that the sermon in the mosque on Friday is in Arabic (rather than in English) which no one understands, that women are not allowed in the mosques while they were in the time of the Prophet. The Indian Muslims developed under the effect of more than one century of persecution a defensive attitude by which they tried very hard to preserve Islam in the mould it had developed in their country, India. The return to Islam of an increasing section of the African population has, however, stimulated the Muslims of Indian origin to look afresh at the problems of their life and the Islamic sources in order to develop a judicious, truly Islamic, lifestyle.

The Muslims have a radio programme, several newspapers and are becoming active in their relationship with the rest of the Muslim world. Their future would seem guaranteed if they succeed in maintaining their unity and improving their educational system by importing more teachers of Islam and providing a better knowledge of Arabic.

## Surinam

Surinam is a South American state which has an area of 163,265 square kilometres and had a total population of 430,000 in 1982. The territory was conquered by Holland in 1667 C.E. It became autonomous in 1954 and gained its full independence on 25 November 1975. A National Military Council took over the government in 1982. Dutch is the official language, but the Surinamese, a local tongue, is the lingua franca of the country. About 44 per cent of the population is of African origin (190,000), 34 per cent are of Indian origin (146,000), 20 per cent are of Javanese origin (86,000) and 2 per cent (8,000) are of diverse origins.

The first Muslims who arrived in Surinam were Africans who were enslaved by the Dutch. They were brought to Surinam to work on sugar cane plantations from 1667 C.E. But most of the descendants of these Muslims have lost their religion due to the harsh conditions under which they lived. Many, however, are at present returning to Islam.

After the abolition of slavery, the Dutch introduced indentured labour by bringing workers from Java to meet their need for manpower. All of these were Muslims of the Shafii school. This immigration started in 1850 C.E. and lasted until 1931 C.E. Islam is still alive in this community.

In 1873 C.E., the Dutch supplemented the manpower from Java by manpower from India as well. This immigration lasted until 1916. Among these Indians there were many Muslims of the Hanafi school. The descendants of these immigrants kept the usage of the Urdu language as well as the Muslim religion.

In 1982, there were about 150,000 Muslims in Surinam, or 35 per cent of the total population. They represent, therefore, the highest Muslim percentage in any American state. Of this total about 90,000 were of Javanese origin, about 50,000 of Indian origin, and the remaining 10,000 Muslims were of diverse origins including African, American-Indian, and Palestinian. The other religions in the country are Christianity (40%), Hinduism (23%) and Paganism (2%).

The percentage of Muslims in the country has increased dramatically during the last two decades. They were only 64,000 people in 1964, or 21.4 per cent of the population. This increase is due to a high rate of natural growth of the Muslim population, immigration, and conversion to Islam. The increase of percentage is dramatized by the large rate of emigration of non-Muslims. Between 1964 and 1971 about 63,000 people left the country permanently. As big a number did the same after 1974, especially just before and after independence.

The Muslims of Surinam have preserved the usages of their religion as well as their languages. But the different ethnic groups did not succeed in fusing into one single Muslim community due to differences in language and school. Many Muslims live in the capital city, Paramaribo, from commerce, others are farmers. Indians are better educated Islamically and their economic level is higher. The differences in language and school between Javanese and Indian Muslims became more serious through a disagreement between the two groups on the direction of Mecca. The Javanese had crossed the Pacific to come to Surinam and kept praying eastward whereas the Indians had crossed the Atlantic and pray westward!

Muslim personal laws are in force in the country. About fifty citizens perform the *hajj* yearly. There are about fifty mosques in the country, the most important being the Paramaribo Jami

Mosque built in 1932 C.E. There are also about twenty Quranic schools and three full-time Muslim schools. There is no Islamic education in public schools however.

In 1973, there were two Muslim ministers in the government out of a total of thirteen and eight Muslims in the Legislative Council out of thirty-nine. Id-ul-Fitr is a national holiday in the country. The country is divided into nine districts and the commissioner of at least one district is Muslim. There are Muslims in the professions as well as in the university. Nevertheless, the colonial regime gave a preferential treatment to Christian churches and Muslims were never treated on an equal footing.

In spite of their diversity, the Muslims of Surinam are well organized in several organizations which are all members of an overall body: the Surinam Islamic Council

## Guyana

Guyana is west of Surinam in South America. It has an area of 214,969 square kilometres and a population of 870,000 in 1982. The territory was conquered by Britain in 1796 C.E. It received its autonomy in 1951 and its full independence on 26 May 1966. The official language is English. About 55 per cent of the population is of Indian origin, 33 per cent of African origin and 12 per cent of diverse origins including 4 per cent American Indians.

Just as in neighbouring Surinam, the first wave of Islamic immigration came from Africa with the enslaved Africans among whom there were many Muslims. A large number of the descendants of these Africans are at present returning to Islam. In 1834 C.E., the British started to bring indentured labourers from India among whom there was a good percentage of Muslims. These were highly persecuted and pressured into leaving their faith. They were able to keep their religion however by forming secret Islamic societies. One manifestation of this persecution was that the Muslims were not allowed to marry outside the Christian Church. It is only in 1860 that Islamic marriage outside the Christian Church was allowed.

Eventually the attitude of the colonizing powers toward Islam relaxed and Muslims were able to build mosques and establish open societies. The different societies united in 1936 to form the United Sadr Islamic Anjuman (USIA). This was unfortunately split in 1972 into two sections: one identified itself with the governmental party, the other with the opposition.

In 1982, there was 130,000 Muslims in Guyana, or 15 per cent of the total population. Of these about 125,000 were of Indian origin, and 5,000 of African origin. There were 48,000 Muslims (11%) in 1951. As for the rest of the population, 37 per cent were Christian, 34 per cent were Hindus, and 14 per cent were of diverse religious convictions.

At present the Muslim community is divided. The roots of the division are political and go back to 1961. This division was evident in the elections of USIA in 1972. Indeed, during that year, two parties fought the elections in the country for power: People's National Congress (PNC) supported in its majority by those citizens of African origin and the People's Progressive Party supported by those of Indian origin. The leaders of the Muslim community in the USIA were divided between those who see Muslims as a third force who are neither Indian nor African. but merely Muslim citizens of Guyana, independently of their ethnic origin, and felt it in the best interest of the Muslims to join the African Party, and those who found greater affinity with the Hindus. The solution would have been to keep an official Muslim neutrality while granting Muslims the freedom to join the party of their choice. Efforts to create an Islamic Party have also failed.

In the face of this division of the USIA, many new Islamic associations were established on a neutral platform. Of these, the General Congress of Islamic Brotherhood (established in 1973), the Muslim Youth League, and the Islamic Centre are among the most important ones.

Nevertheless, the local societies formed around mosques, which were the branches of the USIA, continue to function properly. There are about 120 such societies with an equal number of mosques. Each mosque is usually combined with a Quranic school for the children and a community hall. The Queenstown Jami Mosque in the capital Georgetown is the largest of all mosques. Constructed at the turn of this century, it includes a ladies' annexe, a community hall, a school, and a prayer hall. Saint-Peter's Hall Mosque is the second largest mosque in the capital. Muslim personal laws are in force in marriage and inheritance. But Islam is not taught in the state schools and there are no full-time Muslim schools. The Muslim Trust College in Georgetown has a minority Muslim student body and no Islamic education at all.

Most of the Muslims of Guyana are farmers. Many Muslims who are well-established in the capital are in the professions or in business. Those who are of Indian origin still speak Urdu fluently.

There is a trend toward conversion to Islam among those who are of African origin. In 1978, there were four Muslim ministers in the government, including one African, out of a total of twenty-four ministers. There are about ten Muslim deputies in the National Assembly out of a total of fifty-three members. Both *id-il-Fitr* and the birthday of the Prophet are national holidays.

The Muslims of Guyana never receive much support from the Muslim world and they feel handicapped *vis-a-vis* the Christian community which receives a tremendous help from the Christian world in the form of missions, especially in the field of education.

## Canada

Muslim immigration to Canada started in 1880 C.E., mainly from Greater Syria. This first immigration was followed by immigration from Albania and Yugoslavia after World War I. The number of Muslim immigrants increased speedily after World War II, when they arrived from the four corners of the world, including other minority areas such as Trinidad, South Africa and Fiji. This Muslim immigration still continues.

There were about 120,000 Muslims in Canada in 1982 or about 0.5 per cent of the total population. In 1971, their number barely reached 64,000. Of their total number in 1982, one could estimate about 40,000 were Muslims of Arab origin, 40,000 of Indian origin (including Pakistan, Bangladesh, South Africa, Guyana, Trinidad and Fiji), about 20,000 were of Yugoslav and Albanian origin and the remaining 20,000 of diverse backgrounds, including local converts.

It could be estimated that about half of all Muslims of Canada live in the province of Ontario, with the greatest concentration in the city of Toronto. Most of the Muslims of Canada are Canadian citizens. The new immigrants are often professionals with a high level of education: engineers, physicians, scientists, professors, technicians, etc. Most of the descendants of the old immigrants are in business. Their state of continuous assimilation seems to be arrested and an improvement in their Islamic awareness is perceptible.

The situation of the Muslims in Canada is improving continuously. They are better organized than the Muslims of the US, Argentina, and Brazil, but less well organized than those of Australia. The first Muslim organization was established in Edmonton (Alberta) in the 1920s by the Lebanese immigrants.

This organization built the first mosque of Canada in 1938. After
World War II, new Muslim organizations were established in
London (Ontario), Windsor (Ontario) in 1954, Toronto (Ontario)
in 1955, Lac La Biche (Alberta) in 1957; etc. At present, there are
fifty community Muslim organizations in Canada, of which twenty-
nine are in Ontario, four in Alberta, four in Quebec, three in
Saskatchewan, two in British Columbia, two in Nova Scotia, and one
in each of Manitoba, Newfoundland, New Brunswick and Prince
Edward Island. There were twenty-eight organizations in 1973 of
which seventeen were in Ontario and eleven in the rest of Canada.

By the 1960s the different Muslim organizations which were
concerned mainly with local communities started to feel the need
for overall co-ordination. After years of discussions the Council of
Muslim Communities of Canada was established in 1973. This
council has six committees under it: finance committee, youth
committee, ladies' committee, public relations committee, publications committee and education committee. It publishes a magazine called *Canada-Islam*.

There are eleven mosques/Islamic centres in Canada, including three converted churches. The best known mosques are in
Edmonton (Al-Rashid Mosque, built in 1938); Lac La Biche (1958);
London (1965); Windsor (1969); Toronto (converted Church in
1970); Montreal (1972); and Ottawa (1978). About twelve more
mosques are planned at different places in the country. There are
also about twenty mosques and Islamic centres which are located
in houses and apartments which are sometimes rented.

Islam is not recognized on an equal footing with Christianity
and Judaism in Canada. However, the local Islamic associations
receive some help from time to time from local authorities. Islam
is also taught to Muslim children in some private schools and in all
public schools as one of the 'world religions'. Islamic education is
also imparted in Islamic centres and mosques in week-end classes.
But all this is highly insufficient and a large number of Muslim
children remain without proper knowledge of Islamic principles.
There are no primary or secondary full-time schools. There are
practically no Muslims in the upper echelons of the government,
neither at the provincial nor at the federal level.

## Other Countries

There are about fifty thousand Muslims in Venezuela (1982),
having nearly doubled from thirty thousand in 1971. Of the

present total some twenty thousand are Lebanese, fifteen thousand Syrian, ten thousand Palestinian and five thousand of diverse origins including those from Trinidad. About twenty thousand Muslims lived in Caracas, the rest living in Maracaibo, Maracay, Barcelona, Valencia, Matarin and the island of Santa Marguarita. Most of the Muslims of Venezuela are workers and small retailers. Some are businessmen and professionals. Muslims of Venezuela are not well organized. It was only in 1968 that they formed the first Islamic Society in Caracas, which bought a house in 1972 in Alparaiso, a Caracas suburb, and transformed it into an Islamic centre. This society plans to establish a mosque and an Islamic school in Caracas.

Colombia had in 1982 a Muslim population of about twenty thousand with about five thousand Muslims in the capital Bogota. About half of them are of an old immigration from Syria and Lebanon. The other half came from Palestine more recently. There are large Muslim communities in Paranaica, Cali, Maico and San Andres. Muslims are not organized in Columbia although there is a Palestinian club in Bogota. The old immigrants are in a well advanced stage of assimilation.

The Muslims of Mexico can be estimated at about fifteen thousand. They are in majority of Syrian origin and spread out across the country. They are, however, not organized. Unless they do so soon, they are doomed to be absorbed religiously in the total population.

Muslims reached Jamaica in the nineteenth century from India under the same conditions of indentured labour as those who reached Guyana and Trinidad. But their number was much smaller, which handicapped their efforts to organize. However, by 1982 their number reached about fourteen thousand. With the help of Muslims from Trinidad, they were organized for the first time in the 1950s. They are at present grouped in two organizations and have two mosques, both of them in Spanish Town.

Muslims are organized in thirteen other American countries: Bermuda, Bahamas, Barbados, Curacao, Grenada, Dominica, Puerto Rico, St Christopher, US Virgin Islands (St Croix), Martinique, Panama, Peru and Chili.

The first Muslims who reached Panama are those brought from Bengal for the building of the Panama Canal at the turn of this century. The first Muslim organization was established in 1930 under the name of 'Islamic Mission'. It became in 1967 the 'Indo-Pakistan Islamic Association' and the 'Panama Islamic Association' in 1974. This Association established an Islamic Centre in Panama City as well as a cemetery. There were about one thousand Muslims in Panama in 1982; of whom four hundred were rich businessmen of Indo-Pakistan origin, four hundred were retailers of Palestinian origin and two hundred of diverse origins.

There are about one thousand Muslims in Peru, most of them in the capital Lima and many of them of Palestinian and Syrian origin. They established an Islamic Society in 1975.

Chile has a Muslim population of about a thousand, half of whom are in Santiago. Of these two-thirds are of Syrian and Palestinian origin. They established the first Muslim organization in 1926 in Santiago. This association still exists and operates from rented facilities used as an Islamic centre.

Barbados has a Muslim population of about two thousand, a third of whom are descendants of nineteenth century Indian immigrants. The other part consists of new converts. They are in contact with the Muslims of Trinidad and have four mosques. The number of the Muslims in the Bahamas could be estimated at about one thousand people. Most of them are new converts. They formed an Islamic organization recently called 'Jamaat-us-Islam'. There were about two thousand Muslims in Curacao in 1982 which is part of the Dutch Antilles. Half of these were of Lebanese origin, 25 per cent of Indian origin and the remainder are local converts. They established in 1964 an Islamic Association and built a mosque in the island's capital. There are about five hundred Muslims in Bermuda organized into a Muslim community, most of whom are converts. Several hundred Muslims live in each of Dominica, Grenada, and Saint Kitts. Most of them are new converts and are organized. As for Puerto Rico, it has a Muslim population of about three thousand, most of whom are of Palestinian origin. They formed an Arab Club rather than an Islamic society although one of the elders acts as *imam* for the community. There are about two thousand Muslims in the US Virgin Islands. They are of African and Palestinian origins and have formed an Islamic organization in Saint Croix recently. There were about five hundred Muslims in Martinique. They are mostly converts who were organized in 1982.

There are unorganized Muslim groups in all the other countries of the American continent. One should note in particular about four thousand Muslims of North-African origin in French Guyana, about a thousand Muslims in Cuba, where the Muslim population used to be much larger, and a thousand Muslims in each of

Paraguay and Uruguay. In these three countries the old immigration was Syrian, but the recent one is Palestinian. There are several hundred Muslims in both Ecuador and Bolivia and at least eight thousand Muslims dispersed in the countries of Central America and the Caribbean which have not been mentioned above.

## Conclusions

The Muslim communities of America can basically be divided into two categories: those which are well established and those which are in the formative stage. If one limits comments to those communities where the number of Muslims is larger than ten thousand people, one can see that basically Argentina, Trinidad and Tobago, Surinam, Guyana, Mexico and Jamaica are old communities, whereas the US, Brazil, Canada, Venezuela, and Colombia are in the formative stage.

In the first category the Muslim community results from nineteenth century or early twentieth century immigration. Most of the present-day Muslims were born in those countries. In this category only the communities of Trinidad and Tobago, Surinam and Guyana have a fair chance of growth and survival. The Muslim community of Argentina is in serious danger of complete assimilation in spite of the large numbers involved. Whereas the Muslim community of Jamaica seems to be on the verge of being retrieved, that of Mexico is not even organized and might have reached the point of no return on the path of religious assimilation.

In the second category, at least half of the Muslim population consists of those who were born outside their new countries of adoption. However, the presence of a new Islamic emigration had a beneficial effect on the old immigration and a phenomenon of return to Islam is noticed in these countries. Among these communities, the Muslim community of Canada is best organized, whereas those of the US and Brazil are still without an acceptable overall national body that would legitimately claim to represent the entire Muslim community in a given country. Organization in Venezuela is limited to Caracas, Valencia and Santa Marguerita, and there is no Islamic organization yet in Colombia.

The effort of organization and establishment of new institutions has been enormous. The financing of this effort has come regularly from the Muslim individuals in the different communities. In recent years some financial support has come from Muslim countries, but it has remained negligible compared to the real needs of the communities. It has however, in some special cases, had the effect of encouraging hard-pressed communities to try harder. Islamic literature is well developed in the English language, especially in the US and Canada. The effort in this area of such Muslim organizations at the Muslim Students Association is to be commended. The need for Islamic literature in Portuguese and Spanish is however pressing and unless this need is fulfilled soon the Muslim communities of Brazil and especially Argentina will suffer greatly in so far as they will remain handicapped in transmitting Islamic teachings to the coming generations.

Freedom of religion is at the present enjoyed to a desired degree by all religious communities, including the Muslims, in the US, Canada, and Brazil. Of course, this was not the case in the recent past and this freedom of religion for Muslims is certainly a new development. Had it not been for the preferential treatment the Christian denominations receive and the enormous outside help they obtain, the same could have been said about Trinidad, Guyana and Surinam. In the Spanish speaking countries, Muslims are persecuted and discriminated against statutorily and the attitude of the people, especially outside the capital cities, is one of dislike and discrimination. The level of persecution differs, however, from one country to another. But even in such modern countries as Argentina, the Muslim citizens are not permitted to give Muslim names to their children.

To summarize, while Islam has an old and tragic presence in the American continent, its relative freedom of existence is new. Furthermore, new immigration trends are contributing to a revival and return of the remnants of the old communities especially among those of African origin. Islam is at present strongly rooted in three American states (Trinidad, Surinam and Guyana) and has increasing presence in three others (the US, Canada and Brazil). The only country where Islam seems to have declined is Argentina, but this trend has been arrested in recent years. It seems therefore that the future would guarantee a greater Islamic presence in America.

## References & Further Readings

1. P. I. Etienne, 'A Revolta dos Males' in *Rev. Inst. Geogr. Hist. Bahia*, XIV, No. 33 (Salvador, Brazil, 1907).
2. N. Makdisi, 'The Moslems of America' *The Christian Century*, LXXVI, No. 34 (1959).

3. U. C. Wolf, 'Muslims in the Midwest' *Muslim World*, L, No. 40 (1960).
4. A. A. Elkholy, 'The Arab Moslems in the US' (New Haven, Con., 1966).
5. R. Reichert, 'Muslims in den Guyanas' in *Die Welt des Islams* N.S., X, No. 1-2 (Leiden, Holland, 1966).
6. R. G. Bazan, 'Muslim Immigration to Spanish America' *Muslim World*, LVI, No. 3 (1966).
7. H. B. Barclay, 'The Perpetuation of Muslim Traditions in the Canadian North' *Muslim World,* LIX, No. 66 (1969).
8. R. Reichert, 'Muculmanos no Brasil' *Almena,* I, 1971 (Madrid, 1971).
9. R. G. Bazan, 'Some Notes for a History of the Relations between Latin America, the Arabs and Islam' *The Muslim World*, LXI, No. 4 (1971).
10. E. K. Lovell, 'A Survey of the Arab-Muslims in the US and Canada' *The Muslim World*, LXIII, No. 2 (1973).
11. A. Haley, *Roots* (US, 1976).
12. M. A. Kettani, *Muslims in Europe and America*, II (Beirut, 1976).
13. M. A. Rauf, 'Islam & Islamic Institutions in the Americas' *Impact International* (9–22 April 1976).
14. F. Arbraham, *Early Arab-American Muslim Immigrants* (USA, July 1976).
15. A. W. Hamid, *Muslims in the West Indies* International Seminar on Muslim Communities in Non-Muslim States (London, July 1978).

# 9   Islam in the Pacific

## Introduction

The Western Pacific regions were certainly crossed by Arab
tradesmen on their way from Arabia to China. But Arabs never
settled in the Pacific islands the way they did in Java and Sumatra.
Later, after the sixteenth century and the Islamization of Indonesia
many Muslims from the Indonesian islands visited regularly the
northern coast of Australia, and New Guinea as well as the neighbouring islands. The first European explorers did mention this
Islamic presence, especially in Australia. For instance, when the
Spanish explorer Torres visited New Guinea in 1606, he mentioned a higher civilization in the western part of the island due to
'strong contacts with Muslims of the Molucca islands'. Similarly, when Mathew Flinders visited the north-western shore of
Australia in 1802 he found Muslim fishermen from Timor and
Sulawezi islands. Thus, Islamic presence in the Pacific certainly
pre-dated the European colonization.

The Muslim immigration to the Pacific which has left traces to
this day can be divided into at least eight waves. The first was the
Malay wave which started by 1850, and continued until 1930. It
brought Muslim Malays to the north-eastern, northern and north-
western shores of Australia. The Malays came as pearl divers or as
indentured labourers in sugar cane plantations. Few of the descendants of this immigration remained Muslim. The second wave
was that of 'Afghans' who were brought by the British to Australia
with their camels from 1862 to 1930. This wave of Muslim immigrants originated mainly in the present-day Pakistan. These
'Afghans' helped build up the economy of the desert areas of
Australia. However, only men were allowed to settle in Australia.

The result was that few of those who are of part 'Afghan' origin remained within the Islamic fold. The third wave started in 1872 with the deportation of Algerian freedom fighters by the French to l'Ile des Pins in New Caledonia. The fourth wave was made up by Indian immigration from about 1879 to 1916. Indian Muslims came as indentured labourers in the sugar cane plantations mainly to the Fiji islands, but also to Queensland in Australia. Some traders emigrated from Gujarat to New Zealand. Most of the descendants of these immigrants are still Muslims and form the bulk of the Muslim population of Fiji.

The first four waves could be termed as old immigration. After the World War I, Albanian refugees came to Australia and New Zealand. Their immigration started from 1920 and lasted until about 1950. After the World War II they were joined by a Yugoslav Muslim wave as well as a Turkish Cypriot wave. The immigration of both Yugoslav and Cypriot Muslims started from 1948 and lasted until 1960. Finally a large number of Muslims settled in Australia after 1960. These Muslims came mainly from Turkey and Lebanon, but also from Greece, Pakistan, Egypt and Syria. Most of the Muslims who came after 1920 remained Muslims, albeit at different stages of assimilation in the majority community.

*Table 9.1*    Muslims in the Pacific, 1982

| Country | Population in thousands | | |
|---------|-------|--------|------|
|         | Total | Muslim |      |
| Australia     | 15,100 | 170 | 1.1%  |
| Fiji          | 650    | 50  | 7.7%  |
| New Caledonia | 140    | 14  | 10.0% |
| New Zealand   | 3,130  | 12  | 0.4%  |
| Other         | 4,450  | 14  | 0.3%  |
| Total         | 23,560 | 260 | 1.1%  |

Table 9.1 shows that the Muslims in the Pacific numbered about 260,000 in 1982. In this total are not included the populations of Indonesia (including West Irian) and the Philippines which are considered to be part of Asia. At present (1982), Muslims are organized in six countries of the Pacific: Australia, Fiji, New Zealand, New Caledonia, Tonga and Papua New Guinea. Muslim are also organized in Christmas and Cocos islands which are under Australian jurisdictions (administered by Australia) and

thus are counted with the Muslims of Australia. The highest percentage of Muslims is in New Caledonia (10 per cent) whereas the highest number of Muslims is in Australia (170,000). However, the number of Muslims is increasing fast in all the above mentioned territories and Muslims are expected to organize themselves soon in the other territories of the Pacific.

## Australia: Formation of a Community

The first Muslims to arrive on the coasts of Australia were Arab traders after the tenth century, followed in the fifteenth century by fishermen from the Indonesian islands, especially Makassar, Timor and the Moluccas.

The present Muslim community of Australia, however, traces its origin to 1860 when Dost Mohomet, a Pathan from Kashmir and two other Afghan Muslims arrived in Melbourne with a string of twenty-four camels from Peshawar for use in the Bourke and Wills expedition across the Australian desert. In 1866, twelve more camel drivers were brought from Karachi along with a hundred and twenty camels. Many more came after them and their contribution to the development of Australia was enormous compared to their numbers. Most of the Muslim camel drivers came from present-day Pakistan. Some also came from India, Iran and Afghanistan. But since most of them were Pushtu-speakers they were all called 'Afghans',or just 'Ghans'. In due time, they increased in numbers and became camel owners and breeders, as well as merchants, haulage contractors, hawkers and mailmen throughout the Australian continent.

Their main area of concentration was South Australia. From there they spread out to all parts of the arid inland. They contributed in all explorations of the hinterland. They were employed on the building of the first Overland Telegraph Line across the continent from Adelaide to Darwin, and helped build the Trans-Australia Railway from Kalgoorlie to Port Augusta.

This community produced outstanding personalities such as Abdul-Wadi who operated on such a large scale that he was able to import five hundred camels at a time. Hanji Mahomet Allum was born in Kandahar in Afghanistan in 1858 and emigrated to Australia in 1885. He became famous all over Australia as a great herbalist, healer and teacher of Islam and a great champion of the poor. He died in 1964 in Adelaide at the advanced age of 106.

'Afghans' were treated almost like slaves by the English. Most of them did not come of their free will to Australia. When they came, they were not allowed to bring their womenfolk, a fact which prevented the growth of viable Muslim communities. They were treated with disdain and were made free targets of the Christian prozelytization. The 'Afghans' faced the problem of marriage in many ways. Some of them refused to get married with non-Muslim women; others tried to convert white and aboriginal women and marry them in Islamic manner; still others married any women they met without bothering much about the future of their offspring. The result is that today there are about 15,000 people of part Afghan origin who can be divided into about 3,000 people of white mothers, and 12,000 of aboriginal mothers. About 80 per cent of these Afghans are at present Christian whereas the remaining 20 per cent identify themselves vaguely as Muslims. Notwithstanding their formal profession of Christianity, they all have strong feelings of common Afghan bond. All of them feel completely alienated and many of them are returning to Islam and regaining their lost Islamic identity and dignity.

Since 1860 C.E. the waters from Broome in West Australia, through Darwin in the Northern Territory to, Thursday Island in Queensland produced up to eighty per cent of the world's pearls. Many of the divers were Muslims from Indonesia and Malaysia. Some of them remained Muslims and formed communities. Although they were allowed to bring their wives, there descendants are in an advanced stage of assimilation and only a fraction of them still identifies itself as Muslim. The same could be said about the indentured labourers brought from the Indonesian islands and India to the northern shores of Queensland from Rockhampton to Cairns for the sugar cane fields, around the same period as the pearl divers. However, there is among them a perceptible desire to return to Islam today.

After the World War I a new wave of Muslims reached Australia. They were Albanians, who came with other European immigrants without being noticed as being of the Muslim faith by the then fanatic authorities. Most of the immigrants were men who became active in farming: tobacco in North Queensland and fruit in Victoria. Although they settled down in Australia yet they generally abstained from marrying locally. A great many of them went back in the 1930s to their homelands in Eastern Europe (Yugoslavia, Greece, Albania) and returned to Australia with Muslim wives.

After the World War II, more Albanians immigrated to Australia, especially from Greece and Yugoslavia. Bosniac Muslims arrived also from Yugoslavia and became very active in Islamic organizational efforts in Adelaide, Melbourne and Sydney. Also Turkish Cypriots came in large numbers to Sydney and Melbourne between 1948 and 1952.

Since 1968, a large number of Muslims, especially from Turkey and Lebanon, have been admitted to Australia as factory workers. Many Muslims also arrived from Egypt, Syria, Fiji, India and Pakistan. Some Muslims came from China, Burma and the Soviet Union, and more recently from South Africa. Many Australian converts joined this multinational Muslim community.

In 1982 the number of Muslims in Australia could be estimated at 170,000, among whom about 90,000 Muslims live in New South Wales, 60,000 in Victoria and the remaining 20,000 Muslims in the other states including Christmas Island and Cocos. Muslims are in the majority in these islands, and many of them are being resettled in West Australia. In terms of origin, about 70,000 Muslims are Turkish (from Turkey, Cyprus and Greece); 20,000 are Arab (Lebanon, Egypt and Syria); 25,000 are Albanians and Yugoslavs, and the remainder are of various origins but mainly Malay and Afghan-Indians (India, Pakistan, Fiji, etc.).

Most Muslims are workers in factories; some are farmers; others are professionals and university teachers. There are about 500 Muslim students in the universities and several hundred Muslims in the diplomatic corps in Canberra, the capital of the country.

## Australia: Local Organization

The effective history of Islamic presence in Australia could be dated from 1860, and thus has lasted about 120 years. During this period the Muslims tried to organize themselves twice. The first effort at organization started in the 1880s and was a complete failure by 1948. The second effort started in 1948 and is continuing successfully, increasing in depth, scope and trying to absorb the elements of the first organization.

The first organization was due mainly to the Afghan immigrants who had to live in small outback communities, usually on one edge of the towns. These 'Ghan' towns consisted of an irregular collection of corrugated iron huts, cottages and sheds. Each of these communities had a mosque which was the focal point of the 'Ghan' town. The organization of the community was 'ritualistic' rather than 'idealistic'. In other words, the oldest or most knowledgeable man acted as the *imam* and led the religious activity of the community. Little attention was paid to the education of the offspring. The mosque itself was a place of worship and was often a simple hut, sometimes a stone-built hall for prayers, but could in no way act as a community centre. Most often, the *imam* acted as trustee with full powers over the mosque, but besides the mosque as such there was no organization of the community. The leaders of the community were harsh and rigid, unable to implant Islam in the new environment. They were also quick to expel from the community anyone who violated the ethics of the community. For instance, if a son indulged in drinking or dating, he was brought by the father to the mosque and disowned publicly. Given the fact that all the offspring of the immigrants were of mixed parentage, there was no way for such an organization to survive after the first generation.

The core of the 'Ghan' Muslim community was South Australia with 'Ghan' towns in such places as Oodnatta, Marree, Hergott Springs, Farina, Tarcoola and Port Augusta. Muslims built large mosques in Oodnatta, Marree, Farina, and especially Adelaide, the capital of South Australia. The mosque of Adelaide was among the biggest Afghan mosques. It was built under the leadership of Hanji Mulla Morbin. The land was bought in 1889 and the mosque was built in 1891. From South Australia, the Muslims moved to the other states where they established communities in New South Wales at Broken Hill, Wilcannia, and Bourke. The mosque in Broken Hill was the largest in New South Wales. In Queensland, 'Afghan' communities were established in Cloncurry, Duchess, and Brisbane the capital of the state. The Brisbane mosque, the largest in Queensland, was built in 1907 with the efforts of Abdul Ghiath and Mohammed Hasan. West Australia became the most important state of Muslim settlement with Muslim communities in Marble Bar, Meekatharra, Wiluna, Kalgoorlie, Coolgardie and Perth. The most important mosques were in Coolgardie, a mining town, and Perth, the capital of the state. Construction of the Perth mosque started in 1895 and lasted until 1905 after great efforts by the community.

The Malay community was even less organized. Its main centres were Mackay, Thursday Island (both in Queensland), and Broome (in West Australia). An elderly man was chosen as *imam* in each of these communities, but his only function was to lead the prayers for whoever cared to pray. Only the Muslims of Broome succeeded in building a mosque at the end of the last century.

By 1948, the entire Muslim organizational set-up was a shambles and the Muslims appeared to be a dying breed in Australia. The Perth Mosque became a prey to the Qadiani menace. The Broome Mosque was never rebuilt after its bombardment by the Japanese during World War II, and the Coolgardie Mosque became a museum. In South Australia, newspaper headings read 'Only Two Worship in Mosque Now' or 'Last But One' for Adelaide; the mosques of Oodnatta and Farina were demolished, and the mosque of Marree, was sold in 1951 for £50. Elsewhere, the mosque of Broken Hill became a museum and the mosque of Brisbane was on the verge of being abandoned. By that time those who prayed in Australia could be counted by dozens and those who identified as Muslims were to be counted in hundreds only.

It is at about that time that an Islamic renaissance initiated by the new immigrants, took place providing the initial impulse to the present organizational effort. This effort concentrated more on the community than on buildings; it is based on elections and choice of leaders following the Islamic *shura* principle; it takes greater account of the diversity of the Muslim community and the realities of Australia. It tries to strike roots in the country and thus has more chance of survival.

The first among the newcomers to organize were the Turkish Cypriots in Melbourne in 1948 and in Sydney in 1952. But their organization was purely along national lines and they established clubs rather than mosques. It is only recently that they have tried to reconvert their national organizations into Islamic ones. Then the Muslim communities of Brisbane and Adelaide became organized in 1954 and 1955 respectively along new lines and were able to retrieve the mosques in both these cities, which they renovated later. Then, the Albanians established Albanian Muslim Societies in Mareeba, Queensland (1953); Shepparton, Victoria (1956); and Melbourne, Victoria (1961). They later built mosques in all three locations. Multi-national Muslim organizations were established in 1957 in both Sydney and Melbourne. These organizations built their mosques in the late 1970s. The Muslim Arab communities organized in Sydney (1960) and a multi-national Muslim organization was established in Wollongong (NSW) in 1968. The 1970s saw the greatest increase in the number of organized Muslim communities with nineteen new communities being organized for the first time. This number includes Turkish, Yugoslav amd Malay communities as well as old communities which reorganized Islamically and were joining hands in the great Islamic revival, namely the Afghans of Alice Springs (NT) and the Malays of Mackay (Qld). There are at present fifty-eight organized Muslim communities in Australia; there was one in 1950; four in 1955; nine in 1960; eleven in 1965; thirteen in 1970: twenty-five in 1975; thirty-two in 1978 and fifty-eight in 1983. The distribution of Muslim organizations and mosques is shown in Table 9.2.

*Table 9.2*  Muslim organizations and Mosques in the different states of Australia, 1982

| State or Territory | Mosques | Islamic centres | Muslim organizations |
|---|---|---|---|
| New South Wales | 7 | 10 | 17 |
| Victoria | 7 | 10 | 17 |
| Christmas & Cocos | 1 | 0 | 1 |
| Queensland | 3 | 4 | 7 |
| Northern Territory | 1 | 2 | 3 |
| West Australia | 3 | 5 | 8 |
| South Australia | 1 | 2 | 3 |
| Tasmania | 0 | 1 | 1 |
| ACT | 1 | 0 | 1 |
| Total | 24 | 34 | 58 |

## Australia: National Organization

Until the early 1960s, the Muslims of Australia never formed any national body to unite them, co-ordinate their affairs and amalgamate them into one dynamic Australian Muslim community. An incident occurred in 1961, which under normal circumstances would have been considered just one in a series of humiliations to which the Muslims were subjected until then in Australia. This incident, however, pushed the Muslims into more unity. It concerns Imam Ahmad Skaka, the religious leader of the Muslim community of Adelaide, who is a man of great integrity. He immigrated from Yugoslavia in 1950, earned his living as an electrician, and worked day and night to organize the Muslim community. He was instrumental in establishing the South Australia Islamic Society and in retrieving the Adelaide Mosque for the Muslim community. In 1961, he requested from the Australian Federal Government to be marriage celebrant for the Muslims the way priests were for the Christians. The federal government refused and then the Chief Justice declared: 'I will never allow any Muslim religious person to marry any one in this country'. This was a terrible blow of humiliation to the newly immigrant Muslim community, since the old immigration had, by that time, completely disintegrated. There were in Australia by that time about ten organized Muslim communities in the following cities: Adelaide, Melbourne, Shapperton, Sydney, Brisbane and Mareeba. An intense activity followed between these communities culminating in April 1963 in a general meeting of all representatives of the Muslim organizations. During this meeting the Australian Federation of Islamic Societies (AFIS) was established.

The first act of AFIS was to obtain for the Australian Muslim community the right to have its marriage celebrants denied to the Muslim community of Adelaide. In the beginning, AFIS had a very simple constitution making it more or less a co-ordinating body. In 1968, the constitution was found inadequate and was changed to be on the pattern of the constitution of the Fiji Muslim League, the body which represents the Muslims of neighbouring Fiji Islands. However, such a constitution was of the centralized type, making all societies branches. It was good for Fiji with its small size and homogeneous Muslim population. But it could not be effectively implemented in Australia which is the size of a continent and has an extremely diversified Muslim population. In the 1968 constitution it was said that the Executive Committee of AFIS should be elected every two years by a general assembly consisting of official representatives of member societies. These meetings were held every time in a different city of Australia. The general assembly elected the president and the vice-president, and the president chose five members to form the committee. In practice, the executive committee was always from Melbourne. The first president was Dr Abdul-Khaliq Kazi (University Professor, originally from Pakistan) 1963-67; he was followed by Mr Ibrahim Dallal (journalist, orginally from Cyprus) 1967-71; and Mr Haset Sali (lawyer, Australian born of Albanian parents) 1971-73.

After the visit to Australia of this author, sent by the late King Faisal of Saudi Arabia in November 1974, the Muslims of Australia decided to reorganize their national organizational body on the principles explained in Chapter 1 of this book. Thus, the Islamic organizations of Australia started an effort of reorganization based on the following steps:

the gradual elimination of Islamic societies based on ethnic, national, racial or sectarian ground; the establishment of Islamic societies on purely geographical basis in each state of Australia (the society may use the language of the majority of Muslims present in that geographical area); the local Islamic societies in each state would form an Islamic Council which would represent the entire Muslim population in that state, and the state Islamic Councils would form a Federation of Islamic Councils on a national level.

Intensive work during all of 1975 completely transformed the Australian Federation of Islamic Societies (AFIS) in the Australian Federation of Islamic Councils (AFIC) based on the above three-tier system. Thus, each state and territory of Australia (nine in total) forms now an Islamic Council and each council is made up by a certain number of societies. The status of foreign Muslim students in Australian universities was considered both special and of great importance. Thus, all Muslim student chapters formed the Australian Federation of Muslim Students Associations (AFMSA) which became the tenth Islamic Council of AFIC. The local societies, state councils and AFIC all have constitutions delineating the duties of each. All are based on the free election of office bearers, by the individuals to the local societies; by the local societies for the state council; and by the state councils for the Executive Committee of AFIC. The elected representatives of all the member societies form the Federal Congress whose members meet once a year and decide on the general policy of AFIC. The president and vice-president of AFIC are elected every two years by the ten Islamic councils. The president nominates the other members of the executive committee. Neither the president nor the vice-president could be re-elected more than once. The first president of AFIC under this new system was Dr Abdul-Khaliq Kazi, 1973–76; followed by Dr Qazi Ashfaq Ahmad (University Professor, originally from India) 1976–78; and Dr Mohammed-Ali Wang (Medical Doctor, originally from China) 1978–82; and Mr Ibrahim Atallah (Secondary School Teacher, originally from Egypt) 1982–84; and Dr El-Erian (University Professor, originally from Egypt) since 1984.

Under this new system AFIC embarked on a gigantic task of securing recognition for the Muslims in Australia by the Australian authorities on an equal footing with all other religious bodies; securing recognition for the Australian Muslim community from the Muslim world as a community which is both Australian and Muslim; planning for financial support necessary for the running of Islamic institutions; securing *imams* for all organized

Muslim communities; organizing un-organized Muslim groups (in this respect Afghan and Malay descendants of the first immigration are being brought back to the fold); and securing at a range as short as possible Islamic education for all Muslim children in Australia.

The task that AFIC set before itself is enormous. It has been moving from success to success for the last ten years. On its success in securing Islamic education for the Muslim children and *imams* for all Muslim communities depends the survival of the second phase of the organization of the Muslim community and indeed the survival of Islam itself in Australia.

## Fiji: Formation of a Community

Fiji is an independent state, a member of the Commonwealth of Nations. It is located 2700 kilometres on the north-east of Sydney (Australia) and 1800 kilometres north of Auckland (New Zealand). It is made up of 844 islands of which 106 are inhabited. The total area of the state is 18,272 square kilometres and the total population in 1982 was 650,000 people. The two largest islands, Viti Levu (10,388 square kilometres) and Vanua Levu (5,535 square kilometres), make up 87 per cent of the total area of the state and are the home of 90 per cent of its population.

Tasman discovered the islands for the Europeans in 1643 and Captain Cook visited them in 1774. As soon as Britain conquered the islands in 1874, it introduced sugar cane cultivation and with it indentured labour from India. This indentured labour was brought regularly from 1879 to 1916, so much so that by 1921, the people of Indian origin made up 38.5 per cent of the total populaton of the islands. Because of a higher natural increase among the Indian population compared to the native Fijian population, the Indian percentage kept increasing until it reached a maximum of 50.8 per cent in 1970 to fall to 49.8 per cent in the census of 1976. This fall is due to Indian emigration which became important since 1960. Most of the Fijians have been Christianized by a multitude of Protestant denominations whereas the majority of the Indians are Hindus.

Fiji became independent on 10 October 1970. Its constitution protects the different races. Elections are carried out by racial groups in such a way that the House of Representatives is composed of twenty-two Fijian natives, twenty-two Fijians of Indian origin and eight representatives of citizens of various other origins

(6 per cent of the total population). There is also a senate of twenty-two appointed members. There are two major political parties, the ruling Alliance Party made up mainly of native Fijians and the opposition National Federation Party made up mainly of those who are of Indian origin.

Muslims arrived in Fiji with the Indians as part of an organized migration of indentured labourers to work in the sugar cane plantations. The first Muslims arrived in 1879, and the programme was discontinued in 1916. The labourers were brought on five-year contracts with the option of settling permanently in the new land. The total number of Indians brought under this programme was 62,837. Of these 53,598 were Hindus (85.3%), 9,172 were Muslims (14.6%), and just a handful were Christians. Of the immigrants nearly two-thirds opted for staying on after the end of their contract, or about 41,000 people. But among the Muslims only 47 per cent of the immigrants remained (4,350 persons) the others went back to India. The British allowed the recruiting of forty women for every hundred men, i.e. about 28.5 per cent of the total immigrants were women.

These Muslims who remained in Fiji hailed from different parts of India, but mostly from the north including some of Afghan origin. The greatest majority was of the Hanafi school, a minority from the south of India was of the Shafii school and some families were of the Jaafari school. Those Muslims spoke many Indian languages including Urdu.

The first major problem which faced those who opted to stay was to find wives and raise families. Since among the 4,350 people who remained only about 1,240 were women (28.5%) the problem was a serious one. The Muslims solved this problem by converting Hindu and local Fijian women to Islam and marrying them. Children of these marriages remained Muslim. This explains the tremendous growth rate of the Muslim population from the original 4,350 people to 6,435 in 1921 or 4.1 per cent of the total population, to 45,000 Muslims in 1976 or 7.7 per cent of the total population. The Muslim population in 1982 could be estimated at 50,000. Table 9.3 shows the increase in the Muslim population in the different official censuses since 1921, the percentage of women in the Muslim population, the percentage of the Indian population, and the percentage of Muslims in the total population of Fiji.

The Muslim percentage in the total population increased from nil in 1879, to 4.1 per cent in 1921 to a maximum of about 7.9 per cent in 1970. In the census of 1976, this percentage fell back to 7.7

per cent. This fall in the increase of the Muslim population compared to the total population is due to Muslim emigration which
has become important since 1966. Indeed, about 8,000 Muslims
emigrated from Fiji during the last twenty years, mainly to
Australia, New Zealand, Canada (British Columbia); the United
States (California) and Britain. With their offspring, they form in
these countries a diaspora of no less than 16,000 persons. This
emigration is affecting the Hindus as well, but it seems that pro-
portionally a larger number of Muslims emigrate than do the
Hindus. Indeed, out of an estimated total of 14,000 Indian emigrants from Fiji, there were only about 6,000 Hindus. This Muslim
emigration, although enormous compared to the number of
Muslims, is offset by a high birth rate which is, even in 1976, the
reason for a high proportion of young people in the Muslim population, of which 41 per cent were under the age of fifteen. Recently,
increase of the Muslim population is contributed to by conversion
of Fijian natives as well.

Table 9.3    Evolution of the Muslim population in Fiji

|  | Number of Muslims | Females in Muslim population | Muslims in Indian population | Muslims in total population |
|---|---|---|---|---|
| 1879 | 0 | — | — | — |
| 1921 | 6,435 | 37.9% | 10.6% | 4.1% |
| 1936 | 11,290 | 43.3% | 13.3% | 5.7% |
| 1946 | 16,932 | 46.3% | 14.1% | 6.5% |
| 1956 | 25,394 | 48.8% | 15.0% | 7.3% |
| 1966 | 37,116 | 49.6% | 15.4% | 7.8% |
| 1976 | 45,247 | 49.8% | 15.4% | 7.7% |

At present, most of the Muslims of Fiji are farmers and have
their own sugar cane plantations. Some of them became businessmen in the towns, or active in the professions. All the immigrant
elements have fused to form a Fijian Muslim population of the
Hanafi school and Urdu language but distinctly different from the
Pakistani or Indian Muslims. A small minority is of the Shafii
school.

## Fiji: Organization

Most of the immigrant Muslims were extremely poor and could
not read or write. Like other Indians on arrival in Fiji they were

subjected to a lifeless system, in which human values always mattered less than the drive for production. To this should be added the lack of women leading to the breakdown of moral values; the lack of privacy; non-recognition of Islamic marriages; long hours of work, poor and inadequate diet; and harsh penal regulations for absenteeism. All contributed to a life of virtual slavery and to a complete breakdown of the social system.

In spite of all these circumstances, leaders appeared in the Muslim community who were more educated and more dedicated. The Muslims of Suva were the first to organize themselves around 1910, followed by those of Lautoka; then Labasa in Vanua Levu, then Ba, and Nausori. Each of these local Islamic societies planned to build their mosques, the first mosques being simple wooden structures established around 1922 in Vitogo, Nausori, and Tavua. It should be noted, however, that the Fiji Sugar Milling Company allowed the erection of a wood and iron mosque in 1900 on land they leased to their Muslim workers at Navua. Eventually, by 1930 all Muslim groups were organized locally and established their mosques and Quranic schools.

Already in 1915 the Muslims were trying to organize themselves at the level of all the islands by establishing such associations as Anjuman-e-Hidayat Islam in 1915, Anjuman Ishaat-e-Islam in 1916 and Anjuman-e-Islam in 1919. Although these organizations tried to cater for the Muslim needs for co-ordination and unity, they remained local in their activity and competitive with each other in uniting the Muslims.

The Fiji Muslim League came into existence in 1926 and from the start took positive steps to establish an elected central body to co-ordinate the functions of the various local societies. The Fiji Muslim League was established by the Suva Islamic Society followed quickly by the Islamic Societies of Lautoka, Labasa, Ba, and Nausori. By 1944, the Fiji Muslim League consolidated itself as the representative body of the Muslims of Fiji. Its constitution was rewritten to cater for the new reality. The effort of organization was led by two brothers: Sayyid Hasan and Hasan Hasan as well as Mawlavi Taj Mohammed Khan. The first president of the Fiji Muslim League under this system was Mr Mirza Salim Khan. A new constitution was adopted again in 1957 in which the local organizations became Branch Leagues, thus leading to a more centralized system than that of Australia. The present president is Senator S. M. K. Sherani from Suva. The League has at present nineteen branches as shown in Table 9.4. All the properties of the branches are properties of the League.

Table 9.4  Schools, League branches and Mosques in Fiji, 1978

| Division | League branches | Mosques | Primary schools | Secondary schools | Students |
|---|---|---|---|---|---|
| Central | 5 | 6 | 3 | 2 | 1,600 |
| Western | 13 | 15 | 11 | 3 | 4,810 |
| Northern | 1 | 4 | 2 | 1 | 1,000 |
| Eastern | 0 | 1 | 0 | 0 | 0 |
| Total | 19 | 26 | 16 | 6 | 7,410 |

From the beginning the Fiji Muslim League started a programme of construction of modern schools for Muslim children. The first Muslim primary school was established in 1948 at Lautoka. The first Muslim secondary school was established later in the same town. At present, the Fiji Muslim League manages sixteen primary and six secondary schools and is planning on more schools. Indeed, of the the total 7,410 pupils in the Muslim schools, about 6,200 are Muslim children. This is about only half of the Muslim children of school age, the other half goes to non-Muslim schools and the Fiji Muslim League plans to offer schooling to all Muslim children.

The Fiji Muslim League (FML) is also struggling very hard to finance all Islamic activities. In its education programme it receives some support from the state; otherwise all its activities are financed by donations from the community. These, however, are not sufficient in view of the League's programme of expansion. The other aim of the Fiji Muslim League is to arrange for qualified *imams* in all communities. For this purpose Fiji students were sent to universities in Muslim countries and qualified *imams* were brought from abroad, especially from India. The FML is establishing an *imam* school in the country. It also established the following institutions for treating the different affairs of the community: the board of Islamic affairs; the board of finance and development; the board of education; the Islamic book service; the women's section; the young women's section; the young men's section; Muslim sports association; the family and social welfare; and *The Muslim Voice*, official journal of the FML.

One political problem still nags the Muslim community: it is its present identification as a minority within the Indian 'race'.

Muslims say that they are not a race, that they are a Muslim community of Fiji of diversified ethnic origins. Some of the Muslims request strongly their recognition as a different group from both the Hindus and the Fijian Christians. Although the Muslims of Fiji are on an average poorer than the rest of the population, their unity brought them recognition and respect. Muslims are in the government and in the House of Representatives and the Prophet's birthday is a national holiday in Fiji. The Qadianis have been trying continually to infiltrate among the Muslims since the 1920s. The number of Qadianis is about 3,000 at present. To counteract this danger the FML extended for the first time its contact with the Muslim world in 1973. Indeed, up to then, the only contact with other Muslims was with those of India and Pakistan. These contacts have reached now most of Muslim countries as well as neighbouring Muslim minorities in Australia, New Zealand, and New Caledonia.

## New Zealand

New Zealand was discovered by Tasman for the Europeans in 1642. It was conquered by the British in 1840 C.E. It became then a land of British immigration to the point that the original population has been reduced to a mere 8.4 per cent of the total population of 3,130,000 people in 1982. The country became a fully independent state in 1947, and a member of the British Commonwealth of nations. The total area of the country is 268,675 square kilometres made up of two main islands and a number of smaller ones.

The first Muslim immigrants to New Zealand were Gujarati traders who came on the turn of the century to Auckland, the largest city in the country. Only males came in the beginning and worked as shopkeepers. They later brought their families and established the nucleus of a Muslim community. The most prominent descendants of these first Muslim arrivals are the members of the Bhikoo family who have been active in Islamic organization. By 1950, a new stream of Muslim immigrants was added to the original one. It is mainly made up by Muslims from neighbouring Fiji, but also of Muslims from Albania and Yugoslavia. Most of them settled in Auckland and its area. More recently the capital Wellington has begun to attract some Muslim immigrants, especially the educated and professional ones.

At present (1982) the Muslim population of New Zealand could be estimated at most at 12,000 people, or 0.4 per cent of the total population. However, the census figures are much lower and go as low as a quarter of this figure. The greatest number of Muslims are descendants of the first Gujarati immigrants, but more and more Muslims are immigrating from Fiji. There are also Muslims from Albania and Yugoslavia and a smaller number of Muslims from Turkey, Lebanon and Malaysia. A growing number of Muslims (several hundreds) are converts of European origin (Kiwis). Most of the Muslims are located in the North Island, in Wellington, but especially in Auckland. They are in their majority unskilled or semi-skilled labourers, or small businessmen. More recently, Muslim professionals immigrated in signigicant numbers to New Zealand.

It was in 1952, that the Muslims of New Zealand decided to organize formally for the first time establishing the New Zealand Muslim Association in Auckland. It gathered for many years the Muslim community, acquired a building where Muslims hold their congregational prayers and hired *imams* to come and teach the community. It has also been active in holding week-end classes for children and Islamic education classes for adults. The association purchased a large piece of land on which it plans to build a mosque and Islamic centre. In 1970, a group of Muslims broke away and formed a new association under the name of Anjuman Himayat-e-Islam. In may 1976, Dr Abdullah Al-Zayid, of Muhammad Ibn-Saud University in Riyadh came to Auckland and persuaded the different groups to unite under the New Zealand Muslim Association. Mr Abdul-Samad Bhikoo was elected president. The present president is Mr Abdul-Rasheed, an able lawyer, originally from Fiji. Since the beginning of 1979, the Association went ahead with the construction of its mosque in the Ponsonby area of Auckland where Muslims first settled on the turn of this century, which is now the first and largest mosque in New Zealand.

It was in 1964 when the second Muslim community was organized in New Zealand, the Muslim community of Wellington. The name of the organization is the International Muslim Association of New Zealand. The association is the centre of all the religious activities of the Muslim community in Wellington. It also brings out a small mimeographed newsletter called *IMAN*. The association was established under the leadership of Indonesian and Malaysian students. For many years it was under the able leadership of late Dr Abdul-Majid Khan, Professor of History in

Victoria University, originally from Bangladesh. After the death
of Dr Khan in 1976, the interference of a Muslim embassy went on
on such a large scale that it convinced the community to elect a
second secretary in the consulate of that embassy as president of
the association. He was able to do so by exploiting the naivety of
the community by claiming that he would be able to secure them
financial support for their mosque project. The case of the Muslim
community of Wellington is thus an example to be found in many
capital cities of the unhealthy interference on the part of some
Muslim embassies in the affairs of the Muslim communities motivated by considerations other than the welfare of the local
Muslims. It is only recently that the community is coming out of
this tragic situation and trying to put its activities on the right
track. In 1975, the Association established a cemetery for the
Muslim community, and in December 1978 it acquired a building
in the Newton part of Wellington which it uses as its Islamic
centre.

In 1970, the Muslims in Palmerston North in the Northern
Island organized themselves into Manawatu Muslim Association
with Haji Mohammed Sharief as the first president. The Muslims
in this city are still meeting in homes for their religious activity, but
they are planning to acquire a centre as well.

In 1980, the Waikato-Bay of Plenty Muslim Association was
established in Hamilton where about a hundred Muslims live, and
where some have been present since the 1960s. But they started
their regular prayers only in 1975. The Association meets at
present in homes and their main project is to establish an Islamic
centre.

Immigration to the Southern Island started in 1918 from Gujrat,
especially toward Christchurch, where the Ismail family can be
considered among the first settlers. However, it was only on 5
September 1976 that the Muslims of Christchurch gathered in a
large meeting and formed the Canterbury Muslim Association
with Mr Solayman Ismail as its first president. This association is
now building its mosque, the second of New Zealand. It is turning
out to be the third largest Muslim community in the country.

Other Muslim communities in the South Island are being
formed in Dunedin and other towns.

In April 1979, the organized Muslim communities of New
Zealand (later joined by the fifth) united under the Federation of
Islamic Associations of New Zealand (FIANZ) whose first acting
president was Mr Mazhar Krashigi, a respected Auckland busi-

nessman of Albanian origin. FIANZ developed in an effective co-ordinating body of all the Muslims of New Zealand.

## New Caledonia

New Caledonia is situated between Fiji and Australia. It has a total area of 19,103 square kilometres made up by a large island and several smaller ones including l'Ile des Pins. The territory has the status of a French Overseas Territory. Since January 1976, the state affairs are administered by the High Commissioner and the territorial affairs by a Council of Government of seven elected members. A Territorial Assembly of Thirty-five elected members decides on the important territorial affairs. The territory is represented in the French National Assembly and the Senate by two deputies and two senators.

The total population of the territory was about 140,000 people in 1982. Of this total about 38 per cent were European, mainly French, 48 per cent were local people, mainly Melanesian, but also Polynesian and the remaining 14 per cent were of diversified origins including Vietnamese and Indonesians.

New Caledonia was conquered by the French in 1853. By a decree of 2 September 1863, it was designated by the French government as a territory where penal settlements for hard labour could be established. On 9 May 1864 the first boat carrying condemned men arrived at Noumea with 248 prisoners. Meanwhile, France was in the middle of its war of occupation of Algeria. The first Muslims who were sent to l'Ile des Pins, the penal settlement of New Caledonia, were prisoners of war caught after the collapse of the revolt of Bachagha Mokrani in the Kabyle Mountains of Algeria in 1871. The Muslim prisoners arrived in New Caledonia in 1872, among them were Mokrani, the brother of the Bachagha, and Aziz, one of the tribal leaders.

The first Muslims led a difficult life and tried to keep the teachings of their religion alive. They raised goats to avoid eating pork until 3 November 1874 when the administration of the penitentiary decided by special decree to take account of their religious prohibitions of food. Other Muslim freedom fighters followed the first batch of Algerians as France conquered more Muslim lands. These were Moroccans, Tunisians, and Somalis. Among the freedom fighters there were also some Muslim condemned men banished for a multitude of common law crimes. Banishment was abolished in 1891.

The descendants of these first Muslims eventually emigrated to the main island of New Caledonia where they established communities at Noumea, Bourail and Koumac in the north. They became particularly numerous at Bourail where they settled as farmers. They had their Muslim cemetery at the village of Nessadiou, which has been recently restored due to the efforts of one of the leaders of the Muslims of Bourail, Mr Abdelkader Bouanane. At the turn of the century a new wave of Muslim immigrants arrived from Indonesia. These Muslims settled all over the Island, but they are especially numerous in Kone. After the 1950s, yet another wave arrived from the former French colonies, especially Djibouti, due to the growth of the nickel industry. In 1982, the number of Muslims must have reached about 14,000, or 10 per cent of the total population of the island. Some estimate that as many as 40,000 people are partly of Muslim origin (i.e., 28 per cent of the total population), but most of them do not identify as Muslims any more. Most Muslims are citizens and the majority are financially poor.

The Muslims of New Caledonia organized themselves for the first time on 27 January 1970 by establishing the Association des Arabes et Amis des Arabes de Nouvelle Caledonie et Dependances (Arab and Arab Friends Association of New Caledonia and Dependencies). To the Muslims of New Caledonia, just as to the Muslims of North Africa the word Arab is synonymous to Muslim. On 19 August 1975 the Association des Musulmans de Nouvelle Caledonie (Association of the Muslims of New Caledonia) was established.

The new association started a programme of revival of Islamic institutions and practices. Friday prayers were held in homes where Islamic education is also given to children. The first president of the association was Mr Abdou Mohammed Ragheh, other leaders were Mr Moussa Hadj Bock (of Somali origin) and Mr Mohammed Salaheddine Belleili (of Algerian origin). The association tried very hard to establish contact with the rest of the Muslim *ummah*. First contact was established after a New Caledonian Muslim delegation visited the Fiji Muslims on 28 October 1978. It obtained financial help from Fiji Muslim League for the establishment of the first mosque in Noumea. On 11 November 1978, the Muslim Association bought a piece of land in the quarter of Noumea called Vallee des Colons. The land had a total area of about 1170 square metres on which two old houses were built. These houses are used as a temporary Islamic centre. On 20

January 1979, a provisional Mosque Committee was established, the most important project of the Muslim community being the establishment of its mosque in Noumea. Later two teachers were sent to the Muslim community, one Tunisian from Rabitah of Mecca and one Cambodian from Dawah Organisation of Libya. The Muslims of New Caledonia have been struggling for eighteen years now to establish their mosque. They looked for help from French authorities as well as local authorities, but they got nowhere. They even feel that some local authorities in Noumea still live in the old atmosphere of anti-Islamic fanaticism and do not treat them in the same way as they treat other religious bodies.

Unfortunately, their struggle for survival has been greatly weakened by divisions between old immigration and new immigration and Indonesians, Arabs and Somalis.

## Other Countries

Of the other territories of the Pacific, Papua New Guinea is the most important and largest entity. Administered by Australia, the territory became an independent state in 1973. It has a total area of 475,300 square kilometres and had a population of 3,390,000 in 1982. Its proximity with Indonesia, a Muslim country, with which it shares a long border, favoured Muslim immigration. However, the Muslims remained small in number and scattered. Their number would not be larger than about 500. In 1978, they established for the first time the Islamic Society of Papua New Guinea (ISPANG) with two branches, one in Lae, and the other in Port Moresby; thus making the Muslim community of Papua New Guinea the fifth after Australia, Fiji, New Zealand and New Caledonia to be organized in the Pacific.

Solomon Islands bacame an independent state in 1978 after eight-five years of British rule. It has an area of 29,785 square kilometres and had a population of 250,000 in 1982. It has a small Muslim population in its capital Homara. This community is in contact with the Muslims of Papua New Guinea, but it is not yet organized.

Western Samoa became independent in 1962. It has a total area of 2,842 square kilometres and had a population of 165,000 people in 1982. There are several hundred Muslims in the country but no Muslim organization yet.

French Polynesia has the status of an overseas territory of

France. Its total area is 2,520 square kilometres and its population amounted to 165,000 people in 1982. The most important island in the group is Tahiti. There are several hundred Muslims in this territory but they are not organized.

Vanuatu became independent in 1980. It has an area of 14,760 square kilometres and a population of 125,000 people. They have a small Muslim population which is in contact with the Muslims of Papua New Guinea and those of New Caledonia. There is no Muslim organization yet.

The US Trust Territory of the Pacific Islands has a total area of 1,813 square kilometres made up of several thousand islands and had a population of 120,000 in 1982. There are Muslims but they are not organized.

Guam is an unincorporated territory of the US. It has an area of 450 square kilometres and had a population of 110,000 in 1982. There are many Muslims including those of Malay origin, but they are not organized.

Tonga Kingdom became independent in 1970. It has an area of 754 square kilometres and a population of 103,000 in 1982. Scores of Tongans became Muslims in Fiji and a community was organized in 1984 in this Kingdom.

The other territories of the Pacific had a total population of 112,000 people in 1982. Few among them are Muslims and no Islamic organization is known to exist among these groups.

## Conclusions

The Muslim community in the Pacific can be divided into two categories: an old immigration; and a new immigration. The old immigration succeeded in establishing a viable, living and dynamic community in Fiji but failed in Australia. The new immigration brought life and dynamism to the Muslim community of Australia and through Australia to the entire Pacific. Activity designed to retrieve the elements of the old immigration in the Pacific already started and the signs are those of great hope.

Muslims have organized themselves in six states of the Pacific: Australia, Fiji, New Zealand, New Caledonia, Tonga and Papua New Guinea. Efforts to organize Muslim communities in at least three other states in the area are also afoot. The most advanced community in terms of organization is that of Fiji under the Fiji Muslim League which should be commended for its efforts, especially in the field of education. Next is the Muslim community of Australia under the Australian Federation of Islamic Councils. But the latter is still beset by poor leadership. If, however, it succeeds in establishing full time Muslim schools, the way Fiji did, and combine every mosque with a community centre and primary and secondary schools, then Islam in Australia would have a serious chance of survival and growth.

During the last four years, mutual consultation and help between the six organized communities started. It culminated in 1980 in the formation of The Regional Islamic Council for South East Asia and the Pacific (RISEAP), with headquarters in Malaysia. Such a council helped to pool experience and support. In 1984 the six organized Communities for the Islamic Council of the South Pacific, with headquarters in Suva (Fiji).

The advantage of the new Islamic organizational set-up of the Muslim community of the Pacific is due to the fact that it is based on institutions and not on charismatic leadership of individuals. The result could be lasting and go beyond the short life-span of any single individual. The test of success remains of course the ability of the immigrant generation to pass on smoothly the leadership of the community to the next locally-born generation. This test has been passed in Fiji already.

The freedom of religion applied to Muslims is a new and welcome phenomenon in the Pacific. In the past, Christian religious imperialism left no room for Islamic survival, especially in Australia. At present this imperialism is a story of the past and Muslims are treated with complete equality with other religious groups. This is especially true of Australia and Fiji but also in the other states of the region with the possible temporary exception of Papua New Guinea, where Muslims had in the beginning difficulty in obtaining their religious rights. The only danger remains from groups within the Muslim community who are ignorant of the true spirit of Islam. There is also a danger to the community from other groups who masquerade as Muslims and who are not. These people take advantage of the ignorance prevalent among Muslims to confuse them. These do much harm to the Muslim community from within for they join it on the pretence of being Muslims, even though they have no love or allegiance to it whatsoever.

Finally, an important body of publications has begun to be put out by the Muslims in order to develop better awareness of their own community and to articulate their viewpoint. Prominent among them are the *Australian Minaret*, the official magazine of the Australian Federation of Islamic Councils, and the *Muslim Voice*, the official organ of the Fiji Muslim League. Most community societies and student organizations have their own magazines and newsletters.

## References

Muslim magazines in the Pacific.
Reports of fact-finding missions from different Islamic organizations.
1. M. Allum, *Islam in Australia* (Adelaide, 1932).
2. T. L. McNight, *The Camel in Australia* (Melbourne, Victoria, 1969).
3. M. A. Wang, *Future of Islam in Australia* Cultural Studies Conference, Goulburn College of Advanced Education (Goulburn, NSW, Australia, December 1975).
4. K. Telsch, 'Political Turmoil Upsets Tiny Cocos' *New York Times* (New York, 8 August, 1976) (English).
5. Q. A. Ahmad, 'The AFIC President's Speech' *Muslim World League Journal*, IV, No. 3 (Mecca, January 1977).
6. H. M. Z. Faruque, 'Islam in Australia' *Islamic Herald*, II, No. 9 (Kuala Lumpur, January 1977).
7. M. Ilyas, 'To Put Always in Remembrance' *Impact International* (25 November–8 December and 9–22 December 1977).
8. J. O'Brien, 'The Growing Faith of Islam' *Australia Today*, IV (1977).

# 10 Conclusions

## Number of Muslims in the World Today

It is now possible to draw a table of the number of Muslims around the world including regions where they live in the majority or minority. Muslim majority is defined as those Muslims who live in those countries which define themselves as Muslim by being members of the Organization of the Islamic Conference, whose permanent secretariat is in Jeddah, Saudi Arabia. Table 10.1 gives the Muslim population figures of these forty-five states which are located in Africa (twenty-three), Asia (twenty-one) and Europe (one state), as well as the numerical percentages of Muslims in these states. The total population in these states amounted in 1982 to 715,120,000 people of which 636,720,000 are Muslims (89%). Of these, 181,155,000 are residents of the twenty-two members of the Arab League (167,340,000 Muslims or 92.4 per cent of total population). Thus, the Arab Muslims make up about 26.3 per cent of the total number of Muslims living in states which define themselves as Muslim states.

*Table 10.1* Muslim States, 1982 (* Arab States)

| State | Continent | Population in thousands | | |
|---|---|---|---|---|
| | | Total | Muslim | |
| 1. Indonesia | Asia | 157,230 | 141,500 | 90% |
| 2. Pakistan | Asia | 91,580 | 88,830 | 97% |
| 3. Bangladesh | Asia | 95,710 | 81,350 | 85% |
| 4. Turkey | Asia/Europe | 47,920 | 47,440 | 99% |
| 5. Egypt* | Africa | 44,370 | 40,820 | 92% |
| 6. Iran | Asia | 40,619 | 39,760 | 99% |
| 7. Morocco* | Africa | 22,230 | 22,000 | 99% |

*Table 10.1*   Muslim States, 1982 (* Arab States)
*Continued*

| State | Continent | Total | Muslim | |
|---|---|---|---|---|
| | | Population in thousands | | |
| 8. Algeria* | Africa | 19,920 | 19,720 | 99% |
| 9. Sudan* | Africa | 20,320 | 17,280 | 90% |
| 10. Afghanistan | Asia | 15,740 | 15,740 | 100% |
| 11. Iraq* | Asia | 14,270 | 13,840 | 97% |
| 12. Saudi Arabia* | Asia | 10,980 | 10,430 | 95% |
| 13. Syria* | Asia | 10,700 | 9,100 | 85% |
| 14. Malaysia | Asia | 14,760 | 7,970 | 54% |
| 15. Tunisia* | Africa | 6,760 | 6,690 | 99% |
| 16. Mali | Africa | 7,100 | 6,390 | 90% |
| 17. Uganda | Africa | 14,550 | 5,820 | 40% |
| 18. North Yemen* | Asia | 5,420 | 5,420 | 100% |
| 19. Senegal | Africa | 5,960 | 5,360 | 90% |
| 20. Cameroon | Africa | 8,930 | 5,350 | 60% |
| 21. Niger | Africa | 5,760 | 5,190 | 90% |
| 22. Guinea | Africa | 5,750 | 4,880 | 85% |
| 23. Burkina Faso | Africa | 7,160 | 4,300 | 60% |
| 24. Chad | Africa | 4,810 | 3,850 | 80% |
| 25. Somalia* | Africa | 3,800 | 3,800 | 100% |
| 26. Libya* | Africa | 3,210 | 3,180 | 99% |
| 27. Jordan* | Asia | 2,840 | 2,700 | 95% |
| 28. Palestine* | Asia | 5,300 | 2,330 | 44% |
| 29. Sierra Leone | Africa | 3,540 | 2,210 | 60% |
| 30. South Yemen* | Asia | 2,040 | 2,040 | 100% |
| 31. Lebanon* | Asia | 3,080 | 2,000 | 65% |
| 32. Mauritania* | Africa | 1,660 | 1,660 | 100% |
| 33. Benin | Africa | 3,700 | 1,480 | 40% |
| 34. Kuwait* | Asia | 1,590 | 1,430 | 90% |
| 35. Oman* | Asia | 940 | 930 | 99% |
| 36. United Arab Emirates* | Asia | 1,020 | 920 | 90% |
| 37. Gambia | Africa | 640 | 625 | 98% |
| 38. Djibouti* | Africa | 500 | 500 | 100% |
| 39. Guinea-Bissau | Africa | 670 | 470 | 70% |
| 40. Comoros | Africa | 390 | 388 | 99% |
| 41. Bahrain* | Asia | 370 | 330 | 90% |
| 42. Qatar* | Asia | 230 | 220 | 95% |
| 43. Maldives | Asia | 160 | 160 | 100% |
| 44. Brunei | Asia | 230 | 160 | 70% |
| 45. Gabon | Africa | 670 | 67 | 10% |
| Total | | 715,120 | 636,720 | 89% |

*Table 10.2*    Muslim minorities in the world, 1982

| Country | Continent | Muslim population *thousands* | |
|---|---|---:|---:|
| 1. China | Asia | 107,000 | 10.5% |
| 2. India | Asia | 84,700 | 12.0% |
| 3. Nigeria | Africa | 54,860 | 60.0% |
| 4. Soviet Union | Europe/Asia | 47,330 | 17.8% |
| 5. Ethiopia | Africa | 20,460 | 60.0% |
| 6. Tanzania | Africa | 10,410 | 55.0% |
| 7. Philippines | Asia | 6,250 | 12.2% |
| 8. Thailand | Asia | 6,000 | 12.0% |
| 9. Kenya | Africa | 5,330 | 30.0% |
| 10. Mozambique | Africa | 4,920 | 45.0% |
| 11. Yugoslavia | Europe | 4,225 | 21.5% |
| 12. Ghana | Africa | 4,240 | 33.0% |
| 13. Burma | Asia | 3,560 | 10.7% |
| 14. Ivory Coast | Africa | 3,000 | 35.0% |
| 15. United States | America | 3,000 | 1.3% |
| 16. Zaire | Africa | 2,800 | 9.0% |
| 17. Malawi | Africa | 2,550 | 40.0% |
| 18. France | Europe | 2,500 | 4.6% |
| 19. Albania | Europe | 2,110 | 75.0% |
| 20. West Germany | Europe | 1,800 | 2.9% |
| 21. Bulgaria | Europe | 1,700 | 19.3% |
| 22. United Kingdom | Europe | 1,250 | 2.2% |
| 23. Sri Lanka | Asia | 1,168 | 7.6% |
| 24. Centrafrican E | Africa | 980 | 40.0% |
| 25. Madagascar | Africa | 890 | 10.0% |
| 26. Liberia | Africa | 880 | 45.0% |
| 27. Zambia | Africa | 740 | 12.0% |
| 28. Togo | Africa | 670 | 25.0% |
| 29. Nepal | Asia | 500 | 3.2% |
| 30. South Africa | Africa | 510 | 1.7% |
| 31. Singapore | Asia | 420 | 17.0% |
| 32. Argentina | America | 400 | 1.4% |
| 33. Netherlands | Europe | 400 | 2.8% |
| 34. Rwanda | Africa | 380 | 7.0% |
| 35. Brazil | America | 380 | 0.3% |
| 36. Belgium | Europe | 350 | 3.6% |
| 37. Cambodia | Asia | 335 | 6.0% |
| 38. Outer Mongolia | Asia | 260 | 15.0% |
| 39. Burundi | Africa | 230 | 5.0% |
| 40. Australia | Oceania | 170 | 1.1% |
| 41. Mauritius | Africa | 162 | 20.0% |

*Table 10.2*   Muslim minorities in the world, 1982
*Continued*

| Country | Continent | Muslim population thousands | |
|---|---|---|---|
| 42. Trinidad & Tobago | America | 160 | 13.0% |
| 43. Greece | Europe | 160 | 1.6% |
| 44. Cyprus | Europe | 155 | 24.4% |
| 45. Surinam | America | 150 | 35.0% |
| 46. Guyana | America | 130 | 15.0% |
| 47. Spain | Europe | 120 | 0.3% |
| 48. Canada | America | 120 | 0.2% |
| 49. Italy | Europe | 120 | 0.5% |
| Other | | 1,272 | |
| Total | | 392,707 | 11.6% |

*Table 10.3*   Muslims in the world, 1982

| Continent | Muslims in the world in thousands | | |
|---|---|---|---|
| | *Majorities* | *Minorities* | *Total* |
| Asia | 468,600 | 239,362 | 707,962 |
| Africa | 162,120 | 114,200 | 276,320 |
| Europe | 6,000 | 34,285 | 40,285 |
| America | | 4,600 | 4,600 |
| Oceania | | 260 | 260 |
| Total | 636,720 | 392,707 | 1,029,427 |

Table 10.2 lists the countries with Muslim minorities exceeding 100,000, with their Muslim population and Muslim percentage. There are forty-nine such countries, of which eighteen are in Africa, eleven in Asia, thirteen in Europe, seven in America and one in Oceania. The total number of Muslims in states where they are in the minority amounted to about 392,707,000 people in 1982. Thus, the total number of Muslims in the world was about 1,029,427,000 in 1982. Minorities make up 38.1 per cent of the total number of Muslims on Earth and Arab Muslims form about 16.3 per cent of the Muslim total. Muslims account for about 25 per cent of the world's population.

Table 10.3 shows the Muslim distribution by continent: 68.3 per cent of all Muslims live in Asia, 27.4 per cent live in Africa and the remaining 4.3 per cent live elsewhere. See Figure 5.

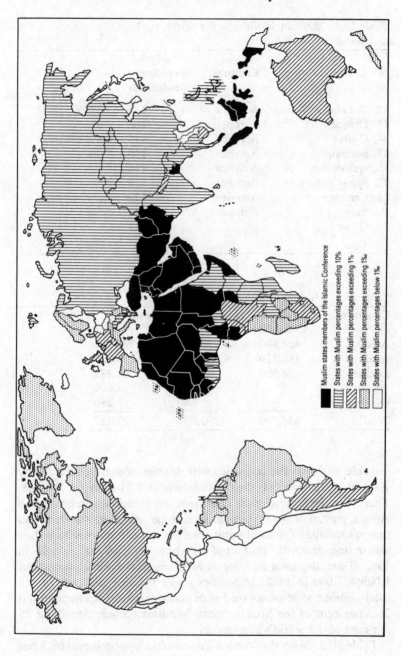

Muslim states members of the Islamic Conference

States with Muslim percentages exceeding 10%

States with Muslim percentages exceeding 1%

States with Muslim percentages exceeding 1‰

States with Muslim percentages below 1‰

Ten Muslim groups form 71.3 per cent of the Muslim population of the world. These are by order of numbers: Indonesia, China, Pakistan, India, Bangladesh, Nigeria, Turkey, Soviet Union, Egypt and Iran. Of the ten, four are Muslim minorities (China, India, Nigeria and Soviet Union) which have a total population of nearly 294 million or about 75 per cent of the total population of Muslims in minority areas. The six Muslim countries include a total Muslim population of about 440 million or 69 per cent of the total population of Muslims in majority areas.

The above tables thus show that Muslims are present in all the countries of the world, that the minorities are of immense numerical importance for the Muslim *ummah*, and that Muslim majorities are as much split in a number of small states as are the minorities. The rate of increase of Muslims is about 3 per cent a year, i.e. every year about thirty million Muslims will be added to the total.

## Role of Muslim Minorities

The basic problem of the Muslims in the world today is that they have no overall organization which might bring them together, adequately express their feelings and aspirations, safeguard their rights and interests, etc. In regard to the Muslims, this is a new situation which has emerged during the last century of Muslim decadence and subjection. Many of the present Muslim minorities were in fact once Muslim states which were forcibly incorporated into non-Muslim entities and are therefore the victims of a subjugation under which the whole Muslim *ummah* suffered and is still suffering in many ways. From the earliest days of Islam to the onset of European colonization about two centuries ago, Muslim unity remained a reality. This is evident from the fact that the Caliphs of Baghdad, then of Cairo and then of Istanbul were not only the temporal and spiritual leaders for the territories which were under their control but also the spiritual leaders of all the Muslims of the world, irrespective of whether they lived as minorities or as majorities.

However, there is no 'papacy' in Islam nor is there any 'clergy', in the sense that no person whoever he may be has the right to pronounce arbitrarily or to act on God's behalf, or to introduce of his own volition any laws on his own authority. A Muslim's relation is directly with God (since there is no priesthood). Muslims do not recognize the authority of an organized church or ordained clerical hierarchy. They rather recognize the authority of the *Quran* and the *Sunnah* of the Prophet. All Muslims are equal in the sight of God, and hence none has the right to make law. Deference is shown only to knowledge and piety, not to hereditary privileges, or 'inherent' spirituality, etc. Furthermore, Muslims are required to stand up to their responsibilities when the need arises and it is stressed that there is no intermediary between God and any person. Thus, the abolition of the *khilafah* by anti-Muslim forces in the 1920s as tragic as it is in principle to Muslims, was no more than the abolition of a regime that was already dead and could in no way have the same effect on the Muslims which could have occurred on the Catholics if the papacy of Rome were abolished.

The real unity of Muslims lies in their attachment to the *Quran* and the *Sunnah* which serve as the rallying point for all Muslims. Muslims around the world feel like one single brotherhood headed by the Prophet himself through his life style (*Sunnah*) and directives (*Hadith*) which serve to elaborate and supplement the *Holy Quran*, embodying the word of God. Muslim states can be established or destroyed, Muslim organizations can be formed or dismantled, but new states are always rebuilt on the ashes of the crumbled ones and new organizations are always formed in one form or another. The secret of this feat of survival is the fact that Islam builds up the individual as a responsible person and builds up his attachment to God Almighty directly without any intermediaries. Islam is not attached to any piece of land. It embraces the whole world. Nor are Muslims attached to any given individual. They follow at a given time the person who proves to be the best Muslim leader and will follow him as long as he remains so.

These are the assets for the survival of Muslim minorities. What are, then, the challenges which occasionally make some Muslim minorities vanish? In this book the story of Muslim minorities is narrated as a long, continuous, and glorious epic of struggle for survival against the most heavy odds. In this rather than in the Muslim military achievements of one period of history or another should be seen the greatness of Islam. The odds can be divided into three categories: ignorance; weak allegiance to Islam; and lack of inner cohesion.

The worst enemy of the Muslim minorities is ignorance, especially ignorance of the true teachings of Islam. This constitutes the basic cause for the disappearance of the Muslim body-politic in

many non-Muslim lands. Ignorance of the basic rules of organization can have also the most damaging effects on the Muslims,
leaving every one to fend for himself with his own limited abilities.
Ignorance in general would also keep the entire Muslim community within the lowest strata of the population.

A true Muslim should make sure that his Islamic identity is one
and encompasses all other identities: his family; his tribe; his
national origin; his race; his occupation; his level of wealth. All of
these considerations should be irrelevant in his dealing with other
Muslims. All Muslims are equal under God. None is better than
any other, except by his effort to be a better Muslim. Tribalism or
nationalism are, therefore, the worst enemies of Islam since they
break up the Muslim *ummah* along lines that are Islamically
irrelevant, let alone are highly destructive. In Muslim minority
areas, we see that Muslims spontaneously gather together independently of their other differences in order to build up one
Muslim community composed of individuals who might have come
to Islam following different routes. Any effort to undermine this
enterprise is essentially an effort that would destroy the Muslim
community.

It often happens that when Muslims emigrate from one land to
another they keep a strong memory of their country of origin. This
memory is essentially good and can be a source of strength to the
Muslim minority if it helps maintain contacts with the rest of the
Muslim *ummah*. However, if the immigrants constantly keep on
thinking of returning to their countries of origin, and refuse to
contribute to the building up of the Muslim community where they
happen to live on the plea that their stay is temporary, they will
discover not before long that they have lost their country of origin
as well as the possibility of a full-blooded Islamic life in their
country of adoption. Worse than that, they would lose their own
children to whom they did not offer enough time to educate them
against the forces of assimilation.

The role of Muslim minorities is to be the representatives of the
Muslim *ummah* in their respective countries. In order to do so they
should organize themselves as a Muslim community. The organization itself is no more than a container. The container is indispensable. It should be a good one. But what matters is the thing to
be contained. The thing is Islamic education. The entire survival of
the Muslim *ummah* is based on that education: education in the
spirit of Islam; education in the meaning of the *Quran*; education
about the *Sunnah* of the Prophet; education about the techniques

of advancement in this world as well as salvation in the hereafter. The role of the organized Muslim minority is to keep contact with all the Muslim communities of the world whether the majority or minority and thus be like one brick in the building that forms the Muslim *ummah*.

## Role of Muslim Majorities

Muslim states have a continuous tradition of defending the right of Muslim minorities and supporting them whenever they are in need of support. It is only with the fall of the different Muslim majorities as prey to European colonialism that the Muslim minorities were left on their own to fend for themselves. As soon as the Muslim states gained their independence, they concerned themselves with the plight of the different Muslim groups around the world. This concern, however, has not necessarily been translated into terms of effective help. No overall philosophy of dealing with Muslim minorities has been developed. The result is too little action, and often that too has been more harmful than useful. This action comes often through diplomatic missions, for the establishment of Islamic centres; by sending *imams*; or by offering financial support. A look at each one of these items would shed some light on their shortcomings.

Many Muslim countries try to help the minorities through their embassies. This should be avoided under all circumstances for many reasons among which is that even if the Muslim legations represented the best example of Muslim behaviour, linking Muslim minorities to them would be most damaging to the minorities. Indeed, they might be looked at by their non-Muslim compatriots as a foreign body in their midst. The relationship between Muslim countries and Muslim minorities should be of a cultural, religious and economical, rather than a political nature. The worst happens when the Muslim ambassadors in a given country establish themselves as an 'Islamic Council' which claims to represent the Muslim minority, decide in its name whatever they wish, each one following the policy of his own country. Such action undermines the minority at the roots and destroys its potential of growth and organization.

Many Muslim countries concentrate their action on establishing 'Islamic Centres' under a 'Mosque Committee' made up by Muslim ambassadors. Often these projects are a colossal waste of money and energy, and when brought into existence are in fact of no help to the minority. Among the most successful, the Islamic Centre of Washington, DC, is at best a nice piece of Islamic architecture. The mosque is not controlled by the Muslim community of Washington DC, nor does it play any role in improving the lot of the Muslims in that city. It is in fact an embassy like many others. The story of the Islamic Centre of Rome is, if anything, more heart-breaking. After World War II, a Muslim community came into being by immigration from Eastern Europe and established 'The Muslim Union in the West'. In 1966 the Muslim embassies established 'The Islamic Centre' which gathered all the attention of their countries on a huge, expensive 'foreign' project. The Muslim community was pushed aside, demoralized, and at the end it is now disorganized. Mosques, schools and Islamic centres should be at the service of the communities and under their control. Those Muslim countries who wish to help the Muslim minorities should help the organized communities establish their institutions. Islamic centres under 'diplomatic missions' might help the personnel of the missions but are not of much use to the Muslim communities.

Each community should have an *imam* who should be well versed with the principles of Islam. He should be the teacher of the community and its leader in all *ibadat*. He should be its spokesman in all its religious affairs. Several Muslim countries realized such a need and sent *imams* to different communities around the world. Some of the *imams* were outstanding examples of dedication and self-denying sincerity. Others had no commitment to the communities they served and created more problems than they solved. Muslim majorities should, therefore, help the communities train their own *imams*, choose their own *imams* and finance their own *imams* without any outside interference.

Financial help can be useful if given to an organized community for a viable project which, in the end, would help the community stand on its own feet. Before extending any financial help to any community, full knowledge of its situation is necessary. It is unfortunate that sometimes help is given to splinter groups, non-representative individuals or for false causes, leading to a situation which is worse than that occurring before the availability of that help. Worse, help was given to institutions such as 'Islamic Departments' in some Western universities which was used in anti-Islamic activities under the cover of 'academic freedom'. Still worse, often Muslim countries help Muslim victims of natural or man-made disasters through international organizations which often pass it on to apparent welfare organizations which are, in fact, in the hands of Christian missions. These often use the money to further their prestige and missionary activity. It is therefore necessary that financial support should be given only to those Muslim communities which are organized and capable of using it through their representative bodies. The help should be tailored in such a way as to enhance the independence of the community as soon as possible from any further help. Any aid to a Muslim group should be given to the Muslims themselves or through another Muslim group.

Furthermore, in their dealings with other countries in the world, the Muslim countries should bear in mind the attitude of such countries toward Islam and Muslims. Only those countries treating their Muslim populations correctly should be considered as friendly nations.

## Basic Tenets of Islam

The basic word in defining Islam is unity. First of all comes the unity of God. God is one, the creator of the universe. He is infinite in space and in time. He was always and will be for ever. He is omnipotent, omnipresent and all-knowing, His love is unlimited and so is His power. The verses describing God in the *Quran* are of a great beauty and have an overwhelmingly convincing power. If God is one and unique, He can have no partners nor can He have parents or sons. Talking about the 'son of God' in Islam is the worst of all blasphemies. The following chapter of the *Quran* is memorized by every Muslim in the world from a tender age: 'Say that God is one, God is self-sufficient, He was not begotten, nor has He begotten, and none is an equal to Him' (Chapter 112).

If God is one, humanity is one as well. All humans are descendants of the same ancestors, Adam and Eve, both of whom were created by God. Differences in colour, language and ancestry are all completely irrelevant. There can be no chosen nation in Islam, or chosen people, or better or lower race. The *Quran* says: 'O mankind! We created you from a single pair of male and a female and made you into nations and tribes, that you may identify each other; the best amongst you in the sight of God is he who is the most righteous of you. And God is all-knowing well-acquainted' (Chapter 49, Verse 13). The Prophet Muhammad translated this into terms of reality by denying the validity of all caste and tribal differences among Muslims. Thus, it is up to the individual to improve himself. And as Umar, the second Caliph said: 'How dare you enslave a people the while their mothers had brought them to this world free?'.

God created man for a purpose. The purpose is to worship God. This life is an abode of trial to prepare for the hereafter which is the abode of eternity. Every individual will be judged for his deeds during the term of his earthly life. For man is responsible and has been created with the capacity to choose between right and wrong. God, however, does make available His guidance through His messengers.

If God is one, man is one too. Likewise God's message is also one and the same. By definition, anyone with whom God has communicated is a prophet; anyone whom God has ordered to deliver a message is a messenger. In the early history of mankind God sent messengers to every nation on the earth to deliver the same message of worship to the One True God. For instance, Moses, and Jesus were messengers sent to Banu Israil at two different periods of time. Muhammad was the first and last messenger sent to all humanity. He was the first because such a universal message was not possible before him due to the early stage of development of the human species. He was the last because through him the message was completed. The last verse in the *Quran* proclaims: 'This day have I perfected your religion for you, completed My favour upon you, and I have chosen for you Islam as your religion' (Chapter 5, Verse 4).

The messages of God to humanity through the messengers are oral as well as written. Written messages to all prophets before Muhammad have been distorted or lost. Only *Quran* preserves the true word of God. Translations can in no way compare with, let alone replace the original; they are mere interpretations and Muslims are urged to learn Arabic to understand the message of God directly in the language in which it was revealed.

Since God sent His message through the prophets and mess-engers to all humanity directly, and without investing anyone with any special sacredotal authority or privilege, there could be no intermediaries between man and God. As such there is no clergy in Islam. Some persons in the Muslim society might be more knowledgeable in one field and some in others. They are urged to communicate their knowledge to others. Their knowledge is highly respected but their role may in no way be the one of law-givers or of intermediaries between man and God.

The Islamic concept of unity encompasses also unity of man's personality. This personality cannot be divided between temporal and spiritual without such dichotomy creating a high degree of hypocrisy in the society. The temporal and spiritual are only two facets of one single aspect. Man should, in all that he does and says in his private or family life, and in the society obey the word of God. There is no concept of 'separation between the state and the church' in Islam. Thus when the word 'religion' is applied to Islam it should not be understood in the meaning given to it in the West. Islam is more than a faith, it is a social and political order as well.

## The Concept of Unity in Islam

In all the teachings of Islam the stress is on strengthening the feeling of togetherness and unity among all those who belong to Islam, independently of anything else. The Prophet said that 'Islam is built on five pillars. One: witnessing that there is no god but God, that Muhammad is the Messenger of God. Two: observing the prayers (*salat*). Three: giving alms (*zakat*). Four: fasting in Ramadan. Five: performing the *hajj* (once in a lifetime) for those who are able'. In another tradition a sixth pillar is considered important, and that is 'struggle in the way of God'.

Each of these 'pillars' has a social value of bridging the gaps of unity between all Muslims. The belief in 'the One True God and in His Messenger Muhammad' is basic and is the condition of entering the brotherhood of the Muslim *ummah*. A non-Muslim, by declaring such a belief, has automatically to be accepted by other Muslims as one them as long as he does not behave in a manner which flagrantly negates this belief. Other Muslims are requested to judge him by his acts whereas God alone can judge what is in his heart. A person who 'believes that there is One True God and that Muhammad is His messenger to all mankind' is a Muslim even if he does not perform any other act. In that case he is, of course, a grave sinner and is liable to God's punishment on the day of judgement, but he is still a member of the Muslim community and Muslims are required to treat him with brotherly love to bring him back to the right path. Moreover, there is a great hope for him compared to the non-believers. God says in the *Quran* 'God forgiveth not that partners should be set up with Him; but He forgiveth anything else to whom He pleaseth; to set up partners with God is to commit a sin most heinous indeed' (Chapter 4, Verse 48).

The most important act after the declaration of belief is prayer. A Muslim is requested to pray to God all the time by remembering Him in all his acts and in all his actions, including the most trivial ones. In these prayers he can communicate directly with God in the manner he wishes and he can use the language he wishes. But five times a day a Muslim should pray in a specific manner, with a strict order and discipline. At these five fixed times (*fajr, zuhr, asr, maghrib* and *isha*) all Muslims of the world turn to one single focal point, the Kaabah which is the mosque built by Ibrahim, the messenger of God, in the city of Mecca. This turning toward one single direction gives a symbolic unity of the greatest importance. A Muslim may pray alone only if there are no other Muslims near him; otherwise prayer is a social act which should be performed in common and in a disciplined order. Whenever there is more than one person praying, an *imam* should be chosen among the faithful to be the leader in prayer. At home, a Muslim is requested to pray with his wife and children. He is requested, however, to make an effort to pray at the five times with his neighbours as well (in a local mosque if possible) so as to strengthen the feeling of unity between all the Muslim neighbours.

Once a week, on Friday, all the Muslims of a quarter in a city or in a rural district should pray the mid-day prayer in one mosque together. Before that prayer, the *imam* gives two sermons relevant to the problems of the community. This common prayer is meant, among other things, to strengthen the unity of the Muslims of that quarter or district. Friday, in Arabic called *jumuah* (or day of gathering), is not a sabbath. It is that day of the week where, among other things, Muslims get together in worship of God. The idea of sabbath is a blasphemy, for God does not need to rest. In the *Quran* God says: 'God, there is no god but He, the Living, the Sustainer, the Eternal. No slumber can seize him nor sleep. His are all things in the heavens and the earths. . . . His throne doth extend over the heavens and the earths, and He feeleth no fatigue in guarding and preserving them, For He is the Most High, the Supreme' (Chapter 2, Verse 255).

Twice a year, the entire population of a city or a rural district gathers outside the town to pray in common in an open field, thus stressing the unity of the Muslims in that entire area. The occasions are the Id-ul-Fitr commemorating the completion of the month of fasting, and falling on the first day of the tenth month of the Muslim lunar year (*shawwal*) and the Id-ul-Adha commemorating the sacrifice of Ibrahim on his son Ismail and falling on the tenth day of the twelfth month of the Muslim lunar year (Dhu-al-Hijjah). During these prayers the *imam* gives a sermon which has a relevance to the problems of the Muslim community during that year.

Once a year, at a specific day, the ninth day of Dhu-al-Hijjah, Muslims of all the world meet at a specific spot, the plain of Arafat, to the east of Mecca, to worship together and to mingle with each other as members of one single world community of Muslims. All differences of class or nations are abolished during this period by the adoption of one single uniform made of simple pieces of white cloth. Every Muslim in the world—male and female—is requested once in his lifetime to participate in this great Islamic convention, unless he is prevented by weakness of health or insufficiency of resources. The institution of *hajj* has proved to be the greatest unifying institution and the most effective melting pot bringing more awareness of togetherness between Muslims of the different corners of the world. In spite of all the hardships—natural or man-made—a man who performs the *hajj* is never the same after he returns home. He becomes the strongest cement of unity between his far-away community and the rest of the Muslims of the world.

The giving of alms is not a kind of give away by the rich to the poor which rests at the sweet will of the rich man. It is a fixed tax (2.5 per cent on most belongings) on the rich man's income and property to be passed on to the needy. It is indeed a social security instituted to strengthen more the unity of Muslims and bridge the gap between rich and poor.

The fast of Ramadan means that during an entire month, every Muslim adult who is in good health and is not travelling should refrain from drinking, smoking, eating and the sex act from before sunrise to sunset. By experiencing hunger the Muslim would get a chance to have empathy with the poor and contribute to the alleviating of their suffering.

Finally, the 'struggle in the way of God' or '*jihad*' is the highest act a Muslim can make in the defence of his community and in its support. The word '*jihad*' which means 'struggle' was most maligned in the western press. Actually, it means that it is a Muslim's duty to care for other Muslims and for the welfare of himself and his children, by defending them against oppression. And thus by giving all that he can including his money and if need arises, even his life. It is the highest level of sacrifice that a Muslim can reach. And this is certainly a necessary act for the building of the unity of the Muslim *ummah*.

## Social Justice in Islam

God is just. He is the Truth. Nothing in the actions of God could violate this rule. In the *Quran* God says: 'Every soul draws the heed of its acts on none but itself: no blame could be put on a person for a crime done by another' (Chapter 6, Verse 164). The concept of 'original sin' is completely abhorrent to the Muslim mind. Indeed, God created Adam and Eve. If they committed the sin of eating from the forbidden tree, they alone are accountable for disobeying an order of God. Their progeny can in no way share in the blame of that sin. In any case, they repented, and God forgave them. The attitude of a Muslim toward Adam and Eve is full of respect, compatible with the respect due to parents from their children.

Thus, man is not only born free. He is also born good. The Prophet Muhammed says: 'Every child is born naturally good (and Muslim). It is his parents who make him Christian, Jew or Pagan.' A person is accountable for his sins only when he is adult, capable of judgement and has heard of the message of Muhammed. If he commits a sin, it is up to him and him alone to redeem himself by repenting, without any intermediary, and by asking forgiveness from God. Thus, the claim that God sent His only son to die on the cross to redeem mankind is, from the Islamic point of view, a great blasphemy. God has no son for He is unique. It is also meaningless since no one can redeem anyone else except oneself.

From this basic rule of justice can be deduced the important concept of responsibility of the individual. Since every person is accountable to God for what he does, that person is responsible to God for all his actions. The Prophet says: 'Every one of you is a shepherd and every one of you is responsible for his flock: the leader is a shepherd and is responsible for those whom he leads; the head of a family is a shepherd and is responsible for his family; the wife is a shepherd and is responsible for her household; the servant is a shepherd and is responsible for his work . . .'.

254    Muslim Minorities in the World Today

Since all men and women are equal in the sight of God, they bow only to him and to no one of their own kind. Wealth itself is irrelevant and is important only on the basis of how much good one can do with it. Basically all wealth belongs to God, a person's property is only a trust in his hands for a defined time. The trust is acquired following a set of rules based on honesty and hard work. The trust is removed by the death of the person or by the community if the person betrays the trust by misusing it. To amplify the trust characteristic of one's property after his death, the property is distributed following fixed rules to his close kin who in exchange for the right to inherit the trust have the duty of caring for the individual during his lifetime in case of need. The individual has no right to play with the rules of inheritance, he can dispose of the third of his property but only to those who are not normally entitled to inherit. During his lifetime, the person has to pay duties on the 'trust' which include *zakat*, but are by no means limited to it. Water, minerals, forests, airspace, open land, and any territory acquired by a common effort of the Muslim community are all the property of the community as a whole.

*Riba* (interest) is strictly forbidden in Islam, for it is morally wrong and militates against the principle of social justice. *Riba* is defined as obtaining an extra fixed sum of money on loans. The reason is that the 'person' who gives the money to another 'person' who works with it should share the risk, and therefore the gain or the loss should be proportionate to the gain or loss obtained by the work done with that money. Therefore, the present capitalistic system is basically at variance with the Islamic concept of 'social justice'. The Islamic economic order is an entirely independent one based on Islam social justice.

Thus, the new Islamic society for which all Muslims yearn should be based in all fields on the basic rules of 'social justice' as announced by the *Holy Quran* and the *Sunnah*.

## The Concept of the Ummah

'Ye are the best *ummah* evolved for mankind,
Enjoining what is right,
Forbidding what is wrong,
And believing in God'
    *Holy Quran* (Chapter 3, Verse 110).

The only link of togetherness acceptable in Islam between individuals is the link of common belief and a common purpose in life. All Muslims are linked in one single bond within one supranational community, the *ummah*. The *ummah* is, therefore, not a nation only, nor it is a religious community only. It is both and more, since Islam is a faith as well as an order.

For a Muslim, therefore, the definition of the 'us' with respect to the 'others' is "the group gathering all the Muslims"; the others are those who are not Muslims. Belonging to the *ummah* is therefore a choice and not an accident of birth. This feeling of togetherness goes beyond links of blood and geography, it is embedded in the Islamic belief itself. Indeed, it is a major sin for a Muslim to consider himself apart from another Muslim because of differences of race, language, class, etc.

The Prophet stressed the brotherhood of all Muslims in so many terms and, above all, in his practice. The Prophet (s.a.w.) said: 'Muslims are like one single body, if one part of it hurts, the entire body hurts with pain and fever'. He also said: 'None of you becomes a true believer unless he wishes for his brother what he wishes for himself.' There could be no excuse whatsoever for a Muslim or a group of Muslims to treat other Muslims discriminatorily, in a manner as if they were different from themselves because of differences such as national origin, which from an Islamic point of view is irrelevant.

From the beginning the *ummah* was meant to encompass eventually the whole world. Its ranks are open to any person who cares to join it without any precondition or prejudice. Within the *ummah*, differences of nationality as denoted by the western concept are of no importance or value. However, it is understood that within this unity of feeling and unity of belief, there may be differences of minor nature such as speech of every day life or habits that do not interfere with the basic tenets of Islam.

The allegiance of a Muslim should go as a first priority and before anything else to the *ummah*. He should strive all his life with his money and his person to defend it and strengthen it. It represents his people with the exclusion of all others and his commitment to it should come first and before all other commitments. Nationality based on community of race is abhorrent to Muslim thinking; that based on community of language or culture is meaningless if not compounded with community of belief; and that based exclusively on common material interest is immoral.

## The Muslim State

The Prophet Muhammed is the messenger of God to mankind. He is also the perfect man, toward whom every person should compare himself in his quest for improvement. Following the *Sunnah* (the way) of the Prophet is a duty of every Muslim and of all Muslim communities. As the perfect man, the Prophet is the perfect father, the perfect husband, the perfect leader, and the perfect head of state. His mission on earth was to establish the *ummah* and secure its sovereignty on at least a small corner of the earth. The *ummah* being that always expanding part of humanity which 'enjoins what is right, forbids what is wrong, and believes in God'. The Muslim state is therefore the embodiment of the sovereignty of the *ummah*. It encloses all those lands which recognize such sovereignty. All those parts of the Muslim *ummah* which find themselves outside the Muslim state are Muslim minorities.

The Muslim state was established by the Prophet himself in Medina in the year 1 A.H. (620 C.E.). And it is this state which is the perfect model state to be followed, just as the Prophet himself is the perfect model man. Since the *ummah* is one there could only be one Muslim state. The Prophet warned against division and against the multiplicity of states within the *ummah*. God says in the *Quran*: 'And obey God and His Messenger; and fall into no disputes, Lest ye lose heart and your power depart, And be patient and persevering: For God is with those who patiently persevere' (Chapter 8, Verse 46).

The principles on which the Muslim state is to be established have been clearly laid down in the *Quran* and the *Sunnah* of the Prophet. These principles have also been effectively put into practice by the Prophet himself in Medina and by the rightly guided caliphs in the early history of Islam between 11 and 40 A.H. (632–661 C.E.). Both periods, the period of the Prophet and that of the rightly guided caliphs are in full light of history and are perfectly well documented.

In the Muslim state, the head of the state is to be elected by the members of the *ummah* among those who are most befitting to be head of the state. The head of the state is not a dictator, since he has to rule by consultation and his powers are limited by the *Quran* and the *Sunnah*. His rule cannot be considered a theocracy since he has no privileges; he is just a first among equals who is subjected to the same law as all members of the *ummah*. He merely has a contract between himself and the *ummah* in which the members of the *ummah* would co-operate with him, support him and obey him as long as he fulfils the terms of the contract which are: the implementation of Islamic Justice and the protection of the *ummah* from internal and external dangers. The condition on the choice of the head of state is that he be a Muslim, completely committed to Islam, knowledgeable of its laws, and having leadership capabilities; no blood or race considerations are acceptable. The Prophet said: 'There is no obedience of a created in the disobedience of the Creator'. And when Abu Bakr, the first Caliph, was elected, he said in his inauguration speech: 'You have chosen me to be your leader and I am not your best. If you see me doing right support me. If you see me doing wrong correct me.'

The social justice in the Muslim state is implemented by the *shura* principle and the complete separation of the judicial legislative and executive powers. The difference between the *shura* principle and democracy as known in the secular west is that in democracy the people are sovereign and can legislate through their representatives. In the *shura* principle, God is Sovereign, the people decide between themselves democratically within the limits of permissibility set by the *Quran* and the *Sunnah*. Legislation in the Muslim state is fixed by the principles laid down in the *Quran* and the *Sunnah*, the power of the legislature is to apply these principles to practical day to day business of the state and society. The execution of the *shar* (justice) in the Muslim state is above the head of state and therefore is independent of him.

The Muslim state binds itself by law to protect minorities. Minorities in such a state are defined as 'those organized groups who do not believe in Islam and who have a set of values of their own which may have originated from a Godly Message'. Traditionally, were placed in this category Christian and Jewish sects and under other circumstances other religious groups as well, including Hindus. This is the only system which protects in its midst those who do not believe in it. In modern day, one cannot imagine a Communist state protecting a group professing a non-belief in communism or a secular democracy protecting in its midst those who are committed to another form of government. The minorities can run their affairs, in exchange for a commitment to not undermining the Muslim state and its members have the same rights and duties as the Muslims, except that they cannot be put in a position where it might be expected of them to do actions that are basically in contradiction with their lack of commitment to the Islamic ideals. Joining the *ummah* is open to all any time and by free will. God says in the *Quran* what it means 'Let there be no compulsion in Religion: Truth stands out clear from error: Whoever rejects evil and believes in God hath grasped the most trustworthy hand-hold, that never breaks. And God heareth and knoweth all things'. (Chapter 2, Verse 256).

As for linguistic minorities they have no existence within the Muslim *ummah*. Speaking one language or another is no cause for any weakening of belonging to the *ummah*. The Arabic language should be mastered by all Muslims and be their *lingua franca* as the language of the *Holy Quran* and the Holy Prophet, but other languages can survive with Arabic, all being treated on the same footing. There should be no difference in treatment between those belonging to one linguistic group or another, not even a line of differentiation.

The ideal of such a state has always attracted the Muslims and has created in them the urge to sacrifice all that is dear to them. For such a state—a state truly devoted to the cause of Islam—is a great blessing and a mercy of God. It ensures that the word of God reigns supreme, that justice governs the relations between man and man, and that the ideal of the unity and brotherhood of the *ummah* is translated into a reality. It is heartening that this ideal continues to inspire the Muslims today. In fact, recently several Islamic countries have shown a renewed commitment and dedication to this ideal, and a defiant insistence to proceed towards the realization of this goal in the teeth of all conceivable opposition and obstruction. Muslims the world over only hope that these efforts would fuse to lead to the nucleus of the long-awaited Muslim state rather than degenerate into a multitude of Muslim contradictory experiences. The same ideal is behind the war of liberation of Afghanistan as well as the burgeoning movements of emancipation in the rest of the Muslim world.

## The Muslim State and the Muslim Minority

Islam does not ask from others more than it imposes on itself. The protection it gives to minorities within its system is expected to be given to Muslim groups living outside the territory of the sovereignty of the *ummah* (i.e., outside the Muslim state). Indeed, an Islamic definition of Muslim minority can be given as 'those parts of the Muslim *ummah* living outside its sovereignty'. Indeed, Islamically, the world is divided into three zones: *Dar-al-Islam* (The land of Islam); *Dar-al-Muahadah* (the land of treaty); and

*Dar-al-Harb* (the land of war). *Dar-al-Islam* encloses all those
territories composing the Muslim state. Outside *Dar-al-Islam*, the
non-Muslim states are part of *Dar-al-Muahadah* or part of *Dar-al-
Harb* depending on their attitude to the Muslims. *Dar-al-
Muahadah* would be made up of those countries which have
treaties of friendship with the Muslim state and which allow the
freedom of existence and of growth to their Muslim communities.
All those countries which deny the existence of Islam and are bent
to its destruction inside its state and outside it are part of *Dar-al-
Harb*.

In modern terms, it is clear that the above division is still valid.
There is a big difference between those states giving full rights to
their Muslim community and those which do everything in their
power to destroy such a community. The attitude of friendliness or
of hostility of every state of the world toward *Dar-al-Islam* is
shown at home with its Muslim community.

As there is a model for the Muslim state in the state established
by the Prophet, there are also two models for Muslim minorities to
follow: One is the model of a Muslim minority in *Dar-al-Harb* and
the other is for the Muslim minority in *Dar-al-Muahadah*. The
example of the existence of a Muslim minority in a territory ruled
by forces that are bent on its destruction has for a model the
Muslim community established by the Prophet himself in his own
hometown, Mecca. The model of the Muslim community in a
friendly territory has for a model the community established by
Muslim emigrants from Mecca to Abyssinia and organized by
Jaafar Ibn Abi Talib, the cousin of the Prophet. In the first case,
oppression led to warfare and eventually to the victory of truth
over falsehood. In the second case, tolerance led to peaceful coexistence and exchange of ideas, making clear to everyone the
truth from falsehood.

## Toward a New Order

The fact of the matter is that by ideal Islamic standards, the
*ummah* finds itself completely disorganized in the twentieth
century. This lack of organization is acutely felt by most of the
thinkers of the *ummah*. And the effort to go back to the ideal,
conciously or otherwise, is indeed the driving force behind political and social forces requiring an improvement of the situation of
the *ummah*.

Deviation from the ideal model of reorganization of the Muslim *ummah* started early in the Islamic history. The first deviation occurred when the Governor of Syria defied the order of the elected head of state (the fourth Caliph Ali) and was able to overthrow the legitimate government by force, thus establishing for the first time in Muslim history in the year 41 A.H. (661 C.E.), a transition of leadership by force, instead of by election. The second deviation occurred, when the same head of the state, decided to pass on the leadership of the state to his son Yazid (in the year 60 C.E.) who was neither qualified nor acceptable to the *ummah*, thus creating a new deviation, that of leadership by heredity instead of election. The Prophet predicted these events when he said: 'The Muslim state (*khilafah*) will last after me for thirty years, then it will become a clannish kingship on the model of the kings of Persia and Byzance'. The third deviation occurred when the popular revolt of the *ummah* to bring back the state to its original ideal was stolen in the years 132 C.E. to establish a new dynasty which was in itself, ideally, no great improvement on the one that had been brought down. This eventually led to the break up of the political unity of the Muslim state leading to several states as one province seceded after another. However, the ideal of one single Muslim state was never denied in theory, since the seceding states either presented their leaders as the true leaders of the entire *ummah*, thus not recognizing any right of the Abbasid Caliph, or they paid lip service to that same Caliph. Opposition to this state of affairs was continuous, spearheaded by the descendants of the Prophet through his grand-sons Hasan and Hussein. In fact the Prophet is reported to have said: 'I left with you those which if you remain attached to them you will never go astray: the Book of God and my descendants. Both will never separate until they reach me in paradise. Watch how you will succeed me in them!' Despite deviations, however, it was only with the fall of the Ottoman Empire that the entire concept of the unity of the *ummah* was put aside to be replaced by the concept of nation-states imported from the nineteenth century Christian Europe. Such a concept is not only foreign to Islamic thinking, it is completely unacceptable to it, since it undermines the very root of the unity of the *ummah*, the very idea that differences in languages and races are absolutely insignificant in comparison with the universality of the unity of belief.

For a full half of this century there was no forum for the different parts of the Muslim *ummah* to meet and discuss their common problems. Not until King Faisal of Saudi Arabia pioneered his call for Islamic solidarity by sending Sheikh Mohammed Al-Muntasir Kettani (the father of this author) to the heads of North African states in 1965 to gather support for the idea. The effort eventually culminated in the creation of the Organization of the Islamic Conference, which is certainly a humble but no less certainly important beginning on the road to the re-unification of the *ummah*.

Balkanization of the Muslim lands and their conquest and colonization by non-Muslim forces are results and not causes of the deviation of the *ummah* from its ideal. The solution of its major problems today is to be searched in the cause and not the result. The Prophet said: 'The latter days of this *ummah* would be improved only by what improved its beginning'. The search of the ways and means of the reorganization of the *ummah* is the duty of all its members. The role in this search of those who are in the minority is no less important than those who might belong to one of the forty-five parts of *Dar-al-Islam*.

## References

1. M. A. Kettani, *Muslims in Europe and America* 2 Volumes (Stuttgart, Germany, 1976) (Arabic).
2. M. Al-Muntasir Kettani, *Fityat Tariq wa Al-Ghafiqi* (the Youth Movement of Tariq and Al-Ghafiqi) (on the Constitution of a Muslim State) (Beirut, 1972).
3. Abdul-Hayy Kettani, *At-Taratib Al-Idariyah fi Al-Hukumah Al-Nabawiyah* (the administrative order in the Government of the Prophet) (Fes, 1936).
4. Muhammad Ibn Jafar Kettani, *Al-Nasihah* (Advice to Kings) (1910) (Arabic) widely spread manuscript.

# Index

Tables and bibliographical references have not been indexed; alphabetization is word by word; acronyms file as words.